Skillstreaming
the Adolescent

A Guide for Teaching Prosocial Skills

THIRD EDITION

Ellen McGinnis

RESEARCH PRESS
PUBLISHERS

2612 North Mattis Avenue ■ Champaign, Illinois 61822 ■ [800] 519-2707 ■ www.researchpress.com

RESEARCH PRESS
PUBLISHERS

Copies of this book may be ordered from Research Press at the address given on the title page.

Composition by Jeff Helgesen
Cover design by Linda Brown, Positive I.D. Graphic Design, Inc.
Printed by McNaughton & Gunn, Inc.

ISBN: 978-0-87822-653-5
Library of Congress Control Number 2011932208

To the memory of Professor Arnie Goldstein, whose work continues to transform lives

Contents

PART 1
Skillstreaming Program Content and Implementation

PART 2
Skill Outlines and Homework Reports

Homework reports follow each skill.

Figures and Tables

Preface

Skillstreaming is now over 30 years old. Starting with its introduction in 1973 as one of the very first social skills training approaches, it has been widely used in the United States and beyond and is now in place in hundreds of schools, agencies, and institutions serving children and youth. This third edition of *Skillstreaming the Adolescent* integrates what has been learned from research investigations over the past 10 years with training recommendations provided by many of the hundreds of teachers, administrators, youth care workers, and other practitioners who have used Skillstreaming.

The origins and development of the Skillstreaming approach afford an interesting context with which to understand the 21st-century incarnation of the program described in this book. The prevailing therapeutic approaches of the 1950s and 1960s (psychodynamic, nondirective, and behavior modification) held that an individual possessed effective, satisfying, or healthy behaviors but that these behaviors were simply unexpressed. In contrast, Skillstreaming represents a psychoeducational approach, viewing the individual in educational terms, as a person in need of help in the form of skills training. Instead of providing therapy, the task of the skills trainer or teacher is the active and deliberate teaching of desirable behaviors to replace those less productive in nature.

Skillstreaming differs from the approaches of behavior theorists such as Albert Bandura (1973), who described the processes of modeling, behavioral rehearsal, and reinforcement implicit in the Skillstreaming approach but who emphasized operant procedures such as prompting and shaping of behaviors. Although a strictly behavioral approach increases the frequency of a behavior, that behavior must already be within a person's repertoire. If the person does not have a grasp of the needed skill, operant procedures are insufficient to add that skill to the person's behavioral options.

The deinstitutionalization movement of the 1960s, which resulted in the discharge of approximately four million persons from mental health and other institutions into local communities, set the stage for acceptance of an alternative way of providing treatment. The realization was that the more traditional therapeutic interventions, which focused on looking inward to correct one's nonproductive actions (i.e., insight-oriented approaches), were ineffective for many individuals from lower socioeconomic environments, who constituted the majority of individuals discharged from institutions. The lack of effective methods to reach this population adolescents led Dr. Arnold P. Goldstein to develop Structured Learning Therapy (Goldstein, 1973), the precursor to Skillstreaming. Structured learning methods approached aggression, withdrawal, and other nonproductive patterns in a new way—as learned behaviors that can be changed by teaching new, alternative skills.

In addition to the growing importance of such structured learning methods in applied clinical work and as a preventive focus in community mental health, parallel developments in education clearly encouraged skills training. Specifically, a number of other approaches grew from the personal development context of certain educational movements—for example, progressive education (Dewey, 1938) and character education (Chapman, 1977). The goal of these approaches was to support the teaching of concepts and behaviors relevant to values, morality, and emotional functioning—in particular, values clarification (Simon, Howe, & Kirschenbaum, 1972), moral education (Kohlberg, 1973), and affective education (Miller, 1976). These three approaches, as well as other personal growth programs, combined to provide a supportive climate and context for skills training. These programs share a concern for personal development, competence, and social effectiveness. Clearly, education had been broadened well beyond basic academic content to include areas traditionally the concern of mental health practitioners.

Since its initial development as an intervention prescriptively targeted to low-income adults deficient in social skills, Skillstreaming has increasingly been used with many other populations. In the 1980s and beyond, Dr. Goldstein's skills training program, now known as Skillstreaming, was adapted to meet the needs of adolescents (Goldstein, Gershaw, Sprafkin, & Klein, 1980; Goldstein & McGinnis, 1997), elementary children (McGinnis & Goldstein, 1984, 1997), and preschool and kindergarten children (McGinnis & Goldstein, 1990, 2003) who exhibited aggression and other problematic behaviors. In addition to its use with children and adolescents, the Skillstreaming approach has been employed successfully with elderly adults, child-abusing parents, industrial managers, police officers, and others. Over more than 30 years of program use, a considerable amount of evaluation research has been conducted and reported. The results of these studies support the efficacy of Skillstreaming and have suggested means for altering and improving its procedures and materials. An annotated bibliography detailing Skillstreaming research is available on the Skillstreaming website (www.skillstreaming.com).

Acknowledgments

During the more than 40 years of his professional life, Arnold P. Goldstein (1934–2002) was a professor at Syracuse University, director of the Center for Research on Aggression, and wrote or coauthored over 90 peer-reviewed articles and 50 books. In the final year of his life, Dr. Goldstein founded the International Center for Aggression Replacement Training (ICART), which leads research and provides information and training to professionals throughout the world. At this point, Dr. Goldstein's work, including Skillstreaming, is used throughout the United States and in at least 16 other countries. Many people, myself included, cannot thank him enough for his efforts to help youth and adults with aggression problems and other challenging behaviors change to improve both their lives and those who interact with them.

Three other persons share major responsibility for bringing Skillstreaming into existence and nurturing its development over these many years. Robert P. Sprafkin and N. Jane Gershaw helped codevelop it originally and were prime contributors to enhancing both its early application and its initial evaluation. Barry Glick fully shared the effort to expand its boundaries to include especially difficult-to-reach adolescents. These colleagues well deserve special thanks and appreciation.

Thanks also to Shawnda Gorish and Julianne Woodhouse from Des Moines Public Schools, who provided many of the real-life scenarios included in the suggested content for modeling displays and to Knut Gunderson, Sandnes, Norway for his thoughtful review and suggestions from his training experience.

Gail Salyards and Russ Pence from Research Press provided the encouragement and understanding needed to complete this revision. Special appreciation and thanks to Karen Steiner, my editor, for her careful and sensitive reviews, changes, and recommendations and for understanding the need to represent Arnie's spirit in this work.

Introduction

With just a click of a computer key, the social and educational worlds for today's adolescents have grown far beyond our imagination. It is understandable, then, that discussions among experts and practitioners in education and school reform center around preparing the current generation of adolescents, often referred to as the "millenial generation" (Marx, 2006), for future jobs and vocations, many of which have not yet been created. The focus of these discussions is on preparing students for the future, not for the school and work worlds of the past.

Although many teachers, school administrators, and teacher trainers search for the best methods to teach 21st-century skills and prepare our young people for a global future, many day-to-day concerns in education remain constant—that is, many adolescents continue to experience anxiety, depression, loneliness, or anger. Most teachers in today's schools must still regularly address classroom disruptions, undesirable peer interactions, and incidents of bullying. They do so in addition to accepting the challenge of moving all students forward academically to meet rigorous state achievement standards.

SOCIAL SKILLS AND THE ADOLESCENT

One of the most hopeful elements in the design of the 21st-century school is its recognition of and support for teaching the social behaviors necessary to work as part of a team, make good decisions, communicate well with others, and engage in problem solving to handle conflict in peaceful ways. As the real-life incidents next described illustrate, aggressive youngsters are often proficient in antisocial ways of responding to real or imagined provocations but weak in carrying out various prosocial alternative behaviors.* It is a curriculum of just such positive alternatives that the Skillstreaming method is designed to teach.

> L. was told several times by several different staff members to take off his hat. He ignored all requests. He would touch his hat each time but not take it off (as if he was taunting us). He began to walk into the office (without permission). I told him that if he didn't take his hat off, I would. He didn't, and I did. He followed me out of the office and down the hall, leaning on me all the way. I told him to back off. He did not. He then said, "Give me my fucking hat." He then pushed me. I began to escort him to the office. He started to wrestle with me by grabbing my legs and pulling me up. We both fell to the floor. He did not release from me until he was pulled away from me. (p. 27)

> O. was rude and disrespectful to me and given a warning. She also refused to do her work. [Two days later] I gave her yet another warning because she wasn't doing any work, was mimicking my instructions and disrupting those who were working. Today O. came into class blowing bubbles, so I asked her to throw the gum away. She did so after telling me not to "get her going."

---

*The events described are drawn from a pool of 1,000 teacher-reported incidents gathered for the book *Break It Up: A Teacher's Guide to Managing Student Aggression* (Goldstein, Palumbo, Striepling, & Voutsinas, 1995).

Immediately, she popped another piece of gum into her mouth, and when I asked her to remove it she called me a "bitch." Her behavior is hampering the learning process of others. (p. 45)

Shortly after my class began, two students (boys) verbally began arguing over the detention and referral one of them had received. The referral occurred in the previous class. One student was making fun of the other's troubles.

A fight broke out. Tables and chairs were being pushed around the room. I tried to get between [the students]. They were not hearing me. I then told the others in [the] classroom to move out of the way. I told one student to push the buzzer to the office and say "fight." We didn't need to say anything—they could hear. Other teachers came over to see if I needed help. Some students from another class had to be told to go back. I let [the boys] fight until the principal and assistant arrived. Both boys were bleeding from the nose. One's face was swollen. When they realized the principal was in the room, they broke themselves up. Each was suspended for 3 days. (p. 89)

The episode that I want to talk about happened in a high school cafeteria. I was on lunch duty and standing near the lunch lines as the students were lining up to get in. The line had just been allowed to go in so that it was moving up rather rapidly to file through the area where you pick up your food. . . . Two ninth-grade girls . . . had a confrontation, and there was a lot of shouting and screaming going on behind me, and as I turned around the first punch was landed. And I was standing behind . . . the puncher, and before she could land another one, I grabbed her arm and tried to keep her away from the other girl. As soon as I grabbed her arm and held her, that was a sign for the other girl to start beating on her. There were no other adults around. What I had to do was to let the one go that I had and try to get in the middle. . . . Another teacher arrived, and actually a couple

more arrived, and one girl was grabbed and subdued by one of the male teachers, and I took the one that was nearer to me. . . . I grabbed her by the left arm, and she hit me three times in the face with the right arm. (pp. 86–87)

Social skills deficits have been the target of considerable research scrutiny, and it is well accepted today that a youth's lack of social competence relates to later negative outcomes (Walker, Ramsey, & Gresham, 2004). For most students, due to the length of time they spend in the school setting, the majority of socialization occurs in school (Schoenfeld, Rutherford, Gable, & Rock, 2008). A positive relationship between social skills and school success has been repeatedly demonstrated (Cartledge & Lo, 2006), and students who are socially competent have a greater likelihood of graduating (Caprara, Barbaranelli, Pastorelli, Bandura, & Zimbardo, 2000). Planned and direct instruction in social skills empowers students to get their needs met in desirable ways, helps them learn important social behaviors to deal effectively with increased social demands, and positively impacts their learning (Cartledge & Lo, 2006; Cook, Gresham, Kern, Barreras, & Crews, 2008; Docksai, 2010). For peers and teachers, social skills instruction results in a more positive school climate and more time for teachers to spend on academic instruction instead of discipline, leading to a more rewarding learning and teaching experience.

WHAT IS SKILLSTREAMING?

Skillstreaming is an evidence-based intervention that involves systematically teaching social skills to address the needs of students who display aggression, immaturity, withdrawal, or other problem behaviors. Skillstreaming is a psychoeducational intervention having its roots in both psychology and education. Although used initially by therapists in the mental health field, its processes focus on four direct instruction principles of learning. These learning procedures—modeling, role-playing, feedback, and transfer—have been used to teach a variety of behaviors, from academic competencies to sports, daily living skills, and vocational skills. These procedures, which allow for flexibility to meet individual students needs, are applied in Skillstreaming to teach students desirable prosocial behaviors.

Before discussing what Skillstreaming is in more detail, it is important to point out what it is not: Skillstreaming is not an affective education strategy that focuses primarily on discussion of feelings and the individual's strengths as a way to foster positive self-concept. Although discussion is a part, Skillstreaming engages students in active learning through role-playing and practice. Skillstreaming will not address all youth's needs in every situation at all times. Instead, it is a well-validated instructional procedure that should be included with other techniques, such as behavior intervention planning, conflict resolution, and cooperative learning. Nor is Skillstreaming a procedure for teaching compliance skills, the focus of some skills-training programs. Although it will teach students the skills needed to follow school rules better, the program is mainly intended to teach students the skills needed to solve problems that occur in their daily lives, to be assertive in handling situations that cause them stress or unhappiness, and to increase the chance that they will have satisfying relationships with others.

A Skill-Deficit Model

The Skillstreaming model makes the assumption that the learner is weak in or lacks a behavioral skill or skills. The goal, then, becomes teaching desirable skills. This assumption is made for several very important reasons. First, the belief that most students do not know how to act productively in given situations lessens the frustration experienced by many teachers when a youth seems continually to react in the same inappropriate way despite efforts to consequate that behavior. This allows teachers to focus on proactive instruction instead of reacting to the youth's misbehavior as if it were done purposefully to create problems. In addition, the assumption of skill deficits sets the stage for instruction in prosocial skills that the student may actually use and that the teacher can therefore prompt and reinforce. The assumption furthermore suggests to the student that the teacher and others will be patient and encouraging during the learning of these sometimes very difficult skills.

In workshops, trainers of prospective Skillstreaming often illustrate or reinforce the skill-deficit model by asking participants to think of a time they agreed to do something asked by a friend, relative, supervisor, or acquaintance but that they really did not want to do. Most participants quickly identify situations in which they as adults have felt pressured into doing something they didn't want to do, whether it was allowing a neighbor to borrow the lawn mower to taking on extra job responsibilities. In a practice environment, group members are asked to respond to such requests by using the skills of Responding to Persuasion (Skill 37) and Negotiating (Skill 25). The majority of participants experience difficulty with these skills, even in the practice setting! Yet many times the expectation is that adolescents will be able to resist peer persuasion quickly and emphatically.

Researchers in the area of social skills training—for example Gresham, Sugai, and Horner (2001); Gresham (2002); and Gresham, Van, and Cook (2006)—advocate that practitioners consider the difference between a skill deficit (can't) and a performance deficit (won't). These authors explain that a youth with a skill deficit lacks knowledge of how to perform a skill or how to select which skill is appropriate in a given situation. Other youth, as in the trainer workshop example, may know how to perform a skill but lack the fluency in skill use necessary to execute the skill in a competent manner. Others may experience competing problem behaviors, such as poor self-control, which inhibit their skill use. Still other adolescents may know how to carry out a skill but fail to do so because of lack of positive reinforcement (i.e., a performance deficit).

Research also suggests that some youth with increased social anxiety have a social information processing deficit (Crick & Dodge, 1994; Raine et al., 2006). In other words, the adolescent experiences errors in thinking about and responding to social cues. In practice, acquisition (can't do), performance (won't do), fluency, and competing problem behaviors will be addressed within the context of a skills deficit, with particular emphasis placed on addressing the type of deficit throughout the instructional process described in subsequent chapters.

Planned, Systematic Instruction

Most educators recognize that the days of defining public education's goal only as teaching basic academic competencies are over. With increased emphasis on increasing student achievement, instruction in social skills and social-emotional learning is gaining in acceptance (Docksai, 2010). Educators, counselors, and therapists have also increased their understanding that students or clients need to be taught desirable behaviors in the same planned and systematic way academic skills are taught (Maag, 2005). Incidental learning (discussing alternatives or telling students what to do) is insufficient for students to learn alternative behaviors, just as it is insufficient to tell students how to solve equations in algebra and expect that they will be able to be successful in algebra. Whatever the reason for a student's skill lack or weakness, schools must establish and implement procedures to teach these skills, just as they would in the case of academic deficits.

A Way to Give Encouragement

Historically, educational interventions dealing with student behavior problems have concentrated on strategies to diminish or extinguish the behavior of concern (e.g., time-out, loss of privileges). Although reinforcement strategies are helpful in increasing positive behaviors, it is necessary to wait until a behavior is displayed before it can be rewarded. Thus, many students with infrequent appropriate behaviors rarely receive positive reinforcement; in most cases, they receive an abundance of negative feedback. Although negative procedures may be a useful part of a comprehensive behavior intervention plan, emphasis on their use may further discourage children with behavior problems.

Teaching prosocial skills provides adolescents with opportunities to be successful in both hypothetical and real-life situations and lends a sense of balance to behavior management programs. Although inappropriate behaviors will continue to need intervention, through Skillstreaming, students have the opportunity to build alternative, socially acceptable behaviors to increase their opportunities for choice. Teachers and others will also find that prompting students to use a previously learned social skill when problematic situations arise in the classroom or in other school settings will often stop the student's inappropriate actions in midstream and channel his or her energies in a more prosocial direction. Like reminding a student to use a reading strategy to master unknown vocabulary, when given in a helpful and encouraging manner, such prompting fosters a positive classroom and school climate.

A Way to Enhance Self-Esteem

A description of adolescents with behavior problems often includes the phrase "poor self-esteem." Counselors, teachers, and others often struggle to design interventions that improve the youth's positive feelings about self. One way of addressing this issue is to teach the student to be more competent. We have traditionally focused on academic competence, recognizing that such competence contributes to a youth's positive feelings about self in relation to achievement. Likewise, increasing competence in a variety of socially related skills will improve an individual's self-concept.

Although behavior management programs are useful, necessary, and very often effective in reducing problem behaviors, we need to be aware that emphasis on such programs alone may reinforce in students the idea that adults are the dispensers of rewards and punishments. Adolescents may learn to believe that whatever they might do or however they might act, the positive or negative results of these actions will be determined by someone else in power—a teacher, parent, or other adult. Such a belief, referred to as an *external locus of control,* can foster feelings of helplessness. When students learn, for example, to handle conflict in ways that yield approval from others, they also learn a sense of responsibility and control. They more easily make the connection between their actions (e.g., use of a skill) and positive consequences. When students learn that they have the skills and ability to effect change, their self-esteem is likely to improve.

Remediation and Prevention

The Skillstreaming approach provides remediation for students who are significantly deficient in prosocial skills whether or not they are receiving special education services. The student with a learning disability may need to learn the skill of Asking for Help (Skill 9), as well as organizational skills such as Following Instructions (Skill 12). Youth with more severe disabilities, those with autism or cognitive disabilities, can learn a variety of social skills to enhance their independence and to make their lives more satisfying. Those with emotional or behavioral disorders— whether characterized by withdrawal, aggression, or immaturity—continue to benefit from learning prosocial skills. Although aggression and violence are very visible and perhaps cause more stress to teachers, school administrators, parents, and others, teaching prosocial skills to the withdrawn child or the student who reacts immaturely or inadequately is also important.

Skillstreaming is also intended for the general education population—students whose behavior is not significantly problematic yet who will increase their personal satisfaction and happiness by learning or improving upon prosocial skills. How many young people do we know who, when they reach adolescence, have significant problems dealing with stress or with interpersonal relationships when no such issues were noticed in earlier grades? Many students may need help with skills to form satisfying interpersonal relationships, participate in problem solving, or deal productively with day-to-day stress. Undertaking instruction with students who do not yet experience significant problems offers the hope of preventing future difficulties. Furthermore, research has demonstrated benefit for students across age and skill levels. For example, instruction in social skills has been shown to positively impact children in the primary grades (Denham, Hatfield, Smethurst, Tan, & Tribe, 2006; Maddern, Franey, McLaughlin, & Cox, 2004), elementary-age students (Gresham et al., 2006; Lane, Menzies, Barton-Arwood, Doukas, & Munton, 2005; Lo, Loe, & Cartledge, 2002), and in adolescence (Cook et al., 2008). Benefit has also occurred for students with disabilities (Maag, 2006), including learning disabilities (Kavale & Forness, 1996) and those with emotional and behavioral disorders (Cook et al., 2008; Gresham, Cook, Crews, & Kern, 2004). Additional evidence supports social skills instruction for individuals with lower incidence disabilities, such as traumatic brain injury (Dykeman, 2003), schizophrenia (Kurtz & Mueser, 2008), and Asperger's syndrome (Lopata, Thomeer, Volker, & Nida, 2006; Tse, Strulovitch, Tagalakis, Meng, & Fombonee, 2007).

A Strategy to Help Prevent Violence and Aggression

The literature related to safe school environments (Public Health Service, 2001; Nickerson & Martens, 2008; Goldstein, Young, & Boyd, 2008; Johnson, 2009) clearly suggests that schools need to address the increase in school violence by teaching students prosocial ways of resolving conflict, proactive problem solving, and the social skills necessary to enhance self-esteem and engender a sense of belonging. Aggressive children, for example, learn quickly and at an early age that they can get what they want by hitting, pushing, biting, and so forth. Because aggression is a remarkably stable behavior and is unlikely to change without intervention, alternatives to aggression need to be taught early. Skillstreaming is an effective method of doing just that.

SKILLS FOR ADOLESCENTS

The 50 Skillstreaming skills listed in Table 1 are derived from a number of sources. Some skills come from examination of educational and psychological studies yielding information on which behaviors constitute successful adolescent functioning in school, at home, with peers, and so forth. These skills include those critical for school success (Lane, Wehby, & Cooley, 2006), social success (Chen, 2006; Spivack & Shure, 1974), and reducing competing problem behavior such as anger and aggression (Coie & Kupersmidt, 1983; Meier, DiPerna, & Oster, 2006). Direct observation of youngsters in various classroom and other real-life settings is a second source. Leaders and group members in the many Skillstreaming groups conducted thus far have been a particularly valuable fund of information.

INCLUDED IN THIS BOOK

This book provides a clear guide to understanding and using the Skillstreaming program with adolescents, organized into two parts. Part 1 includes chapters devoted to program content and implementation. Part 2 provides skill outlines and homework reports for each of the 50 skills in the curriculum.

Chapter 1, "Effective Skillstreaming Arrangements," describes the procedures necessary to plan and begin Skillstreaming with adolescents. Discussion concerns specific arrangements to maximize the effectiveness of Skillstreaming instruction and the settings in which it occurs. Specifically discussed are group leader selection and preparation; student selection and grouping; the role of support staff and parents in instruction; and specific instructional concerns such as skill selection, setting, materials, and instructional variations.

More than 30 years of research supports the individual components of modeling, role-play (behavioral rehearsal), feedback, and generalization training, as well as the positive results when the four components are implemented together. Chapter 2, "Skillstreaming Teaching Procedures," examines these four core teaching procedures of Skillstreaming, along with the nine-step sequence constituting the Skillstreaming teaching method.

Chapter 3, "Sample Skillstreaming Session," offers an edited transcript of an introductory Skillstreaming session. This transcript depicts the leaders introducing students to the group's purpose and procedures and follows the Skillstreaming teaching procedures discussed in chapter 2. The skill used for instruction is Dealing with Group Pressure (Skill 42).

A challenge in intervention work is to match the intensity of the group member's need to the type and amount of intervention. Chapter 4, "Refining Skill Use," describes factors that increase the effectiveness of Skillstreaming, as well as other skill-building strategies that may be incorporated for students with more intense behavioral concerns. Real-world use of this skill curriculum, especially in the face of difficult and challenging interpersonal circumstances, will require that students be skilled in employing skill sequences and combinations, also described in this chapter.

As evidence regarding Skillstreaming's effectiveness has accumulated, it has become clear that skill acquisition is a reliable finding. The main concern of any teaching effort is not how students perform in the teaching setting but how well they perform in their real lives. Chapter 5, "Enhancing Skill Generalization," examines approaches to improve transfer and maintenance of skill learning.

Chapter 6, "Managing Behavioral Concerns," addresses issues in the group reflecting deficient motivation and heightened resistance and describes a framework of universal, targeted, and individual strategies for enhancing motiva-

Table 1: Skillstreaming Curriculum for Adolescents

Group I: Beginning Social Skills

1. Listening
2. Starting a Conversation
3. Having a Conversation
4. Asking a Question
5. Saying Thank You
6. Introducing Yourself
7. Introducing Other People
8. Giving a Compliment

Group II: Advanced Social Skills

9. Asking for Help
10. Joining In
11. Giving Instructions
12. Following Instructions
13. Apologizing
14. Convincing Others

Group III: Skills for Dealing with Feelings

15. Knowing Your Feelings
16. Expressing Your Feelings
17. Understanding the Feelings of Others
18. Dealing with Someone Else's Anger
19. Expressing Affection
20. Dealing with Fear
21. Rewarding Yourself

Group IV: Skill Alternatives to Aggression

22. Asking Permission
23. Sharing Something
24. Helping Others

25. Negotiating
26. Using Self-Control
27. Standing Up for Your Rights
28. Responding to Teasing
29. Avoiding Trouble with Others
30. Keeping Out of Fights

Group V: Skills for Dealing with Stress

31. Making a Complaint
32. Answering a Complaint
33. Being a Good Sport
34. Dealing with Embarrassment
35. Dealing with Being Left Out
36. Standing Up for a Friend
37. Responding to Persuasion
38. Responding to Failure
39. Dealing with Contradictory Messages
40. Dealing with an Accusation
41. Getting Ready for a Difficult Conversation
42. Dealing with Group Pressure

Group VI: Planning Skills

43. Deciding on Something to Do
44. Deciding What Caused a Problem
45. Setting a Goal
46. Deciding on Your Abilities
47. Gathering Information
48. Arranging Problems by Importance
49. Making a Decision
50. Concentrating on a Task

tion and reducing resistance. Examination of individual strategies includes discussion of functional behavioral assessment (FBA) and steps in creating a behavior intervention plan (BIP).

Establishing positive relationships between families and the school is necessary to improve student behavior, as well as academic skills. A positive working relationship with parents is important to Skillstreaming success. Therefore, this is the subject of chapter 7, "Building Positive Relationships with Parents."

Finally, chapter 8, "Skillstreaming in the School Context" reviews issues surrounding school violence and discusses Skillstreaming as a viable schoolwide intervention for reducing aggression and other behavior problems in schools. Specifically examined are such topics as integrating Skillstreaming in the curriculum and the role of Skillstreaming as it relates to inclusion, multitiered systems of support, Positive Behavior Intervention and Support (PBIS), and Response to Intervention (RTI).

Following these chapters, Part 2 presents Skillstreaming's 50 skills for the adolescent child. Provided for each skill are a skill outline and two different homework reports. The skill outline includes the behavioral steps of the skill, notes for group leaders further explaining the steps, suggested situations for modeling displays, and related skill-supporting activities. Outlines and reports may be reproduced from this book or printed from the accompanying CD.

Three appendixes complete the book. Appendix A includes forms helpful in running the program in addition to the skill outlines and homework reports included in Part 2. These may be photocopied or printed from the CD at the back of this book. Recent research has pointed to the need to monitor the consistency and accuracy of program implementation. Appendix B therefore includes implementation checklists for leaders and those who supervise them, as well as for ensuring generalization integrity. Appendix C examines behavior management techniques based on behavior modification principles helpful in the Skillstreaming group and in general.

PART I

Skillstreaming Program Content and Implementation

CHAPTER 1

Effective Skillstreaming Arrangements

This chapter describes specific arrangements to organize and maximize the effectiveness of the Skillstreaming instructional environment. In particular, discussion concerns group leader selection and preparation; student selection, grouping, and preparation; the role of support staff and parents; specific instructional concerns such as skill selection and negotiation, setting, and materials; and instructional variations.

GROUP LEADER SELECTION AND PREPARATION

Who is the ideal Skillstreaming group leader? In the decades since Skillstreaming began, hundreds of persons with a wide variety of backgrounds and credentials have served as effective leaders. Teachers, counselors, and psychologists in school settings; youth care workers in delinquency centers; social workers in mental health and other community agencies; and correctional officers in prisons are primary examples.

Qualities of Effective Leaders

Four related qualities seem to characterize effective leaders. First, they are at ease with adolescents and comfortable working with them in groups—whether doing Skillstreaming or other activities. The concerns youth share are taken seriously; group members are listened to respectfully and never looked down on. In short, whether dealing with youth individually or as a group,

skilled leaders show sensitivity to the fact that adolescence is a stormy time of life composed of unpredictable expressions of both adult and childlike behaviors.

At times this mix of youthful qualities causes problems manifested in Skillstreaming groups in aggressive, resistive, or otherwise difficult behaviors. When these behaviors occur, the skilled group leader is able to respond effectively. Chapter 6 presents techniques for avoiding and reducing such problem behaviors. Effective leaders are competent in the use of these techniques, provide consequences fairly, and are able to maintain the skills training agenda of the group.

The third quality of effective Skillstreaming group leaders is that they deliver the skills training agenda well. They are competent teachers whether or not they possess formal teaching credentials. Their teaching styles are alive, energetic, and responsive to different learning styles. The content of lessons and skill modeling displays is clear and relevant to participants' real-world needs and aspirations. They are able to work with individual group members during sessions without losing the group-oriented focus of Skillstreaming. There is little downtime, transitions are made easily, and, in a variety of ways, the leader communicates a "can do" sense of positive expectancy.

The ideal Skillstreaming leader not only is sensitive to the needs of adolescents, possesses techniques to manage group instruction, and is a skilled teacher but is also motivated to implement the Skillstreaming teaching agenda as it is designed. Although some flexibility in Skillstreaming delivery is recommended to individualize the agenda to the particular student needs, program components must be implemented consistently and comprehensively. This fourth quality, motivation to follow the training protocol, is necessary to ensure implementation integrity. If the leader is mandated by someone else to provide Skillstreaming instruction and does not believe in its effectiveness, implementation integrity and student improvement will suffer. Motivation may be increased by providing leaders with the background and rationale for Skillstreaming presented in the introduction and by developing knowledge and skill in program implementation.

Leader Preparation

Preparation for the role of effective leader of Skillstreaming groups optimally follows an apprenticeship training sequence. Prospective leaders must first familiarize themselves with the procedures and content of the Skillstreaming method. Reading this program book is a good first step. *The Skillstreaming Video* (Goldstein & McGinnis, 1988) is helpful as an adjunct training tool. At this stage in the dissemination of Skillstreaming, competent and experienced trainers regularly employ the method in schools and other locations in the United States and other countries. Observing an ongoing Skillstreaming group, discussing implementation with an experienced group leader, or attending a workshop provided by an expert trainer will augment the training materials.

Following provision of information from text, video, and/or observation, a good next step in leader training is participation in a mock Skillstreaming group led by experienced trainers and made up of leaders-to-be taking on the role of adolescent group members. After one or more such role-play training opportunities, the prospective leader can take part in an actual adolescent group as an observer, then co-lead such a group with the experienced lead, and, finally, lead the group alone or as part of a pair of apprentice leaders while the experienced leader observes. This incremental training sequence has proven to be a most satisfactory means for training Skillstreaming group leaders.

Cultural Compatibility

Which specific behaviors define a given Skillstreaming skill, which skills are optimal for use in any given setting, and the very teaching–learning processes by which such skills may best be acquired vary from culture to culture. Culture may be defined by geography, ethnicity, nationality, social class, gender, sexual orientation, age, or some combination thereof. And "Cultural proficiency is a way of being that allows individuals and organizations to interact effectively with people who differ from them" (Robins, Lindsey, Lindsey, & Terrell, 2006, p. 2). For Skillstreaming to be meaningful, it must be viewed in a multicultural context and practiced in a manner responsive to such a context. With the increase in diversity in our country, Perea (2004) has accurately observed that there is no longer a single American culture to assimilate into.

When leader and participant are members of different cultural groups, identities, definitions, and prescriptions may conflict. Training goals may fail to be met. Cartledge and Johnson (1997) state this concern well:

> Cultural differences may cause children from diverse backgrounds to respond to environmental events in different or nonproductive ways and cause their actions to be misperceived by peers and adults who do not share the same cultural orientation. School personnel are challenged to interpret accurately the behaviors of culturally different learners, to distinguish social skill differences from deficits, and to employ instructional strategies effective in helping those learners maximize their schooling experiences. (p. 407)

Teachers and other group leaders must be aware of cultural differences so they can determine which behaviors are in actuality social skills deficits and which behaviors are a part of the child's culture and should either be appreciated as they are displayed or modified according to specific situations (Cartledge & Lo, 2006; Cartledge & Milburn, 1996). Typical examples of such differences include acceptability of assertiveness and nonverbal communication. For example, children from African American backgrounds tend to be more assertive, whereas those from Hispanic American, Native American, and Asian American backgrounds tend to be more passive. Anglo American students need more physical space between speakers than do the other groups (Elksnin & Elksnin, 2000). When teacher and student are members of or are only minimally familiar with different cultural groups, definitions and prescriptions may conflict. Actions may be misperceived (Cartledge & Kourea, 2008). Learning goals may not be met. For example, youth may engage in verbal bantering that appears to observers from a different cultural orientation to be aggressive. Yet these behaviors may be common and acceptable in their culture. In such an instance, the behaviors themselves do not need to be changed; instead, instructional emphasis may need to focus on when and where such verbal exchanges are appropriate. When we fail to address cultural differences, students certainly suffer. For instance, African American students are more frequently perceived by educators to have social difficulties (Harry & Klingner, 2006) and are more often identified for special education (Donovan & Cross, 2002) than are other students.

Cartledge and Feng (1996) encourage teachers to "validate cultural background, making sure learners understand that certain situations will call for different responses, not that their ways of doing things are inferior" (p. 112). Classrooms in this country are increasingly characterized by different languages, cultures, and learning styles. To reach all students, administrators and teachers

will to the degree possible employ materials that are consistent with a diversity of backgrounds and learning styles (i.e., "appropriate") and that have been selected in active and continuing consultation with persons representing the cultural groups concerned (i.e., "appreciative").

Appropriate and appreciative programming also applies to interventions designed to reduce student aggression. In discussing social skills interventions and what educators can do to interact with a culturally diverse student population, Cartledge and Johnson (1997) state:

> Social skill interventions are not to be viewed as a means for controlling students for the comfort of teachers or for homogenizing students so they conform to some middle-class prototype designated by the majority group in this society. Inherent in the concept of culturally-relevant social skill instruction is a reciprocal process where the educator: (a) learns to respect the learner's cultural background, (b) encourages the learner to appreciate the richness of this culture, (c) when needed, helps the learner to acquire additional or alternative behaviors as demanded by the social situation, and (d) similarly employs and practices the taught behaviors. (p. 404)

Leader knowledge, skill, and sensitivity will be required if responsive assistance is to be provided. Culturally proficient instructional strategies may include multiple response techniques, appropriate pacing, establishing a community of learners, use of models from the learner's cultural group, incorporating the learner's language into instructional scripts, and involving parents in support of the instruction (Cartledge & Kourea, 2008).

Leader Motivation

What is the best way to motivate potential leaders to participate in this training effort? After all, most teachers and other professionals working with unskilled and often aggressive adolescents are frequently overworked, underpaid, and overwhelmed by other interventions they are urged to implement. It is the rare school or other institution that is able or willing to pay staff for participation in activities such as Skillstreaming. Other forms of external reward or recognition—titles, awards, compensatory time, or relief from other duties—are similarly uncommon. In the final analysis, volunteering to learn this approach is most typically motivated by the prospective leader's desire to enhance his or her own level of competence and be more helpful to the adolescents for whom he or she is responsible. In the absence of external rewards, internal goals usually drive the decision to participate.

PARTICIPANT SELECTION AND GROUPING, PREPARATION, AND MOTIVATION

Skillstreaming teaches an extended curriculum of interpersonal, aggression management, and related skills to youth who are weak or lacking in these competencies. Although in the present book we emphasize program use with youth who frequently employ aggressive behaviors, in practice in schools and elsewhere Skillstreaming has been successful with adolescents having other types of skill deficiencies: shy or withdrawn teenagers, those who are immature, those who have developmental delays, and others harder to categorize but who display nonaggressive inadequacies in their interpersonal skill attempts.

Participant Selection and Grouping

The core assessment task in screening adolescents for participation is determining their degree of skill proficiency and deficiency. Those already relatively competent in the skill curriculum are excluded; those deficient in what Skillstreaming is prepared to teach are included. This selection process may make use of a number of assessment techniques—interviews, sociometric procedures, skill games, trial groups, direct observation, and skill checklists.

Direct observation and skill checklists are most helpful. Direct observation is especially valuable if the group leaders (teachers, youth

care workers, etc.) are the same persons who are with the youth all day and who routinely see them in interaction with others. In such circumstances, behavior observations can be frequent, take place in the youngster's natural environment, and, because skill deficiencies are often situation specific, reflect each youth's skill competence across peers, adults, challenges, times, and physical conditions. In other words, when the Skillstreaming leader is also in a position to observe behavior, a valuable sample of observational opportunities becomes available.

Adequate assessment is, in addition, both multimodal and multisource. *Multimodal* means that more than one type of assessment approach (such as observation) is employed to minimize assessment biases associated with the type of measure being administered. Checklists in versions for teacher, parent, and student (see Appendix A) are a straightforward screening and selection device, on which all 50 Skillstreaming skills are listed and defined. It is a frequency-of-use response format, on which the rater simply circles a number corresponding to "almost never," "seldom," "sometimes," "often," or "almost always."

Multisource assessment means that more than one type of person is asked to complete a checklist for each youth to minimize assessment biases associated with the rater. In most Skillstreaming programs, assessments involve each youth's teacher and parent, as well as the youth himself or herself. In some instances, siblings, peers, or other significant adults have been involved. In carrying out multisource assessments, it is common for persons such as teachers and parents to report considerably more skill deficiency for the youth than does the youth. Teacher and mom or dad may circle "almost never" or "seldom" for 25 skills when the youth does so for only 6 or 7. Whether such a discrepancy reflects overconfidence, denial, blaming others, or some other process in the youth's self-perception, it is still important to assess each youth's perspective because, as discussed shortly, teaching participants the skills in which *they* feel they are deficient has proven to be a successful motivational tactic.

Once selected for program participation, how are youth grouped? Two grouping criteria are valuable. The first is *shared skill deficiency*—in other words, grouping youth together who share similar skill deficiencies and skill deficiency patterns. The Grouping Chart included in Appendix A can be used to summarize skill scores across all Skillstreaming skills for entire classes, units, or other large groups of individuals and is helpful in identifying shared skill deficiencies. The second grouping criterion is responsive to the generalization-enhancing principle of *identical elements,* discussed in depth in chapter 5, which examines means for facilitating generalization. Briefly, this principle states that the greater the similarity between training session and real-world setting in which the youth can use the skill, the greater the likelihood of transfer of training effects. One means of maximizing transfer is having the same people involved—in other words, placing in the same Skillstreaming group adolescents from the same class, living unit, neighborhood, and the like. In short, if they live together, hang around together, even fight together, put them in the same group together.

Participant Preparation

Once participants are selected and grouped, the next task is preparing them for Skillstreaming participation. Such efforts are conducted first individually, then repeated as appropriate in the group context as the youth come together for the first group meetings. Such structuring typically includes discussion of the group's purpose, procedures, rules, and any incentive system that may be in place.

Purpose

The leader describes the purposes of the Skillstreaming group as they relate to the youth's skill deficits. For example, the group leader might say, "Remember last week, when you got into a fight with Russ and got two days in-school suspension? Well, in these meetings you'll be taught skills to help you keep out of that kind of trouble and stay out of in-school suspension." Note how a statement such as this can serve both group preparatory and motivational purposes.

Procedures

The leader next outlines the Skillstreaming process and sessions, saying something like the following:

> To learn how to handle such difficult situations well, we'll first show you some good examples of the skills needed for that purpose, then you and the other members of your group will take turns trying it here. Then we'll all let each other know how well we did in our rehearsals. Finally, you'll have a chance to go practice each skill on your own, where and when you need it.

This brief structuring statement is only an introduction to Skillstreaming's modeling, role-play, feedback, and generalization procedures. Group members will understand the full nature of sessions much better once they have participated in a round or two of actual skills training.

Group Rules and Incentive System

Skillstreaming depends not only on teaching procedures and content but also on core qualities of the group itself. Is it a safe place, one free of put-downs, intimidation, and even subtle bullying? In addition to being competent teachers, are leaders also competent protectors? Has the group come up with a useful set of operating rules, and are members functioning in accord with them? No matter how well crafted the modeling displays, how true-to-life the role-plays, and how accurate the feedback, if participants feel threatened, skill learning will not go forward. It is highly desirable that each group's rules be established by its own members. Ownership enhances compliance. In doing so, the group leader may wish to suggest that the group consider such matters as attendance, participation, confidentiality, management of disagreements, and any other issues unique to the particular setting. Some "rules for the use of rules" are described in chapter 6.

If an incentive or level system of any kind is in place, the leader explains the tangible or token rewards that are its currency, as well as the specific rules by which they may be gained or lost. Details can be provided at the first group meeting.

Participant Motivation

Motivating attendance and meaningful participation in Skillstreaming is sometimes not an easy task. Many of the youths offered the opportunity to participate in Skillstreaming—a technique for training *prosocial* skills—are highly competent in the regular use of *antisocial* behavior. Further, their antisocial behavior is frequently encouraged, supported, and rewarded by significant people in their lives—family, peers, and others.

Extrinsic and Intrinsic Motivation

Two types of motivation are relevant to the discussion: extrinsic and intrinsic. *Extrinsic motivators* are tangible rewards provided contingent upon performance of desired behaviors. In the early years of the behavior modification movement, the use of extrinsic and tangible motivators was often denounced as "bribery." The youth, it was asserted, should *want* to engage in the desired behavior for its own sake and not for the external rewards it would bring. Most now agree that use of a combination of external and internal motivators is typically the most effective strategy.

Tangible motivators are, in fact, widely used in American schools and other institutions and facilities for adolescents. The points, checks, stars, and stickers of elementary school may have given way to pizza parties, movie privileges, club clothing, special activities, or other events or objects, but the use of extrinsic rewards is widespread. They seem especially useful in eliciting initial involvement, when the Skillstreaming program is still unfamiliar.

Although extrinsic incentives may be necessary to manage the Skillstreaming group in its initial stages, resting one's motivational effort strictly on a foundation of external rewards—whether in the form of tangible reinforcers, a token economy, a level system, or other extrinsic incentives—is insufficient over time. In Skillstreaming, substantial payoffs are inherent in the skills themselves, especially those group members select and use successfully in their real-world settings.

Skill Negotiation

Experience suggests that one of the most potent intrinsic motivators is negotiation of the skill curriculum. Many of the youths for whom Skillstreaming is appropriate chronically ascribe responsibility for their antisocial acts to others. They externalize; rarely is something *their* fault. As noted earlier, a teacher or parent may indicate on the checklist that the youth seldom or almost never uses two or three *dozen* of the prosocial skills listed. Yet the youth checks but a few of the skills as deficient! However inaccurate and inadequate such a self-picture may be, the group leader's knowledge of those self-admitted deficiencies is golden. Teaching these skills (in addition to those selected by the leader) has proven to be especially motivating. In a "consumer model," the "customer" is provided with what he or she feels is most needed. As frequently as every other Skillstreaming session, we begin the meeting not by announcing and enacting a modeling display for a skill chosen by leaders but instead with "How is it going?" or "What's been happening to you all since our last meeting?"

Out of such openings often comes information about difficulties at home, in school, on the street, or elsewhere—difficulties that can be resolved by the Skillstreaming skill leaders and group members then jointly select and portray. The earlier in the group's life such negotiation of the curriculum commences the better. In fact, in the group's very first session, when open discussion of life difficulties by group members may still be uncomfortable, the leader can initiate such negotiation by tallying the skills checked on the Participant Checklist by *all* the members of the group, without revealing who checked which ones, and then by teaching the one or ones checked most often.

Giving youth the opportunity to negotiate the curriculum and select the skills *they* feel they need is a major step toward motivating positive attendance and participation. When participant-selected (and, perhaps to a lesser degree, leader-selected) skills yield positive interpersonal outcomes in interactions with family, peers, or significant others, motivation is further enhanced.

Provision of Alternatives

In addition to regular negotiation of the skill curriculum, a second tactic helps increase intrinsic motivation. It is to communicate to group members, both during the introduction to the Skillstreaming process and periodically as sessions unfold, that the goal of Skillstreaming is to teach alternatives, not substitutes. Many of the adolescents referred to a Skillstreaming program have been reprimanded and punished perhaps hundreds of times for behaviors their parents, teachers, or others deemed inappropriate. In one or another way, they have been told, "Stop doing that, and do this *instead!*"

Although it is certainly desirable to decrease a youth's antisocial or other inappropriate behavior, a more successful means of doing this is to provide alternatives by expanding the youth's behavioral repertoire—the range of possible responses available. This is the goal of Skillstreaming. If, for example, someone falsely accuses the youth of stealing something and the only response the youth has learned, practiced, and been rewarded for is to lash out, he or she will do so again. The youth has, in effect, no choice because there are no choices. Skillstreaming teaches the youth that other responses to an accusation include explanation,

investigation, negotiation, walking away, and other means. The fact that reprimands and punishment have had to be used hundreds of times in the past is testimony to their lack of enduring success. However, if the youth has skill response choices, some of the time he or she is likely to use them.

The following excerpt shows a way to convey the idea that alternatives are available to a Skillstreaming group.

Participant: This won't work.

Leader: What do you mean, it won't work?

Participant: Come on, get real, get out of that university, get out on the street more. We can negotiate up the wazoo in here, but you can't negotiate out on the street. Out on the street, you got to hit the guy before he hits you.

Leader: Now wait a second—what do you think we're doing in here? We're not teaching substitutes, we're teaching alternatives.

Participant: I don't understand those words.

Leader: All right, I'll give you a sports example. There's a team with a good quarterback, the only quarterback on the team, but for one reason or another, injury or whatever, one particular Sunday he can't throw long and he can't run. All he's got working for him is his short pass, and he's good at it. So on the first down, he goes out and he throws that short pass, and it's good. Same thing on the second down, another good short pass, but after that the defense in their huddle say, "Two short passes on two plays—maybe that's all the guy's got today. Let's look for it." Third down he throws it again, they knock it down. Fourth down, it's his only play, he throws it again and they intercept it. You're like that quarterback. You have only one play—it's your fist. You've got a fist in every pocket. Someone looks at you, you hit them, they don't look at you, you hit them. They talk to you, you hit them, they don't talk to you, you hit them. That's why you've been in so much trouble. How about we try to help you become like a skilled quarterback, who has a variety of plays? Now you keep your fists, and if you need to hit someone, you hit them. I wish you wouldn't, but I can't follow you around to stop you, and I'm not going to teach you how to hit. You're already better at that than I am. But keep the fist in one pocket only instead of every pocket. Back here, in the back pocket, another play. It's called negotiation. We'll not only teach you how to do it, but as a group we'll figure out where and when it fits. And back here, a miracle play. I think you're going to call it a miracle play—I actually wouldn't. I think you'll call it a miracle play because once I tell you what it is you're going to say to me it's a miracle if I can do that. But you know what, I've seen kids do it, and like any good football play, it fits some situations and it doesn't fit others. It's called walking away without losing face. There are times that adolescents like you can do it. Let's figure out together where and when. And in the fourth pocket, yet another play. So like a good quarterback, you have a variety of plays.

SUPPORT STAFF AND PROGRAM COORDINATOR ROLES

Support Staff

Skillstreaming training never goes forward in isolation: Group leaders and groups are part of a school, a delinquency center, a residential facility, or some other institution peopled by both youth and staff—teachers, youth care workers, and so forth. Means for preparing staff members who will serve as Skillstreaming trainers have been described. What about the rest of the staff?

Programs that try to change the behavior of aggressive adolescents often succeed only at a certain time and in a certain place. That is, the program works but only at or shortly after the time it occurred and only in the same place where it occurred. However, a few weeks later or when in the schoolyard, out on a field trip, home visit, or elsewhere outside the school, a youth who has mastered skills in group may be as aggressive and prosocially unskilled as ever. Temporary success followed by a relapse to old, negative ways of behaving is a failure of generalization. Generalization failures are much more the rule than the exception with aggressive youth. During Skillstreaming, adolescents receive a great deal of support, enthusiasm, encouragement, and reward for their efforts. Between sessions and after the program terminates, many may receive very little support, reward, or other positive response.

The common failure of generalization is not surprising. Yet this outcome can be minimized. Newly learned and fragile skills need not fade away after Skillstreaming. If attempts by adolescents to use such skills in the real world are met with success—support, enthusiasm, encouragement, reward—skill use will be much more likely to continue. Teachers, school staff, community workers, parents, friends, peers, and employers are in an ideal position to provide support and reward. In the following ways, these individuals can serve in the powerful role of *transfer coach,* helping make sure that the Skillstreaming curriculum turns into long-term, even permanent learning.

Prompting

Under the pressure of real-life situations both in and out of school, adolescents may forget all or part of the Skillstreaming skills they learned earlier. If their anxiety is not too great or their forgetting too complete, prompting may help them perform the skill correctly. Prompting involves reminding the person of *what* to do (the skill), *how* to do it (the steps), *when* to do it (now or the next time the situation occurs), *where* to do it (and where not to), and reasons to use the skill here and now (describing the positive outcomes expected).

Encouraging

Offering encouragement to adolescents to use a skill assumes they know it well enough (thus, they do not need prompting) but are reluctant to use it. In other words, encouragement may be necessary when the problem is lack of motivation rather than lack of knowledge. Encouragement can often best be given by gently urging youth to try using what they know, by showing enthusiasm for the skill being used, and by communicating optimism about the likely positive outcome of skill use.

Reassuring

For particularly anxious youth, skill attempts will be more likely to occur if the threat of failure is reduced. Reassurance is often an effective threat reduction technique: "You can do it," "I'll be there to help if you need it," and "You've used the other skills well, so I think you'll do fine with this one, too" are examples of the kinds of reassuring statements the transfer coach can provide.

Rewarding

The most important contribution by far that the transfer coach can make is to provide or help someone else provide rewards for using a skill

correctly. Rewards may take the form of approval, praise, or compliments, or they may consist of special privileges, points, tokens, recognition, or other reinforcers built into a behavior management system. All of these rewards will increase the likelihood of continued skill use in new settings and at later times. The most powerful reward that can be offered is the success of the skill itself. If a youth prepares for a stressful conversation and the conversation then goes well, the successful conversation itself will help the skill transfer more than any external reward can. The same conclusion—that success increases transfer—applies to all of the Skillstreaming skills. Whenever possible, it is important to reward a youth's skill use by promoting skill success. Respond positively to a complaint if it is reasonable and try to have others also respond positively. Try to react with whatever behaviors signal awareness of effective and appropriate skill use. If you do so and encourage other important people in the adolescent's environment to do so, fragile skills will become lasting skills, and Skillstreaming will have been successful.

Program Coordinator

Even if teachers, students, and support staff are prepared and motivated to begin a Skillstreaming program, the participation of one more professional helps ensure a successful outcome. Many effective programs involve the appointment of a program coordinator or master teacher. It is unfortunately common for Skillstreaming programs to begin with appropriate organization, good intentions, and adequate enthusiasm only to wind up being discarded a few months later because of a lack of oversight. The barrage of other responsibilities often placed on teachers and other frontline staff makes intervention programs more likely to fail in the absence of such guidance.

The program coordinator or master teacher should be well versed in both Skillstreaming and program management. His or her responsibilities may include providing staff development, observing sessions, monitoring schoolwide progress, setting up specific generalization-increasing efforts, motivating staff, facilitating the gathering and distribution of materials, and handling the many other details on which program success depends.

SKILLSTREAMING GROUP MECHANICS

The following "nuts and bolts" issues—essentially the mechanics of the Skillstreaming group—deserve consideration.

Number of Leaders

Though many Skillstreaming groups have been effectively led by one trainer alone, where possible, two trainers should work together. Skill-deficient adolescents are often quite proficient in generating behavior management problems that make successful instruction difficult. To arrange and conduct a role-play between two youths while at the same time overseeing the attention of a half dozen easily distractible others is a challenge for even the most experienced teacher. A much better arrangement involves one leader in front of the group, guiding the role-play, the second sitting in the group, preferably next to the youth or youths most likely to behave disruptively. In school settings in which two instructors are not available for group co-leadership, the effective use of teacher aides, parents, volunteers, or other adults has been reported. Use of two leaders may be particularly valuable in the early sessions of a Skillstreaming group. As group members become more familiar with the group's required activities, conducting sessions with one leader may become more feasible.

Number of Group Members

Typically, the Skillstreaming session lasts a class period—perhaps 45 to 50 minutes. It is common that a modeling display by the leaders and role-plays by most or all of the six to eight group members can be accomplished within that time period. Though this is our usual recommended group size, smaller numbers (as low as two) may be necessary, such as when the youth involved are very aggressive and out of control. Here, one would start with a smaller group size and slowly increase membership—perhaps at the rate of one new member per week—as the group comes under control and a positive group culture begins to build. At other times, namely, the successful management of larger groups is the challenge. If a class or unit consists of a dozen youth, one might conduct a group of six to eight while another group of similar size observes "fishbowl style." The following week, they reverse. But what if it is a class or unit of 20 to 25 or more youths? Here the problem is greater. Leaders should avoid putting on modeling displays to groups this large without providing following role-play opportunities. Skillstreaming is an experiential activity; the rehearsal of the role-playing is vital. In large groups, some leaders have created subgroups of five or six and had each subgroup role-play simultaneously as the two leaders rotate from subgroup to subgroup. Others have gotten additional help for this purpose—two aides, two parent volunteers, and so forth. Yet others have tried with some success to work with the larger group as a whole, using the standard Skillstreaming procedures but seeing to it that group members all have some role in the process. This may be attempted by having several group members serve as co-actors in the role-play; by instructing members who are not role-playing to watch for and give feedback on the main actor's performance of specific skill steps; and by assigning other helper roles (e.g., pointing to skill steps on the skill poster as the role-play unfolds, helping arrange props to make the role-play more realistic). Still other leaders have chosen to provide Skillstreaming for only the half dozen or so most skill-deficient youth in the larger group. Skillstreaming, like so much else in schools and other institutions, often is the doing of the possible.

Session Frequency

For Skillstreaming sessions to be more than an in-group exercise, participants must have the time and opportunity to try out the skills they have role-played outside the group. These practice or homework attempts are more likely to occur if ample time is provided between sessions. A schedule of two sessions per week is optimal.

Program Duration

Skillstreaming programs have lasted as briefly as two days, as long as three years, and just about all lengths in between. The two-day programs generally are in in-school detention centers, in which students are taught a single skill during their brief stay. Three-year and other lengthy programs are open Skillstreaming groups, adding new members one at a time as older members "graduate," drop out, or otherwise leave. A more typical program duration is the school year.

A second way of defining duration of program, beyond days or months of meetings, is by number of skills taught. The goal of Skillstreaming is teaching prosocial skills in such a manner that the skills are not only learned (acquired) but also used (performed) in an effective manner, in a variety of settings, for an enduring period of time. It most definitely is not a curriculum to charge through to get to its end. Although the full curriculum consists of 50 skills, no expectation exists that all will be taught in any given Skillstreaming group. Because the goal is to teach only skills in which group members are deficient and that will be useful in their daily lives, a full curriculum for some groups may be only a few skills. For other groups, it may be several skills.

Whether few or several members are involved, group leaders should not move on to a second skill until the first is well learned (as evidenced by successful role-play within the group) and regularly performed (as evidenced by successful homework outside the group). These training goals will usually require that the same skill be taught (modeling, role-playing, etc.) for more than one session. Even if group members express boredom, skills should be taught until they are nearly automatic or "overlearned"—a process described in more detail in chapter 5, dealing with generalization.

Materials Needed

Other than the cost of staff time, Skillstreaming is not an expensive program to implement. Necessary checklists and other program forms are provided in Appendix A and may be reproduced as needed. These materials may also be printed from the CD that accompanies this book.

A whiteboard or easel pad, skill cards listing the skill steps, and skill step posters to hang in the classroom and school are the core materials needed. Preprinted skill cards like the sample shown and skill posters are available from the publisher, but group leaders or group members may also make these cards and posters themselves.

Figure 1: Sample Skill Card

Skill 1

Listening

1. Look at the person who is talking.
2. Think about what is being said.
3. Wait your turn to talk.
4. Say what you want to say.

Physical Arrangements and Placement in the School Curriculum

Figure 2 depicts a common horseshoe-shaped room and furniture arrangement often employed for conducting Skillstreaming sessions.

As noted, mounting an intervention program in a school or other setting is most often the doing of the possible. Class scheduling and administrative and personnel realities must be taken into account and accommodated. These facts of institutional life have resulted in Skill-streaming's taking place at a wide variety of times and locations—from homeroom at the beginning of the day to after-school detention at its end and just about every other possible time in be-tween. The program has been incorporated into social studies, English, physical education, and life skills classes. Other frequent placements have been homeroom, resource room, in-school sus-pension, after-school detention, and more.

Naming the Group

What should the Skillstreaming group be called? Most often, it is just called "Skillstream-ing." But concerns expressed in the education-al literature on the negative effects of labeling children and adolescents should be taken into account. Such effects may occur when young-sters are selected for even benignly titled in-terventions such as Skillstreaming. Some have sought to avoid the labeling problem by re-naming Skillstreaming something even more positive (e.g., Positive Skill Building Group, Fantastics, etc.). This may not solve the prob-lem because youth peer groups are quick to recognize those selected as being singled out for deficit remediation. One way of avoiding the issue entirely is to include *all* members of a given class or unit in the training so that no one is singled out, as has often been done at the preschool and elementary levels.

Figure 2: A Functional Room Arrangement for Skillstreaming

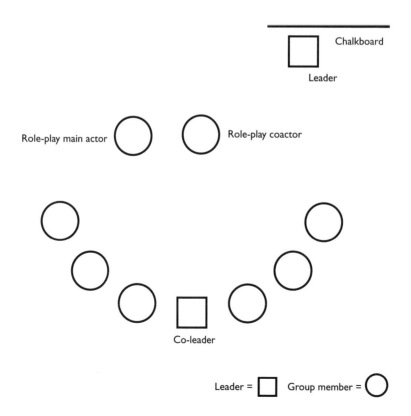

CHAPTER 2

Skillstreaming Teaching Procedures

The four core training procedures that constitute Skillstreaming are described here, along with the sequence of steps illustrating how these procedures are incorporated into instruction. Discussion of methods for ensuring program integrity completes the chapter.

CORE TEACHING PROCEDURES

Modeling

Modeling is defined as learning by imitation. Imitation has been examined in a great deal of research and under many other names: copying, empathic learning, observational learning, identification, vicarious learning, and matched-dependent behavior among them. Research has consistently shown that modeling is an effective and reliable technique for both the rapid learning of new behaviors and the strengthening or weakening of previously learned behaviors.

Three types of learning by modeling have been identified: Observational learning refers to the learning of new behaviors that the person has never performed before. Adolescents are great imitators. Almost weekly, new idioms, new clothing styles, and new ways of walking, dancing, and doing emerge and take hold in the world of adolescence. Many of these events are clear examples of observational learning effects. Inhibitory and disinhibitory effects involve the strengthening or weakening of behaviors previously performed only rarely by the person due to a history of punishment or other negative reactions. Modeling offered by peers is, again, a major source of inhibitory and disinhibitory effects. Youth who know how to be altruistic, sharing, caring, and the like may inhibit such behaviors in the presence of models who are behaving more egocentrically and being rewarded for their egocentric behavior. Aggressive models may also have a disinhibitory effect and cause observing youngsters to engage in aggressive behavior. Behavioral facilitation refers to the performance of previously learned behaviors that are neither new nor a source of potential negative reactions from others. One person buys something he seems to enjoy, so a friend buys one, too. A child deals with a recurring household matter in an effective manner, so a sibling imitates her behavior. A classmate tries talking over a class problem with her teacher; when she succeeds, a second student decides to approach the teacher in a similar way. These are all examples of behavioral facilitation effects.

Behaviors that can be learned, strengthened, weakened, or facilitated through modeling include acting aggressively, helping others, behaving independently, planning careers, becoming emotionally aroused, interacting socially, displaying dependency, exhibiting certain speech patterns, behaving empathically, self-disclosing, and many more. Yet it is also true that most people observe dozens and perhaps hundreds of behaviors every day that they do not imitate. Television, newspapers, and the Internet expose people to very polished, professional modeling displays of someone's buying one product or another, but these observers do not later buy the product. And many people observe expensively produced and expertly acted instructional films, but they remain uninstructed. Apparently, people learn by modeling under some circumstances but not others.

Modeling Enhancers

Laboratory research on modeling has successfully identified modeling enhancers, or circumstances that increase the degree to which learning by imitation occurs. These modeling enhancers are characteristics of the model, the modeling display, or the observer (the learner). These variables affect learning, as does use of a coping model.

Model Characteristics

More effective modeling will occur when the model (the person to be imitated) (a) seems to be highly skilled or expert; (b) is of high status; (c) controls rewards desired by the learner; (d) is of the same sex, approximate age, and social status as the learner; (e) is friendly and helpful; and, of particular importance, (f) is rewarded for the given behaviors. That is, we are all more likely to imitate expert or powerful yet pleasant people who receive rewards for what they are doing, especially when the particular rewards involved are something that we too desire.

Modeling Display Characteristics

More effective modeling will occur when the modeling display shows the behaviors to be imitated (a) in a clear and detailed manner, (b) in the order from least to most difficult behaviors, (c) with enough repetition to make overlearning likely, (d) with as little irrelevant detail as possi-

ble, and (e) performed by several different models rather than a single model.

Observer (learner) characteristics

More effective modeling will occur when the person observing the model is (a) told to imitate the model; (b) similar to the model in background or in attitude toward the skill; (c) friendly toward or likes the model; and, most important, (d) rewarded for performing the modeled behaviors.

Coping model

Further, modeling is more effective when a coping model, or one who struggles a little to achieve the goal of competent skill performance, is presented. If learners perceive the skill is "easy" and can be performed without any feeling, they may be less likely to try the skill when caught up in the emotion of a real-life event. When demonstrating Using Self-Control (Skill 26) or Responding to Teasing (Skill 28), for example, it is important to struggle a bit when performing the behavioral steps. This coping model must be demonstrated in a low-key manner and in an acceptable way so the struggle does not detract from the modeling display. Depicting coping models will further enhance students' ability to identify with the model and will likely give them more courage to try the skill themselves.

Stages of Modeling

The effects of these modeling enhancers, as well as of modeling itself, can be better understood by examining the three stages of learning by modeling.

Attention

Group members cannot learn from watching a model unless they pay attention to the modeling display and, in particular, to the specific behaviors being modeled. Such attention is maximized by eliminating irrelevant detail in the modeling display, minimizing the complexity of the modeled material, making the display vivid, and implementing the modeling enhancers previously described.

Retention

To later reproduce the behaviors a group member has observed, he or she must remember or retain them. Because the behaviors of the modeling display itself are no longer present, retention must occur by memory. Memory is aided if the behaviors displayed are classified or coded. Another name for such coding is covert rehearsal (i.e., reviewing in one's mind the performance of the displayed behaviors). Research has shown, however, that an even more important aid to retention is overt rehearsal. Practice of the specific behavioral steps is crucial for learning and, indeed, is the second major procedure of Skillstreaming, role-playing. It should be noted at this point that the likelihood of retention through either covert or overt rehearsal is greatly aided by rewards provided to both the model and/or the learner.

Reproduction

Researchers interested in human learning have typically distinguished between learning (acquiring or gaining knowledge about how to do something) and performance (doing it). If a person has paid attention and remembered the behaviors shown during the modeling display, it may be said that the person has learned. The main interest, however, is not so much in whether the person can reproduce the behaviors that have been seen but in whether he or she does produce them. As for retention, the likelihood that a person will actually perform a behavior that has been learned will depend mostly on the expectation of a reward for doing so. Expectation of reward has been shown to be determined by the amount, consistency, recency, and frequency of the reward that the group member has observed being provided to the model for performing the desired behavior.

Verbal Mediation

Verbal mediation, or saying aloud what would normally be thought to oneself silently, is a valuable and necessary part of both modeling and role-playing. Saying the steps aloud as the model enacts the behavioral steps demonstrates the cognitive processes underlying skill performance and facilitates learning. For example, in Dealing with an Accusation (Skill 40), the model might say something like "The first step is to think about what the other person has accused me of. My friend just accused me of saying nasty things about her online. I don't know why she would say that. I was online last night, but I didn't say a word about her. The second step is to think about why the other person might have accused you. I was in kind of a bad mood last night because of a fight with my mom. Maybe I did say that Latisha seemed to be ignoring me." And so on. This type of accompanying narration increases the effectiveness of the modeling display (Bandura, 1973), draws attention to the specific skill steps as they are being portrayed, and helps to reduce behaviors or emotions that may compete with skill performance. Self-talk further enhances the effectiveness of the coping model.

Role-Playing

Role-playing has been defined as when an individual is asked to demonstrate specific behaviors not typical for him or her or to respond to certain situations with behaviors within his or her repertoire (Mann, 1956). Learning appears to be improved when the learner has the opportunity and is encouraged to practice, rehearse, or role-play the behaviors and is rewarded for doing so. The use of role-playing to help a person change many types of behavior or attitudes has been a popular and useful approach for many years. However, as for modeling, behavior or attitude change through role-playing will occur and be more lasting only if certain conditions are included in this process. If the role-player has enough information about the content of the role-play to enact it, and if sufficient attention is paid to the factors that enhance its effectiveness, it is more likely that behavior or attitude change will occur. These role-play enhancers include (a) choice on the part of the group member regarding whether to take part in the role-play; (b) public commitment to the behavior; (c) improvisation in enacting the role-played behaviors; and (d) reward, approval, or reinforcement for performing the behaviors.

Seeing the modeling display teaches students what to do, but repeated practice in a variety of contexts is needed to increase skill fluency. However, in most attempts to help a person change behavior, neither modeling alone nor role-playing alone is enough. Combining the two is an improvement, for then the group member knows both what to do and how to do it. But even this combination is insufficient because the group member still needs to know why he or she should behave in new ways. That is, a motivational or incentive component must be added. Performance feedback provides this incentive.

Performance Feedback

Performance feedback involves providing a group member with information on how well he or she has done during role-playing. It may take such forms as constructive suggestions for improvement, coaching, reteaching, material reward, and, especially, social reinforcement such as praise and approval. Social reinforcement has been shown to be an especially potent influence on behavior change. In addition, positive feedback from peers has been shown to increase peer acceptance, as well as appropriate behavior (Jones, Young, & Friman, 2000; Moroz & Jones, 2002; Skinner, Cashwell, & Skinner, 2000).

Peer feedback has been shown to have positive effects on prosocial behavior. For example, Moroz and Jones (2002) implemented a positive peer reporting program that taught students to describe and provide praise to socially isolated classmates during structured sessions. Results showed a decrease in negative behaviors and an increase in positive social interactions in the classroom. Jones et al. (2000) also instructed peers in giving positive feedback to delinquent, socially rejected adolescents. This protocol included looking at the learner, smiling, saying a positive thing the learner did or said, and giving verbal praise. Their results indicated improved peer acceptance for the target youth.

Because peer feedback has been found to be instrumental in improving the behavior of group members, it is an important element in Skillstreaming. To be most effective, group leaders should follow these guidelines:

1. Provide reinforcement only after role-plays that follow the behavioral steps.

2. Provide reinforcement at the earliest appropriate opportunity after role-plays that follow the behavioral steps.

3. Always provide reinforcement to the coactor for being helpful, cooperative, and so forth.

4. Vary the specific content of the reinforcements offered (e.g., praise particular aspects of the performance, such as tone of voice, posture, phrasing) and plan this feedback with the group members prior to the role-play.

5. Provide enough role-playing activity for each group member to have sufficient opportunity to be reinforced.

6. Provide reinforcement in an amount consistent with the quality of the given role-play.

7. Provide no reinforcement when the role-play departs significantly from the behavioral steps (except for "trying" in the first session or two).

8. Provide reinforcement for a participant's improvement over previous performances.

The types of feedback group members provide should be planned in advance and include the following four elements:

1. The steps: Does the main actor follow each skill step? How do you know? (for example, "He said it" or "She used thinking aloud to let us know").

2. The way the skill is performed: What were the main actor's nonverbals (facial expres-

sions, distance, gestures, tone of voice)? Did the main actor show concern or empathy for the coactor?

3. Context: Was this skill appropriate to this situation? Was the skill used at a good time, a good place, and with the appropriate person?

4. Coactor: How did the coactor respond? Was this response helpful?

These four feedback elements should be adapted to the age and maturity level of the group members and to their experience giving positive or constructive feedback.

Generalization

The main interest of any intervention program and where most programs fail is not the group member's performance of behaviors during the instruction but to what degree he or she uses newly learned skills in natural settings and experiences improved quality of life. The goal of Skillstreaming is successful social functioning in school, at home, and in other places. Generalization, or use of the skill in a variety of novel situations or environments, assists the individual in identifying where and when skill use is desired or necessary. A variety of generalization and maintenance strategies are suggested in chapter 5.

STEPS IN THE SKILLSTREAMING SESSION

To carry out the modeling, role-playing, performance feedback, and generalization procedures, leaders guide the group through the following nine steps:

▶ Step 1: Define the skill

▶ Step 2: Model the skill

▶ Step 3: Establish participant skill need

▶ Step 4: Select the first role-player

▶ Step 5: Set up the role-play

▶ Step 6: Conduct the role-play

▶ Step 7: Provide performance feedback

▶ Step 8: Select the next role-player

▶ Step 9: Assign skill homework

The following text describes these steps and illustrates the Skillstreaming procedure in operation. Table 2 provides a detailed summary of the steps for ongoing reference.

Step 1: Define the Skill

This session-opening activity is a brief group discussion of the skill to be taught in that meeting. Whether the skill was selected by the leader or through periodic negotiation between leader and group members, helpful in all Skillstreaming groups, this activity is necessary. Its purpose is orientation to both the abstract meaning and concrete examples of the chosen skill. This goal can typically be met quite rapidly, in perhaps a few minutes, and does not require protracted discussion over definitional minutiae. The following dialogue shows a leader briefly defining Skill 19, Expressing Affection.

Leader: OK, let's get started. Today's skill is quite an important one, one that lots of people have trouble doing well—or even at all. It's called Expressing Affection. Can anyone tell me what you think Expressing Affection means? Latoya? Yes, what do you think?

Latoya: Like, when you love somebody.

Leader: Good, a good part of it. Anyone else? Chico, you had your hand up.

Chico: Kissing, hugging.

Leader: OK again. Those are two ways of doing it. Good examples. What is the general idea of what expressing affection means, its definition? Emily?

Emily: Letting someone know how you feel about them, when you feel really good about them.

Table 2: Skillstreaming Session Outline

Step 1: Define the skill

1. Choose skills relevant to the needs of the students as they perceive them.

2. Discuss each skill step and any other relevant information pertaining to each step.

3. Use skill cards and/or poster or whiteboard or easel pad on which the skill and steps are written so all group members can easily see the steps and illustrations.

Step 2: Model the skill

1. Use at least two examples for each skill demonstration.

2. Select situations relevant to the student's real-life circumstances.

3. Use modeling displays that demonstrate all the behavioral steps of the skill in the correct sequence.

4. Use modeling displays that depict only one skill at a time. (All extraneous content should be eliminated.)

5. Show the use of a coping model.

6. Have the model "think aloud" steps that ordinarily would be thought silently.

7. Depict only positive outcomes.

8. Reinforce the model who has used the skill correctly by using praise or encouraging self-reward.

Step 3: Establish participant skill need

1. Elicit from the students specific situations in which the skill could be used or is needed.

2. List the names of the group members. The co-leader may then list the situations identified by each student and record the theme of the role plays.

Step 4: Select the first role-player

1. Select as the main actor a student who describes a situation in his or her own life in which skill use is needed or will be helpful.

2. Provide encouragement and reinforcement for the student's willingness to participate as the main actor.

Step 5: Set up the role-play

1. Have the main actor choose a coactor who reminds him or her most of the other person involved in the problem.

2. Present relevant information surrounding the real event (i.e., describe the physical setting and events preceding the problem).

3. Use props when appropriate.

4. Review skill steps and direct the main actor to look at the skill card or the skill steps on display.

5. Assign the other group participants to watch for specific skill steps.

Step 6: Conduct the role-play

1. Instruct the main actor to "think out loud."

2. As needed, assist the main actor (e.g., point to each behavioral step as the role-play is carried out; have the co-leader, if available, sit among the group members, directing their attention to the role-play).

Step 7: Provide performance feedback

1. Seek feedback from the coactor, observers, leader(s), and main actor, in turn.

2. Provide reinforcement for successful role-plays at the earliest appropriate opportunity.

3. Provide reinforcement to the coactor for being helpful and cooperative.

4. Praise particular aspects of performance (e.g., "You used a brave voice to say that").

5. Provide reinforcement in an amount consistent with the quality of the role-play.

Step 8: Select the next role-player

Ask, "Who would like to go next?"

Step 9: Assign skill homework

1. Assign homework to the main actors who have successfully role-played the skill.

2. Provide the main actors with the appropriate homework report.

3. Discuss with each main actor when, where, and with whom he or she will use the skill in real life.

From *Skillstreaming the Adolescent: A Guide for Teaching Prosocial Skills* (3rd ed.), © 2012 by E. McGinnis, Champaign, IL: Research Press (www.researchpress.com, 800-519-2707).

Leader: Agree. You've given good definitions, all of you. That's the skill we're going to learn today.

At this point, the specific behavioral steps composing the skill are presented and discussed (or reviewed if the skill has been introduced in a previous session). Aspects of how a specific step could best be performed such as looking at the person, speaking in an assertive voice, and giving a brief explanation of the reason for your decision should also be discussed.

Step 2: Model the Skill

In planning and conducting modeling displays, leaders must attend to the specific modeling enhancers that are characteristics of the model and the modeling that make learning most effective for the observer. Displays that relate to the group's real-world concerns will always be most effective, as long as they incorporate the following guidelines:

1. Use at least two examples for each demonstration of a skill. If a skill is used in more than one group meeting, develop two more new modeling displays.

2. Select situations that are relevant to participants' real-life circumstances.

3. The main actor (i.e., the person enacting the behavioral steps of the skill) should be portrayed as a youth reasonably similar in age, socioeconomic background, verbal ability, and other characteristics salient to the group.

4. A coping model should be portrayed with skills that typically elicit strong emotion.

5. The model should "think aloud" what would normally be said to oneself as the modeling display unfolds.

6. All displays should depict positive outcomes. There should always be reinforcement to the model who is using the skill well.

7. All modeling displays should depict all the behavioral steps of the skill being modeled, in the correct sequence, without extraneous or distracting content.

8. Modeling displays should depict only one skill at a time.

The modeling displays should be planned ahead by the group leaders and be brief and clear in their depiction of the skill steps. While the behavioral steps are modeled, it is helpful for the co-leader to point to the steps as the modeling display unfolds. The coactor in the modeling may initially show resistance to the model's performance if doing so enhances a realistic portrayal. For example, when modeling the skill of Dealing With Group Pressure (Skill 42), typically the individual's initial response to resist will likely be met with increased pressure from the group. However, when the model performs the skill steps effectively, the coactor should then show acceptance. At the conclusion of the modeling scenario, the coactor should then be complimented for accepting the decision in a helpful way.

At times it is also useful for the model to "step out of role." Doing so is appropriate when input from the group is desired regarding good alternative actions or when additional explanation of why an action is being taken will contribute to the group's understanding. When stepping out of role, it is helpful to visually depict this change—for example, by physically taking an exaggerated step away from the coactors and facing the group members. Stepping out of role should occur only occasionally and for a brief period in order for the modeling display to clearly illustrate the skill steps.

Step 3: Establish Participant Skill Need

Before group members commence role-playing the skill they have seen modeled, it is necessary to openly discuss each group member's current need for the skill. After all, behavioral rehearsal is the purpose of the role-play—that is, enactment of the skill as it relates to a current or anticipated situation or relationship in the group member's present life, not a situation provided by the leaders or a reenactment of a past problem that is no longer relevant. Skill need may have been established earlier as part of the selection and grouping process. Nonetheless, open discussion in the group is needed to establish relevant and realistic role-plays. Each participant, therefore, is asked in turn to describe briefly where, when, and especially with whom he or she would find it useful to employ the skill just modeled. Questions such as "Can you use this skill at school? At home? With your friends?" and "When is it difficult to use this skill?" are helpful to prompt identification of situations needed in the group members' real lives.

To make effective use of such information, it is often valuable to list on the whiteboard or easel pad at the front of the room each group member's name, the name of the persons with whom the group member wishes to use the skill, and the theme of the role-play associated with that person. Following each situation, the participant should answer "Why is this skill important to you?" Doing so will help all group members reflect on the value of using the skill in a variety of situations. Because an ironclad rule of Skillstreaming is that every participant must role-play every skill, with no exceptions, having such information at hand will be useful if a group member expresses reluctance to participate.

Step 4: Select the First Role-Player

Because all members of the Skillstreaming group role-play each skill, in most instances it is not important who does so first. Typically, the selection process can proceed by the use of volunteers. If for any reason the act of role-playing a particular skill seems threatening to certain group members, it is helpful not to ask them to role-play first or second. Seeing others role-play first can be reassuring and help ease their way into the activity. For some, reluctance may turn into outright resistance and refusal. Means for dealing with such behavior are described at length in chapter 6. Although the "no exceptions" rule still applies, it is generally best to involve reluctant participants in role-playing through support,

encouragement, reassurance, and highlighting the utility of the skill for their own personal needs, rather than through penalties or other coercive means.

Step 5: Set Up the Role-Play

Once a group member has described a real-life situation in which skill use might be helpful, that individual is designated the main actor. The main actor chooses a coactor to play the role of the significant other person (e.g., mother, peer) involved in the skill problem. The group member should be urged to pick as a coactor someone who resembles the real-life person in as many ways as possible.

The group leader then elicits from the main actor any additional information needed to set the stage for role-playing. To make role-playing as realistic as possible, the leader should obtain a description of the physical setting, the events immediately preceding the role-play, and the mood or manner the coactor should portray, along with any other information that would enhance realism.

Preparing and coaching the coactor, in addition to the main actor, is important in setting up the role-play. For the role-play to have a positive outcome, the coactor must respond in a prosocial way for instance, accepting the main actor's effort. Many times, this acceptance is demonstrated by using another skill. For example, if the main actor is to role-play the skill of Making a Complaint (Skill 31), then the coactor may respond by using the skill of Answering a Complaint (Skill 32), Understanding the Feelings of Others (Skill 17), or Deciding What Caused a Problem (Skill 44). In this sense, then, both the main actor and the coactor are practicing prosocial skill use and become models for the other group members.

Step 6: Conduct the Role-Play

Before role-playing begins, leaders should remind all of the participants of their roles and responsibilities:

► Main actor: Follow the behavioral steps and "think aloud" what would normally be thought silently.

▶ Coactor: Stay in the role of the other person.

▶ Other group members: Watch carefully for the enactment of the behavioral steps.

It is useful to assign one behavioral step to each observer and have that observer track it during the role-play and report on its content and quality afterward. For the first several role-plays, observers can be coached as to what kinds of cues to observe. Specifically, leaders can encourage them to consider the four elements of feedback: (a) Was the step followed? (b) What were the main actor's nonverbals? Did he or she show empathy for the coactor? (c) Was this skill appropriate to this situation? and (d) How did the coactor respond? Was this helpful?

Role-players are then instructed to begin. At this point, the leader provides the main actor with whatever help or coaching he or she needs to keep the role-playing going according to the behavioral steps. At this time in the main actor's learning, the group leader provides the help necessary for the skill to be successful, gradually reducing these prompts as the student progresses in skill proficiency. Such help may include reminding the main actor to "think aloud," drawing attention to a specific skill step, or whispering a suggestion. Main actors who "break role" and begin to explain their behavior or make comments are urged to get back into the role and explain later. If the role-play is clearly going astray from the behavioral steps, the leader stops the scene, provides needed instruction, then restarts the role-play. One leader should stand near the skill poster and point to each of the behavioral steps, in turn, as the role-play unfolds, helping the main actor, as well as the other group members, follow each of the steps in order.

Role-playing should be continued until all participants have had an opportunity to take the role of main actor at least once and, depending on the quality of the role-plays and skill homework, perhaps two or more times. Sometimes this will require two or three sessions for a given skill. As noted, each session should begin with two modeling vignettes for the chosen skill, even if the skill is not new to the group. It is important to note that, although the behavioral steps of each role-play in the series remain the same, the content can and should change from role-play to role-play. The problem as it actually occurs, or could occur, in each youth's real-life environment should provide the content of any given role-play. When the role-play has been completed, each group member will be better able to act appropriately in a real situation requiring skill use.

A few further procedural matters relevant to role-playing will increase its effectiveness. Role reversal is often a useful role-playing a skill if a participant has a difficult time perceiving the coactor's viewpoint (or vice versa). Having the two exchange roles and resume the role-play can be very helpful. On occasion, the leader can assume the coactor role to give participants the opportunity to handle types of reactions not otherwise role-played during the session. For example, it may be crucial to portray a difficult adult coactor role realistically. The leader as coactor may also be particularly helpful with less verbal or more hesitant group members and to avoid having group members model negative behaviors.

Step 7: Provide Performance Feedback

A brief feedback period follows each role-play. Feedback helps the main actor find out how well he or she followed or departed from the behavioral steps, examines the psychological impact of the enactment on the coactor, and provides the main actor with encouragement to try out the role-played behaviors in real life. To implement this process, the group leader asks the main actor to wait until everyone else has commented before responding.

1. The coactor is asked to react first. Questions such as "How did you feel when she said that to you?" and "What do you think about the way she talked to you?" or "Will you mention one thing she did well?" may be needed to prompt the coactor's feedback.

2. Next the observers comment on whether or not the skill steps they were assigned to watch for were followed and on the other relevant aspects of the role-play. When asking for this feedback, it is helpful to ask questions such as "Did he follow the first step, did he think about what he was asked to do?" "How do you know he did this?" Other aspects of the performance—including the way the skill was performed, the context of skill use, and feedback to the coactor—should be provided next.

3. Then the group leaders comment in particular on how well the behavioral steps were followed and provide social reinforcement (praise, approval, encouragement) for close following of the skill steps. Because adolescents exhibiting behavioral issues may misperceive others' motivation, it is helpful to ask the main actor questions such as "Tell us more about your reason for making that choice" and "What do you think the coactor meant when she said . . ." Doing so will clarify how the main actor perceived the actions of the coactor. This is also a good time for the group leaders to emphasize character traits demonstrated by the main actor (e.g., "You were courageous to go against what the group wanted") and the coactor (e.g., "You were a good friend to accept what he said when he told you he did not want to do that").

4. After listening to the feedback from the coactor, observers, and group leaders, the main actor is asked to make comments regarding the role-play and, if appropriate, to respond to the comments of others. In this way the main actor can learn to evaluate the effectiveness of his or her skill performance in light of others' viewpoints. In addition, the main actor should provide reinforcement to the coactor in the role-play. Questions or comments to prompt the main actor in giving positive feedback to the coactor (such as "How did your action affect your coactor?" and "Tell us one thing your coactor did that was helpful to you") will facilitate such necessary positive comments.

In all aspects of feedback, it is crucial that the leader maintain the behavioral focus of Skillstreaming. Leader comments must point to the presence or absence of specific behaviors and not take the form of vague evaluative comments or broad generalities. Feedback, of course, may be positive or negative. A negative comment should always be followed by a constructive comment as to how a particular fault might be improved. At minimum, a "poor" performance (a major departure from the behavioral steps) can be praised as "a good try" at the same time that it is being criticized for its real faults. If at all possible, participants failing to follow the behavioral steps in their role-play should be given the opportunity to replay these same steps after receiving corrective feedback. However, group leaders have found that focusing on the positive aspects of the role-play both encourages the main actor to try the skill again and motivates other group members to take the risk to role-play.

Whenever possible, youth failing to follow the behavioral steps in the role-play should be given the opportunity to repeat the same behavioral steps after receiving corrective, constructive criticism. At times, audio- or videorecording entire role-plays can serve as a further feedback procedure. Giving group members opportunities to listen and observe themselves in this way can be effective in enabling them to reflect on their own verbal and nonverbal behavior.

Because a primary goal of Skillstreaming is skill flexibility, role-play enactment that departs somewhat from the behavioral steps may not be "wrong." That is, a different approach to the skill may in fact work in some situations. Leaders should stress that they are trying to teach effective alternatives and that group members would do well to have the behavioral steps being taught in their repertoire of skill behaviors, available to use when appropriate.

Step 8: Select the Next Role-Player

The next student is selected to serve as main actor, and the sequence just described is repeated until all members of the Skillstreaming group are reliably demonstrating in-group and out-of-group proficiency in using the skill.

Step 9: Assign Skill Homework

Skill homework constitutes the generalization component of Skillstreaming. Following each successful role-play, the main actor is instructed to try, in real life, the behaviors practiced during the session. The name of the person(s) with whom the participant will try the skill, the day, the place, and so on are all discussed and entered on Part 1 of the Homework Report 1 form (see sample in Figure 3). Part 2 of the report requests information about what happened when the group member attempted the homework assignment, how well he or she followed the behavioral steps, self-evaluation of performance, and thoughts about what the next skill assignment might be.

It is useful to start with relatively simple homework behaviors and, as mastery is achieved, work up to more complex and demanding assignments. This provides the leader with an opportunity to reinforce each approximation of the more complex target behavior. Successful experiences at beginning homework attempts are crucial in encouraging group members to attempt further real-life skill use.

The first part of each Skillstreaming session after the first is devoted to presenting and discussing these homework reports. When group members have made an effort to complete their homework assignments, leaders provide social reinforcement. Leaders may express their disappointment if group members fail to do homework. When most participants are demonstrating skill proficiency through successful role-plays of the skill in the group and successful use of it in homework assignments outside of the group, it is time for the group as a whole to move on to

another skill. But what of group members who are not yet competent in the skill most have mastered? They move on with the rest of the group to the new skill but continue to do their homework on the old skill, recording their efforts on Homework Report 2 (Figure 4). Group members submit these reports, and leaders provide feedback either verbally or by jotting a note—in either case using little or no group time in the process.

By the time a group is a few months into the Skillstreaming program, all its members will be doing homework on whatever new skill is being addressed, but most will also be on one or another skill they have yet to master. A skill contract like the sample shown in Figure 5 may help participants, either individually or as a group, follow through with skill practice.

Leaders can encourage independent skill practice by distributing skill sheets like the one shown in Figure 6 and asking group members to copy the steps of any skill or skills they intend to practice in the future. Self-recording forms like the samples in Figures 7 and 8 can also facilitate continued skill use. Self-Recording Form 1 is intended as a record of individual skill use; Self-Recording Form 2 documents the results of students' use of multiple skills.

Generalizing and maintaining newly learned skills is difficult, and these homework assignments are one step toward generalizing skill use. It cannot be stressed too strongly that without these or similar attempts to maximize transfer, the value of the entire training session is in severe jeopardy.

IMPLEMENTATION INTEGRITY

Recently, increased attention has been drawn to implementing intervention programs with integrity. Implementation integrity—also called implementation fidelity, treatment integrity, and procedural reliability—is defined by Lane et al. (2005) as "the extent to which the intervention plan is implemented as originally designed" (p. 22) and is concerned with both the consistency

Figure 3: Sample Homework Report I

Name _____Tammy_____ Date _____9/20_____

FILL IN NOW

1. What skill will you use? _____Dealing with Group Pressure (#42)_____

2. What are the steps for the skill?

    1. Think about what the group wants you to do and why.

    2. Decide what you want to do.

    3. Decide how to tell the group what you want to do.

    4. Tell the group what you have decided.

3. Where will you try the skill? _____Hanging out with friends—walking home____

4. With whom will you try the skill? __Marcy, Todd_____

5. When will you try the skill? _____After school_____

FILL IN AFTER YOU PRACTICE THE SKILL

1. What happened when you did the homework?

    Marcy kept pressuring me for a while. Then she gave up. It was

    hard to stay with my decision, but I did.

2. Which skill steps did you really follow?

    I followed all the steps, but I need to do step 4 better.

3. How good a job did you do in using the skill? *(check one)*

    ☐ excellent   ☑ good   ☐ fair   ☐ poor

Figure 4: Sample Homework Report 2

Name_____Michelle_____ Date_____9/20_____

FILL IN NOW

1. What skill will you use? _____Giving a Compliment (#8)_____

2. What are the steps for the skill?

    1. Decide what you want to compliment about the other person.
    2. Decide how to give the compliment.
    3. Choose the right time and place to say it.
    4. Give the compliment.

3. Where will you try the skill? _____At home_____

4. With whom will you try the skill? ___My sister_____

5. When will you try the skill? _____On the weekend_____

6. If you do an excellent job, how will you reward yourself? ___Go to a movie___

7. If you do a good job, how will you reward yourself? _____Listen to music___

8. If you do a fair job, how will you reward yourself? _____Call a friend_____

FILL IN AFTER YOU PRACTICE THE SKILL

1. What happened when you did the homework?

    _____My sister smiled and said thanks. She asked me if I wanted_____

    _____to go to the mall._____

2. Which skill steps did you really follow?

    _____I did all the steps._____

3. How good a job did you do in using the skill? *(check one)*

    ☐ excellent   ☑ good   ☐ fair   ☐ poor

4. What do you think should be your next homework assignment?

    _____Give a compliment to my mom_____

Figure 5: Sample Skill Contract

Name _____ *Beth* _____

Date(s) of contract _____ *11/15 – 11/20* _____

I agree to use the skill of _____ *Using Self-Control (#26)* _____

when _____ *Someone disses me during passing time.* _____

_____

If I do, then _____ *I can invite someone to eat outside.* _____

_____

Participant signature _____ *Beth* _____

Leader/staff signature _____ *Mr. Burrows* _____

Review date(s) _____ *11/16, 11/20* _____

Figure 6: Sample Skill Sheet

Name _____ *Beth* _____ Date _____ *II/2* _____

Skill _____ *Using Self-Control (#26)* _____

SKILL STEPS

1. *Tune in to what it is going on in your body that helps you know you are about to lose control of yourself.*

2. *Decide what happened to make you feel this way.*

3. *Think about ways in which you might control yourself.*

4. *Choose the best way to control yourself and do it.*

NOTES

Step 1 — My face gets red. I make fists.

Step 2 — Say "It's not woth losing control."

Step 3 — Count to 10. Take 3 deep breaths. Say "Slow down."

Figure 7: Sample Self-Recording Form 1

Name _____A.J._____ Date ___10/17_____

INSTRUCTIONS: Each time you use the skill, write down when and how well you did.

Skill _____Keeping Out of Fights (#30)_____

| **When?** | **How well did you do?** |
| | *(excellent, good, fair, poor)* |

1. Billy said we would fight
   after school.   fair

2. My brother started punching
   me.   good

3. A kid bumped me in the
   hallway.   excellent

4. Enrique hit on my girl.   good

Figure 8: Sample Self-Recording Form 2

Name _____Chico_____ Date___2/20_____

INSTRUCTIONS: Each time you use any of these skills (or skill combinations), write down when and how well you did.

SKILLS

Using Self-Control (#26), Answering A Complaint (#32), Negotiating (#25)

When?	**How well did you do?** (excellent, good, fair, poor)
1. _When my mom said I couldn't hang out because of my grade in math._	_good_

What happened as a result of your skill use?

I didn't get grounded like I usually do. I hung out with friends. Then I studied.

When?	**How well did you do?** (excellent, good, fair, poor)
2. _When my bro said I couldn't use his iPod._	_good_

What happened as a result of your skill use?

We agreed I could use it after I helped him work on his car.

and accuracy of implementation (Gresham, Sugai, & Horner, 2001). Sanetti and Kratochwill (2009) go beyond this standard definition, stating that "treatment integrity is the extent to which essential intervention components are delivered in a comprehensive and consistent manner by an interventionist trained to deliver the intervention" (p. 448). This concept considers the competence of the interventionist (What is the skill level of the interventionist? Does the interventionist believe in the strategy or required by another to do this?); the quality of intervention delivery (How well was the intervention implemented?); the quantity of the intervention (How much of the intervention was delivered?); and the process of intervention delivery (for example, were all components of the intervention included?) (Gresham, 2009; Sanetti & Kratochwill, 2008). Although acknowledged as a critical factor in assessing the usefulness of interventions, implementation integrity is rarely measured (Gresham, 2009; Gresham, Macmillan, Beebe-Frankenberger, & Bocian, 2000) and instead is often just assumed (Cochrane & Laux, 2007). We expect that the intervention will be implemented as originally planned; when change occurs, we assume the changes were due to the intervention. When there is no change, we assume this was due to an inappropriate or ineffective intervention (Gresham & Gansle, 1993). Instead of drawing one of these faulty conclusions, it is probable that the intervention in applied settings (e.g., school, clinic) was changed in some way (Gresham, 2005). Therefore, it is important that we attend to this concept when implementing Skillstreaming as an intervention to change the problematic behavior of adolescents.

Measuring implementation integrity is necessary to derive accurate conclusions regarding the effectiveness of the intervention and to help understand its outcomes, such as behavior change in target individuals (Lane et al., 2005; Wood, Umbreit, Liaupsin, & Gresham, 2007). Stated another way, "Intervention is effective only to the

degree to which it is reliably measured" (Kulli, 2008, p. 145). To know whether Skillstreaming or any other intervention is producing the desired behavior change, monitoring the quality and quantity of the instruction, as well as the motivation of the interventionist, must occur.

Sanetti and Kratochwill (2009) offer several considerations when addressing treatment integrity:

1. Typically, most intervention components are not equally important.

2. Rigid implementation may not be most desirable, and flexibility may be needed.

3. Evaluation and documentation are needed to assess the successfulness of multi-tiered models.

4. For some interventions, there may be a threshold, beyond which increased use does not provide a meaningful impact.

5. As requirements change for research proposals and publications, attention to treatment integrity may increase.

A process recommended by Jung, Gomez, Baird, and Keramidas (2008) is most useful for Skillstreaming purposes. This process includes providing a short checklist identifying the critical features of the strategy, providing concrete examples of how this objective is addressed using the strategy, modeling use of the selected strategy, and offering to watch other team members using the selected strategy and provide feedback.

In addition to implementing the intervention with integrity, it is important that the intervention be an appropriate one for the needs of the youth. Therefore, some flexibility in implementation may be required (Maag, 2006; Sanetti & Kratochwill, 2009). Relative to Skillstreaming, this flexibility includes selecting modeling and role-play scenarios relevant to the needs of group members, as well as changing the language of the skill steps to reflect cultural factors and individual needs of the participants. For example, Sanetti and Kratochwill (2009) emphasize that "deviations may add effective strategies or make the intervention contextually relevant" (p. 451). These authors suggest that emphasizing "flexibility with fidelity" and distinguishing between intervention adaptation (intentional adaptation of the intervention to meet individual needs of the recipient, such as context and culture) and intervention drift (unplanned, gradual changing of the intervention).

Ways to measure implementation integrity include both direct and indirect methods. Direct methods include direct and video observation. Indirect methods include self-reports, permanent products, interviews, and component checklists. The Leader's Checklist and Observer's Checklist, included in Appendix A, are used to ensure implementation integrity. The Leader's Checklist is completed by leaders at the completion of each session when first beginning Skillstreaming groups. When leaders consistently implement all of the steps, this checklist may then be used every two or three weeks. The checklist may also serve as a planning guide to coach leaders through a Skillstreaming session. The Observer's Checklist is designed for use by a highly skilled master teacher or supervisor who observes a newly trained group leader to provide feedback to improve the leader's performance in implementing Skillstreaming instruction. This observation form should be used frequently when a leader first begins groups. This feedback to the leader is most valuable early on to ensure procedures are being implemented as intended. This form has also been used by leaders to observe each other, thereby providing feedback to enhance their skills.

CHAPTER 3

Sample Skillstreaming Session

The following transcript, adapted from the training resource *The Skillstreaming Video* (Goldstein & McGinnis, 1988), depicts the core Skillstreaming procedures discussed in chapter 2. The first portion of the dialogue illustrates the way the group leader structures the first Skillstreaming group. The second portion shows how the Skillstreaming teaching procedures are applied with Skill 42, Dealing with Group Pressure.

The goal of the introductory session is to remind participants in the group of the concept of social skills, illustrate the activities that will be performed, define group expectations (rules), and emphasize that in this group they will learn the things they want and need to learn. The group leader uses a whiteboard or easel pad to illustrate the Skillstreaming procedure and record group members' homework situations, as well as a skill step poster and skill cards on which steps are written.

INTRODUCTION TO SKILLSTREAMING

Introductions

Leaders introduce themselves if the students do not already know them, then ask students to introduce themselves if they do not know one another.

Explanation of Prosocial Skills and Group Purpose

Leader: Welcome, all of you, to today's Skillstreaming group. I've met with all of you individually, so you remember this is a skills-learning group. When I say our purpose is learning skills, what does the word *skill* make you think of? What are examples of skills that people learn?

Larry: Riding a motorcycle.

Beth: Playing a piano.

A.J.: Sinking a basket, in basketball.

Michelle: Cooperating, like with other people.

Leader: Good examples. Riding a motorcycle, playing the piano, sports skills. Those are all skills, but so is Michelle's example, cooperating. It's one kind of what might be called "people skills." There are many others, and they are the type of skills we'll be working on. Things like how to handle failure when something you try doesn't work out, responding to teasing, what do you do when another person accuses you of something that maybe you didn't do.

Overview of Skillstreaming Procedures

The leader illustrates the four-step process by discussing learning another type of skill (in this case, an athletic skill).

Leader: These are just a few examples of what's called people skills. But whether it's people skills, or cooking skills, or athletic skills, all skills are learned the same way. Let's talk for a minute about how you all are going to learn the skills that are going to be taught in this group. Let's say that A.J. here is a good athlete, but he never played basketball and he wants to learn it. I'm the coach, and I'm going to teach him. Let's say lesson one is on shooting a foul shot. What's the first thing that happens? Who does what?

Chico: You show him. You shoot some first.

Leader: Right, I show him. *(Modeling)* I'm the expert. He doesn't know what to do. So I ask him to watch carefully, and I go up to the foul line, stand in a certain way, I hold the ball in a certain way, bend my knees, take a breath, look at the front rim, and I shoot the ball. Because I'm the coach, it goes right in. Is that it? He watched me do it, right? Does that make A.J. ready for the NBA? No, he's got to do something then, too. What does he have to do?

Sue: He's got to try it, to try to do it like you did.

Leader: Exactly! He has to do it. *(Role-playing)* So he goes to the foul line. He stands in a certain way, breathes in a certain way, bends his knees, and shoots it. Too bad, he misses. I showed him the right way, and he tried, but it didn't go in. What do I have to do then?

Sue: Help him.

Leader: Yes, I help him. I give him what's called feedback. *(Performance feedback)* I tell him what he did right, what he didn't do as well, and how to do it better. I say, "A.J., it was terrific the way you stood, the way you held the ball, took a nice deep breath, but you weren't quite facing the basket squarely, and you shot it too fast." I give him feedback on the parts of the skill he did right and the parts where he needs to improve. I would probably show him again the right way of doing the skill. Then what? There's one more step to teaching a skill. Nobody? Well, he's got to practice. *(Generalization)* Practice, practice, practice.

So, that's how you learn the skills of basketball. Someone shows you, an expert, a coach. You try it. You get feedback on how you did, and then you practice what you learned. These steps—show, try, feedback, practice—are how you learn any skill. Shooting a basket, cooperating with others, dealing with group pressure, and any other skills that involve one person with another.

Explanation of Reinforcement System and Discussion of Group Rules

Leader: *(Showing the group a packet of paper tokens)* When you take part in the Skillstreaming group in the ways we just discussed—by trying the skill, giving your feedback or accepting feedback from others, and practicing the skill—you may earn a skill coupon. These are a bit like the coupons for discounts you may find online. In this case, you can exchange the coupons for privileges. When I hand out a coupon, I'll also say why you earned it.

A.J.: So we'll get a coupon for each thing we do?

Leader: Good question. At first, when a new skill is being learned you may earn several coupons in the group. Later on, though, as you perform the skill better and better, you won't need quite as many coupons to know that you are performing the skill well. When you return to your desks after the group, be sure to write your name or initials on the back of each coupon and keep these in an envelope I'll give to you. You may also earn coupons for following our guidelines, or rules, for our group.

Larry: Ah, man. More rules.

Leader: Well, the purpose of behavioral guidelines—or rules—is to make sure everyone in the group has the opportunity to learn the skills that will help get your needs met but still stay out of trouble. It's only fair that everyone understands these expectations. But first we need to decide as a group what these behavioral expectations are. What guidelines, or rules, do we need for our group to run smoothly? For example, what if everyone talked at once? Could we hear what everyone is saying?

Chico: Don't talk when someone else is talking.

Leader: That seems like a very fair expectation to me. Let's phrase this in a positive way, in a way that tells us what to do instead of what not to do. Chico?

Chico: Listen when someone else is talking.

Leader: I like the way you phrased this. Can we all agree on "Listen to the person who is talking" as one of our group rules?

The dialogue continues until the group has defined the following rules: 1. Listen to the person who is talking; 2. Only one person talks at a time; 3. Speak respectfully to others; 4. Follow instructions; and 5. Take part in the group. The co-leader lists the rules on chart paper as they are developed.

Leader: So in addition to role-playing, feedback, and doing homework assignments, you may also earn coupons for following the group expectations that we just defined. What are some privileges you would like to trade your coupons for? I know that some of you have asked to use one of the computers to do an assignment. What do you think about this as a privilege to earn?

Marcy: Sounds good to me.

A.J.: Cool.

Leader: I've listed some classroom privileges the coupons may be used for on this chart. We can add to these or change some as our group progesses.

The group leader shows the students a chart listing privileges, such as using a classroom computer, leaving for lunch two minutes early, extra locker pass, purchasing school supplies, two-minute break from work, library pass, and so on, along with the number of coupons needed to earn each privilege.

Leader: Do each of you see something on the list you'd like to earn? *(Students nod.)* You may turn in your coupons for privileges on Fridays. Be thinking about which privilege you'll choose, and you're free to change your mind and choose a different privilege or even save your coupons for a larger privilege later on.

Conclusion

Leader: Thank you all for listening and participating! I'm excited to start our group tomorrow. This will be a helpful group to learn different choices you have when you're dealing with difficult situations.

Subsequent sessions begin with review of students' homework reports.

SKILL INSTRUCTION

Step 1: Define the Skill

Leader: Today we're going to learn a really important people skill. It's one that several of you told me you needed—Dealing with Group Pressure. What do you all think that means?

Larry: Group pressure, like when my friends want to go cruising or something, and I don't.

Tanya: Or your family. My parents and sometimes my older sister sometimes try to make me do stuff I don't want to do.

Leader: Again, good examples from you folks. Yes, it's when people ask you or push you to do things that maybe you don't want to do or have mixed feelings about doing. Chico, Michelle, do you get a sense of this, of what Dealing with Group Pressure means? *(Participants respond affirmatively.)* Good.

Here are the steps that make up Dealing with Group Pressure. A.J., would you please pass these skill cards around?

A.J. hands out the skill cards while the leader directs the group's attention to the skill step poster in front of the group.

Leader: Thanks. The steps for this skill are also on this poster. I'd like to read them to you.

> ### Dealing with Group Pressure
>
> 1. Think about what the group wants you to do and why.
> 2. Decide what you want to do.
> 3. Decide how to tell the group what you want to do.
> 4. Tell the group what you have decided.

Step 2: Model the Skill

Leader: These four steps, together and in this order, make up one good way of dealing with group pressure. Bess and Al *(co-leaders)* and I are going to model it for you. Like the basketball coach, we'll show you the skill being done in an expert way. Try to pick out the steps as we do them because when we're through doing it, I'm going to ask each of you to get up and go through the same steps.

Leader: Here's the situation. Bess and Al are my old buddies. I haven't seen them for a long time because I've been away at a delinquency center for some stuff I did and got in trouble for. Now I'm back out on the street, my first couple of days out. I'm walking down the street, and here come my two friends, tooling along in this great-looking car. They're going to pull over and urge me to get in the car and go for a ride with them. But I don't think it's their car. I don't want to get back in trouble, but I don't want to lose their friendship. That's my dilemma. So Bess and Al are going to put pressure on me to get in the car, and I'll deal with it by going through these steps. *(To Bess and Al)* Hey, how are you guys doing? Good to see ya.

Bess: Hi, Arnie, how are you? Been a long time.

Leader: I'm good. What's up?

Bess: Al got this car started, and we're going for a ride. Maybe over to the park.

Al: Get in, man. We gotta catch up with you.

Leader: Well, that's one nice car. I gotta admit it.

Al: You getting in or what?

Leader: *(Thinking aloud)* Well, let me see what to do here.

(Pointing to Step 1) They want me to get in and go for a ride with them. I guess the "why" is just because I'm an old buddy and they'd just like my company. *(Pointing to Step 2)* Decide what I want to do. I'd like to go for a ride with them. I mean, it's a nice car, and it's nice to go cruising. But I don't want to get in trouble again, and I'm kind of embarrassed to ask about the registration, but I'm 'bout sure it's not their car. No, I'm not going to do it. I've got to take a risk here and not get in.

(Pointing to Step 3) I could lie to them and say I've got something else to do. I could just walk away and make believe I didn't hear them, but they'd think I was crazy if I did that. I think I'm just going to have to tell them straight out what's going on here and hope for the best.

(Pointing to Step 4, speaking to Bess and Al) Thanks for inviting me, you guys, I appreciate it. It is a neat car, but I don't know who owns it, if you know what I mean. And the food wasn't too great up at the center, so I'm gonna have to pass. How about I head over to the park and meet you there—Lot D—in about 25 minutes. OK?

Bess: Well . . . OK. If you want to walk over. Driving is a lot easier, but we'll catch you there.

Al: I don't get it, man, ain't nobody going to stop us. But, like she says, if you want to walk.

Leader: Good, see ya there.

Step 3: Establish Participant Skill Need

Leader: That's our demonstration of the skill. What is an example each of you have, in your current life, of people putting pressure on you to do things you don't want to do and why is this important to you?

Michelle: There are three kids in my math class. Whenever there's a test, they want me to give them answers. I just don't want to do that, but they really press me a lot. I don't want to cheat.

Sue: Dwayne and Christy want me to go across the street, cut out of class and go behind the drugstore to smoke. It's regular cigarettes, but if I get caught I'll be in big trouble with the truancy officer. Off school grounds and smoking.

Leader: Tammy, how about you? What would be a good example for you?

Tammy: Well, last week Marcy and Todd asked me to go somewhere with them. But I was afraid I'd be grounded, and I told them I couldn't go. They said I should tell my mom I was just going next door and that I'd be back soon, and then go with them. I know my mom would find out and I'd get grounded.

A co-leader lists group members' situations as they are generated.

Step 4: Select the First Role-Player

Leader: Good examples for all of you of tough group pressure you have to deal with. Who would like to role-play this skill first? Tammy, how about you? C'mon up and let's do it.

Tammy: OK.

Step 5: Set Up the Role-Play

Leader: Great, let's give it a try. Could you, Tammy, tell us a little bit more about the situation so that we could help you feel that you are really actually back in the pressure situation you faced? Let's see, two of your friends, Marcy and Todd, were urging you to lie to your mom. Tell us more.

Tammy: They wanted us all to go to the campus so we could drink. My mom's really against my going there because she says it's not for high school kids. There's more. They wanted me to tell my mom we wanted to go to a movie and ask her to drive us there!

Leader: An interesting twist. They not only wanted you to lie to her but also to have her provide the transportation! Who in the group reminds you most of Marcy, either by the way she looks, or talks, or any other important way?

Tammy: I think Sue. I'm not sure why but probably her hair, blond also. And you're both pretty tall.

Leader: What about Todd? Who in the group seems to be like him or remind you of him?

Tammy: Larry. Larry is closest of the boys in the group. I'm not sure why, but it just feels that way.

Leader: Sue and Larry, would you two please come up here and play the parts of Tammy's two friends? You've got a

pretty good idea by now, I think, of what they were pressuring her to do. Tammy, where might you see them next?

Tammy: I don't have classes with either of them this term, but most days we meet after eighth period and walk home together. They both live near me.

Leader: Where do you usually meet?

Tammy: In the schoolyard.

Leader: OK, in the schoolyard. Larry. Sue. Would you both pretend you are in the schoolyard at the end of the day. Here comes Tammy. But before you start, I want to give all of you sitting and watching an assignment. I'm going to ask each one of you to watch the role-play carefully so that you can give Tammy feedback when she's done on how well she followed the steps. A.J., would you take Step 1? When the role-play is over, tell Tammy and the rest of us just what she did to act out Step 1 and how well you think she did it. Chico, would you take Step 2? Beth, Step 3? Michelle, please handle the last step. OK? Don't forget, Sue and Larry, put pressure on her to go with you just the way you think the two friends of hers, Marcy and Todd, laid it on her. Let's go.

Step 6: Conduct the Role-Play

Sue: Hey, Tammy, me and Todd here were just talking, and we decided we want to go to campus tonight and we thought you'd really want to go, too, so how about it?

Larry: Yeah, everyone will probably be there. What do you say? Don't worry about being grounded—you can lie your way out of that. So, what do you say? About 8:00?

Leader: Good. Now hold the action. They've put real pressure on you, now it's your turn. *(Pointing to Step 1)* What did the group want you to do and why?

Tammy: They want me to go up on campus with them and go partying and hang out and drink and stuff.

Leader: *(Pointing to Step 2)* Decide what you want to do. Before you decide, think about different choices, and then pick one.

Tammy: Well, I could figure out some lie and tell it to my mom.

Leader: That's one alternative. What else? Before you pick one, what else?

Tammy: I could lie to them. Tell them I had something else to do.

Leader: Lie to them.

Tammy: I could say, in my situation, that my mom would really get mad and she really wouldn't want me to be up there.

Leader: All right *(pointing to Step 3)*, why don't you go ahead and do it *(pointing to Step 4)*.

Tammy: Well, you guys, I really can't go because if my mom found out that I went up there she would ground me forever. I'd be kept from going out for who knows how long, so I'm not going to go this time.

Sue: Well, you know there's lots of other people who'd like to go.

Tammy: I think I'd like to go, too, but I really can't. Sorry.

Step 7: Provide Performance Feedback

Order of feedback is co-actor(s), observers, main actor, leader(s).

Leader: OK, let's get some feedback for Tammy. First you two. Sue and Larry, if you were the real Marcy and Todd, how do you think you'd respond to how Tammy handled you?

Sue: I'd probably pursue it further. Pressure her more to see if I could convince her. Or tell her to tell her mom she's spending the night at my house, and then we'd go to campus.

Larry: Yeah, and remind her again that other people will be there.

Leader: In other words, both of you would put still more pressure on her. She'd have to keep resisting if she wanted to not do it. OK, A.J., what did Tammy do for Step 1, and how well did you think she did it?

A.J.: Go to campus and get drunk. That was pretty clear.

Leader: How do you know she followed Step 1, A.J.?

A.J.: She used thinking aloud so we would know what she's thinking about.

Leader: OK, how about Step 2? Chico?

Chico: She said she thought about lying. To her mom or her two friends. Or just telling them no, I ain't going.

Leader: Beth?

Beth: She picked the last one, to tell them her mom wouldn't really want her to do that and that she'd be grounded to the next century if her mom found out.

Leader: All right, Step 4. Michelle, you had that one: "Tell the group what you have decided." How'd that come out?

Michelle: She told them what she decided, what she wanted to. They put more pressure on her, but she stuck with what she decided.

Leader: What about her nonverbals?

Chico: She didn't seem sure at first. But, when they kept pressuring her, she stood up straighter.

Larry: Yeah, and her voice sounded stronger, not as quiet as the first time she said no.

Leader: What about the context? Was the skill appropriate, the appropriate place and time?

Observers: *(Nod and agree.)*

Beth: She could have said she'd let us know later. But I think it was good that she told us right away. If she had said she'd let us know later, we might have thought she was in with us.

Leader: What about the coactors? Were they helpful?

Michelle: I thought so, yes. First they pressured. Then they accepted that she wasn't going to go drinking.

Leader: How did you think you did on this skill, Tammy?

Tammy: It was hard to do. I was afraid I'd lose them as friends. But I did all the steps, and I was honest with them. I think I need to practice some more!

Leader: What did your coactors do that was helpful to you?

Tammy: Well, they pressured me. But, finally, they accepted what I said. That helped a lot.

Leader: There's your feedback, Tammy. They all seem to be saying you did a good job, and I think you did also. You followed all of the steps, seemed sensitive to what your friends wanted you to do, but you stuck with what was best for you. I wonder if we work on seeming more assertive when you use the steps. Maybe this will help you feel more confident?

Tammy: Yeah, I didn't feel very confident.

Step 8: Select the Next Role-Player

Leader: Who is next? Who would like to role-play next?

The process continues until all have had a chance to role-play the skill.

Step 9: Assign Skill Homework

The leader helps group members identify a time to try out the skill and coaches them through the process next described for Tammy.

Leader: *(To Tammy)* I know that this isn't just play acting for you, that it's a situation you probably will have to face again soon. If we work on an assertive voice, do you think you're up to doing this with the real Marcy and the real Todd?

Tammy: I think so. I think I could do it. Could I practice again first?

Leader: Absolutely! But go ahead and take this homework form. Fill out the top half right now—it's your promise that you'll try the skill where and when it's needed, after another practice. After you try the skill in real life, you'll complete the bottom half. The bottom half is your chance to put down how well your try went. And then we'll talk about everyone's homework at the beginning of our next meeting.

CHAPTER 4
Refining Skill Use

For many youth, relationships with adults and peers present difficult interpersonal challenges—challenges that draw heavily upon their repertoire of interpersonal skills. The interpersonal challenges of adolescence are for both young people moving through "normal" adolescence and those identified as having behavioral problems. This is a time when young people are faced with an increased number of choices as they begin to develop autonomy ("Leave me alone"), while still being dependent on adults ("Take care of me"). The goal of Skillstreaming is to increase the prosocial options adolescents may choose.

Although Skillstreaming is a psychoeducational intervention derived primarily from social learning theory, cognitive-behavioral interventions such as problem solving, anger control, stress management, and verbal mediation are embedded in its instructional format and can enhance its effectiveness. This chapter briefly examines the role of these approaches in Skillstreaming, as well as that of strategies to increase a student's social performance, including reducing competing problem behaviors, supportive modeling, empathy, nonverbal behaviors, and skill shifting/skill combinations.

For more intensive interventions for adolescents in the areas of problem solving, anger control, stress management, empathy, situational perception, and supportive modeling, readers are encouraged to consult the courses included in *The Prepare Curriculum: Teaching Prosocial Competencies* (Goldstein, 1999b).

COGNITIVE-BEHAVIORAL STRATEGIES

Kaplan and Carter (2005) explain the concept of cognition relative to behavioral intervention strategies as including cognitive processes, cognitive structures, and inner speech. Cognitive structures relate to our beliefs and ideas and involve "more the way we think as opposed to what we think" (p. 381). Gresham (2005) explains this concept in this way:

> Cognitive-behavioral theory is based on the premise that thoughts, emotions and actions are inextricably linked and that changing one of these necessarily produces changes in the others. These reciprocal relationships between thoughts, emotions, and actions serve as the fundamental basis of all cognitive-behavioral intervention strategies. (p. 213)

Incorporating elements of the cognitive-behavioral approach into Skillstreaming will promote the self-control needed by many adolescents to change their typical manner of reacting, thus better enabling them to reduce competing problem behavior, recall skill steps, and generalize the skills they learn. Knowledge of the following areas—problem solving, anger control, stress management, and verbal mediation will guide group leaders in enhancing Skillstreaming instruction.

Problem Solving

Adolescents and younger children may, as Ladd and Mize (1983) point out, be deficient in such problem-solving competencies as knowledge of appropriate goals for social interaction, knowledge of appropriate strategies for reaching a social goal, and knowledge of the contexts in which specific strategies may be appropriately applied. An analogous conclusion flows from research on interpersonal problem solving conducted by Spivack, Platt, and Shure (1976). During early and middle childhood, as well as in adolescence, chronically aggressive youth are less able than their nonaggressive peers to function effectively in most problem-solving subskills, such as identifying alternatives, considering consequences, determining causality, and engaging in means-ends thinking and perspective taking. Skillstreaming skills specifically related to improving problem solving include Deciding What Caused a Problem (Skill 44), Gathering Information (Skill 47), and Making a Decision (Skill 49).

Anger Control

Anger Control Training was developed by Feindler and her research group at Adelphi University (Feindler, 1979, 1995; Feindler & Ecton, 1986) and modified in separate programs involving incarcerated juvenile delinquents (Goldstein, Glick, Carthan, & Blancero, 1994; Goldstein, Glick, Irwin, Pask-McCartney, & Rubama, 1989; Goldstein, Glick, Reiner, Zimmerman, & Coultry, 1986). In contrast to the direct facilitation of prosocial behavior in Skillstreaming, Anger Control Training facilitates such behavior indirectly by teaching means for inhibiting anger and loss of self-control. Participating youth are taught, over an eight-week span, how to respond to provocations to anger by (a) identifying their external and internal anger triggers; (b) identifying their own physiological/kinesthetic anger cues; (c) using anger reducers to lower arousal via deep breathing, counting backwards, imagining a peaceful scene, or contemplating the long-term consequences of anger-associated behavior; (d) using reminders, or self-statements that function opposite to triggers (i.e., to lower one's anger arousal level); and (e) self-evaluating, or judging how adequately anger control worked and rewarding oneself when it has worked well.

When instructing adolescents with anger control issues, instruction in skills that are used under stressful conditions, particularly those in Group IV, Skill Alternatives to Aggression, should include an anger control strategy—counting to 10 or taking three deep breaths, for example.

Stress Management

Individuals may possess an array of prosocial skills in their repertoires but may not employ them in particularly challenging or difficult situations because of anxiety. Many adolescents may know the desired and expected behavior and may, in fact, be likely to behave in this manner in many situations. However, when angry, anxious, or otherwise upset, they are unable to see beyond the emotion-producing event. Before these adolescents will be able to recall the steps of a specific skill, they must use strategies to stop themselves from reacting with a well-established pattern of aggression or another unproductive behavior. Such impulse control procedures are often referred to as *coping skills* or *self-regulation strategies.*

A youth may have learned well the Skillstreaming skill Responding to Failure, but his embarrassment at receiving a failing grade in front of his teacher or at missing a foul shot in front of his friends may engender a level of anxiety that inhibits skill use. Another may possess the problem-solving competency to plan well for a job interview but may perform poorly in the interview itself because anxiety takes over. Anxiety and resulting inhibition are strong sources of prosocially incompetent and unsatisfying behavior in the highly peer-conscious adolescent years. Skillstreaming includes a variety of skills for dealing with stressful situations typical of adolescence. However, the youth who needs more intense instruction in stress management would benefit from additional and more intense intervention. Meichenbaum's stress inoculation training, as presented by Maag (2006), describes three phases of stress management training. First, the individual receives information about the components of interpersonal functioning and the impact of stress on his or her behavior. Second, the individual learns social skills relevant to the problem behaviors (e.g., dealing with the emotion causing the stress). Third, the individual practices using the stress reduction or coping skills in both role-play and real-life situations while regulated stressors are introduced (application and follow through). These stressors are significant enough to create stress for the individual but are not so intense that they inhibit newly learned social skills.

Verbal Mediation

Much of the early work on children's use of language to regulate their own behaviors was done by the Russian psychologist Luria (1961). As Mayer, Lochman, and Van Acker (2005) point out, many aspects of cognitive behavioral modification are based on a premise that inner speech mediates behavior and that by using language to alter cognition, behavior can change. This pattern of development is described by Little and Kendall (1979):

> The process of development of verbal control of behavior . . . seems to follow a standard developmental sequence. First, the initiation of motor behavior comes under control of adult verbal cues, and then the inhibition of responses is controlled by the speech of adults. Self-control emerges as the child learns to respond to his own verbal cues, first to initiate responses and then to inhibit them. (p. 101)

Verbal mediation techniques have been used to teach impulse control in children with hyperactivity (Kendall & Braswell, 1985), anger control in adolescents, impulse control in aggressive youngsters (Camp & Bash, 1981), and academic behaviors through self-instruction training (Meichenbaum, 1977). By practicing talking themselves through a skill or saying aloud ways to control the impulse to react in an undesirable way, children and adolescents learn to regulate their actions until the actions become nearly automatic.

FACTORS IN SUCCESSFUL SKILL USE

Social skills deficits may be due to a skill deficiency (can't do), performance deficit (won't do), a competing problem, or lack of fluency in skill performance (Gresham, 2002). Clearly, Skillstreaming is successful in teaching participants how to perform prosocial skills. In addition to strategies relating to the cognitive-behavioral approach, factors that impact successful skill use include skill fluency, social perceptions, reduction of competing behaviors, nonverbal behaviors, empathy, and supportive modeling.

Skill Fluency

Fluency in performing selected social skills is largely achieved by the generalization principle of overlearning. As is the case for other skills, such as learning to read or playing a sport, prosocial skill performance is often somewhat artificial and rote in its initial stages. The more practice group members have in using the skill in a variety of different situations and settings and with different coactors, the more fluent and natural performance will become. A positive relationship between amount of social skills training and successful results has been found (Gresham et al., 2006; McIntosh, Vaughn, & Zaragoza, 1991). When skill fluency is at issue, more intense and frequent skills training is called for.

Perceptions of Social Situations

A major thrust in psychology concerns the role of the situation or setting, as perceived by the individual, in determining overt behavior. Morrison and Bellack (1981), for example, state that individuals must not only possess the ability to enact given behavioral skills but must also know when and how these responses should be applied. Accurately reading the social environment includes awareness of the norms and conventions in operation at a given time and understanding of the messages given by the other person.

Crick and Dodge (1994) have proposed that individuals with social information-processing deficits have errors in interpreting social cues or events and process these cues in a series of six steps: encoding the cue, interpreting the cue, selecting the desired goal, accessing a response, evaluating the response, and enacting the behavior. The individual is presented with a problem (encoding the cue), thinks aloud or is coached while processing what has occurred (interpreting the cue) and thinking of reasons to use the skill (selecting the desired goal), and engages in a role-play of behavioral steps (accessing a response, evaluating the response, and enacting the behavior). Further evaluation of the response occurs through the feedback process. Clearly, parallels exist between this model and Skillstreaming's instructional format. Individuals access responses that have been stored in their long-term memory. As children and adolescents with social information-processing deficits learn new social behaviors and skills, they will expand their options for responding to a variety of social events and problems.

Therefore, even if adolescents have learned the interpersonal skills necessary to respond prosocially to others, chronically skill-deficient youth may still fail to behave prosocially. Emphasis must be placed, therefore, not only on Skillstreaming skill performance but also on such questions as the following:

▶ What is the situation or problem?

▶ What outcome do I want?

▶ What is the expected behavior in this setting?

▶ How should I perform the skill with this person, considering his or her role?

What signs are there that this is a good time and place to use this skill? Inviting group members to consider such questions will result in more successful skill use and guide students in developing the flexibility needed to adjust skill use across settings, situations, and people. In addition, in-

struction in skill combinations and skill shifting, discussed later in this chapter, will help address this need.

Reduction of Competing Problem Behaviors

Competing problem behaviors may be either externalizing (acting out) or internalizing and impede either acquiring new skills or in performing newly learned skills (Gresham et al., 2006). Gresham (1998) explains that the problem behavior may be more efficient for the youth. In other words, the outcome the adolescent desires is easier to obtain through using the problem behavior than through using an alternative, more socially acceptable behavior or skill. The problem behavior is also likely to be reliable, consistently leading to obtaining reinforcement. A goal, then, is to reduce the efficiency and reliability of the problem behavior. For adolescents whose emotional responses inhibit or prevent skill performance, Elliott and Gresham (1991) suggest that instruction in the prosocial skill be paired with strategies to reduce the interfering problem behavior. Three such strategies include anger control, stress management, and verbal mediation, discussed previously.

Nonverbal Behaviors

Nonverbal communicators such as body posture and movements, facial expressions, and voice tone and volume give others messages either consistent with or contradictory to verbal content. Consider, for example, the group member who was asked to lower his voice in the school cafeteria. He did not make a verbal response, but instead turned back to his friends. He was then told to leave the cafeteria for breaking the rules. Often it is not the breaking of the rule per se that results in an adult's negative reaction. Rather, one hears comments about such students like "He was defiant" or "He was disrespectful." Understanding the influence of nonverbal language is an important factor in learning prosocial behaviors. Fox and Boulton (2005), for example, researched the behaviors that discriminated between victims of bullying and nonvictims. These results found 50 percent of the behaviors that best predicted victimization were nonverbal behaviors, including looking scared, standing in a way that looks weak, and looking like an unhappy person.

Nowicki and Duke (1992) illustrate six areas of nonverbal communication:

1. Paralanguage (voice tone, speech rate, variation of speech, nonverbal sounds)

2. Facial expressions

3. Postures and gestures

4. Interpersonal distance (space) and touch (intimate, personal, social, and public zones)

5. Rhythm and time (e.g., being on time, spending time with friends)

6. Objectics (hygiene, style of dress)

Skill-deficient group members will need to be made more aware of the ways in which nonverbal communicators send clear and definite messages.

Empathy

Even very young children possess the capacity to show empathy. Denham (1998) states that "children as young as two years of age are able to broadly interpret others' emotional states, to experience these feeling states in response to others' predicament, and attempt to alleviate discomfort in others" (p. 34). Chronically aggressive or other skill-deficient youth have been shown to display a pattern of personality traits high in egocentricity and low in concern for others (Slavin, 1980).

Expression of empathic understanding can serve both as an inhibitor of negative behaviors and as a facilitator of positive actions. Results of numerous studies inquiring into the interpersonal consequences of empathic responding show that empathy consistently promotes interpersonal attraction, dyadic openness, conflict resolution, and individual growth (Goldstein & Michaels, 1985). In addition, Grizenko et al. (2000) found more lasting improvement in social skills instruction with the addition of social perspec-

tive taking. In other words, adolescents who are able to show empathy are far less likely to act out aggressively toward others, are more accepted and sought after in social situations, are more able to participate in resolving interpersonal disputes, and are more satisfied with themselves.

Some helpful methods of encouraging empathy include (a) instructing adolescents in Understanding the Feelings of Others (Skill 17); (b) providing opportunities for role reversal during role-plays followed by actors' expression of feelings; (c) providing opportunities for observers to take the perspective of others (e.g., that of the main actor) during feedback sessions; and (d) encouraging empathy toward others through modeling and discussion of appreciation for individual differences.

Supportive Modeling

Aggressive youth typically are exposed regularly to aggressive models in their interpersonal worlds. Parents, siblings, and peers are frequently chronically aggressive individuals (Knight & West, 1975; Loeber & Dishion, 1983; Robins, West, & Herjanic, 1975). Simultaneously, relatively few countervailing prosocial models are available for these youth to observe and imitate. When prosocial models are available, however, they can make a tremendous difference in these adolescents' daily lives and development. In support of this assertion are community models such as Big Brothers, Big Sisters, the Police Athletic League, Scouts, and the like. Research also consistently shows that rewarded prosocial behaviors (e.g., sharing, altruism, cooperation) are often imitated (Bryan & Test, 1967; Canale, 1977; Evers & Schwartz, 1973). Even more direct evidence suggests the value of supportive models. For example, Werner and Smith (1982), in their longitudinal study of aggressive and nonaggressive youth *Vulnerable but Invincible,* clearly demonstrated that many youngsters growing up in a community characterized by high crime, high unemployment, high secondary school dropout rates, and high levels of aggressive models were able to develop into effective, prosocially oriented individuals if they had experienced sustained exposure to at least one significant prosocial model—parent, relative, teacher, coach, neighbor, or peer.

Classroom teachers and other school staff can be powerful models for students. Needless to say, a powerful negative effect can be exerted on students if teachers model prosocial skill deficiencies. Throughout the school day, teachers and others should model desirable, prosocial behaviors and use the behavioral steps for selected skills when it is appropriate to do so. When frustrated or angry with an individual student's behavior, for example, a teacher can greatly affect the student's learning by modeling the steps of Using Self-Control (Skill 26) in a clear and deliberate manner.

Because such models may be scarce in these youths' real-world environment, efforts must be made to help them identify, attract, and at times even create sources and attachments to others who function prosocially themselves and who also can serve as sustained sources of direct support for the youths' own prosocially oriented efforts.

SKILL SHIFTING, COMBINATIONS, ADAPTATION, AND DEVELOPMENT

Skill Shifting

Sometimes during the course of a Skillstreaming session devoted to one skill, the need may arise for instruction in another. When this occurs, the leader should either shift to teaching the new skill on the spot or make note of the need to do so in the near future. For example, in a session devoted to Dealing with Embarrassment (Skill 34), one participant developed a role-play related to Dealing with Being Left Out (Skill 35). Although this group member obviously felt embarrassed when she was not included in an event with peers, Dealing with Being Left Out would have likely better met her needs.

Group members often find it valuable to know when and how to shift from one skill to another. Skillstreaming instruction should help them discern when a skill is unsuccessful, when an alternative skill should be attempted, and which specific skill to try. In a homework assignment, Sam tried using the skill of Convincing Others (Skill 14) when he wanted two of his friends to come over to play video games. Instead, the peers wanted to hang out at the mall. Sam was baby-sitting his sister and knew he couldn't go along. Sam continued to try to convince them and became frustrated and angry. At that time, when his current skill was unsuccessful in meeting his need, it would have been helpful for Sam to then use the skill of Using Self-Control (Skill 26) and then try the skill of Negotiating (Skill 25) or Deciding on Something to Do (Skill 43).

Skill Combinations

Often, competence in single skills will prove insufficient. For example, Bob correctly tries to convince his mother of his views on a matter (Skill 14, Convincing Others), but Mom remains unconvinced. A teacher accuses Benita of cheating on a test. Benita responds with appropriate behavior (Skill 40, Dealing with an Accusation), but the teacher does not believe her. Kyle is called a "fat slob" by three agemates in his neighborhood, and they refuse to stop badgering him. He responds to their teasing well (Skill 28, Responding to Teasing), but they continue making nasty comments. One youth at school has drugs in his possession and asks a second to hold them for him until a school locker search is completed. The second youth refuses (Skill 37, Responding to Persuasion), but the pressure from the first continues and escalates.

These are all examples of the common experience that many youth have in response to difficult and often complex interpersonal challenges. Single-skill responses, even when carried out correctly, prove inadequate. More effective skill combinations and sequences are necessary. Fortunately, after a Skillstreaming group has been meeting for several months, members have learned several skills. At this point, group leaders can shift some of the group's time away from learning single new skills to practicing how to select, sequence, and enact combinations of previously learned skills. The following transcript, an edited excerpt from *The Refusal Skills Video* (Goldstein, 1990), illustrates the modeling and role-playing portions of an advanced Skillstreaming session in which participants rehearse a combination of skills. Group leaders first model the three skills in the sequence—Dealing with Someone Else's Anger (Skill 18), Dealing with Fear (Skill 20), and Standing Up for Your Rights (Skill 27)—then two participants role-play the skills. The steps for these skills are presented in Table 3.

Leader: OK, you guys, if I can get your attention, let's get started. Today is going to be a little different from what we did last week. Remember last week we just did one skill. It seemed to be enough in most refusal situations. Sometimes it's not enough. You try, but it doesn't seem to work. That's the kind of difficult situation we're going to practice today, how you handle, put together, a sequence or a group of skills. I'm going to do a modeling demonstration in a minute with Vernessa. She's going to offer me something that I don't want. I'm going to refuse. But this time, it's not going to work—in fact not only isn't it going to work, but she's going to get pissed off at me. She's really going to get angry at me, and I have to deal with her anger *(Skill 18)*. So I try to do that. That turns out not to be enough. As a matter of fact, just about the time I'm through trying to deal with her anger unsuccessfully, along come two more friends. I've asked two more members of the group to get up there and join Vernessa. Now I've got to deal with three people, and I'm getting a little frightened because the stakes have kind of gone up. So I think about how to deal with that fear *(Skill 20)*, and I decide that the answer is to stand up for my rights *(Skill 27)*. That's the sequence we're going to demonstrate, and that's what I'll get some of you to come up to actually try. Vernessa, let's do it. Hey, how you doing there?

Table 3: Sample Skill Sequence

Skill 18: Dealing with Someone Else's Anger

1. Listen to the person who is angry.
2. Try to understand what the angry person is saying and feeling.
3. Decide if you can say or do something to deal with the situation.
4. If you can, deal with the other person's anger.

Skill 20: Dealing with Fear

1. Decide if you are feeling afraid.
2. Think about what you might be afraid of.
3. Figure out if the fear is realistic.
4. Take steps to reduce your fear.

Skill 27: Standing Up for Your Rights

1. Pay attention to what is going on in your body that helps you know that you are dissatisfied and would like to stand up for yourself.
2. Decide what happened to make you feel dissatisfied.
3. Think about ways in which you might stand up for yourself and choose one.
4. Stand up for yourself in a direct and reasonable way.

Vernessa: Hi.

Leader: What's that, gin?

Vernessa: Yeah, go ahead and take some. You know you've been here all of three hours and you haven't done nothing.

Leader: What is it? I don't want that.

Vernessa: Hey, this is the fifth time. Come on now, we're not going to invite you anymore. You're really pissing me off.

Leader: She is really angry. There's no doubt about this first step. *(Pointing to Step 1)* "Listen to the person who is angry." I've tried to just sort of listen and stay calm and not interrupt her, try to understand what she's feeling. *(Pointing to Step 2)* "Try to understand what the angry person is saying and feeling." I'm not sure I understand that. Could you tell me why you're so angry at me? Why are you so pissed off?

Vernessa: You're giving me a bad reputation with my folks, OK? Everyone here is live except you, you know.

Leader: *(Pointing to Step 3)* "Decide if you can say or do something to deal with the situation." She's still angry. I could just keep listening to her. I could let her blow off steam. I could try to ignore her.

Vernessa: Arnie, all the guys are going to come into the kitchen. They're going to see you standing there with a cup of water! You can't fool them with a cup of water. Arnie, take a sip. OK, see. The home boys are coming. They are going to be looking at you, and you're going to be left out in the mud. You won't even take a sip.

Leader: OK, now it's clear that this has not worked—she's still angry. I haven't been able to deal with it, and now there's three of them, and I'm getting a little more concerned. I got to move to this next skill *(Skill 20)*, Dealing with Fear. *(Pointing to Step 1)* "Decide if you are feeling afraid." I've got that feeling in the pit of my stomach, and it's bothering me. I got those butterflies. "Think about what you might be afraid of" *(pointing to Step 2)*. They might make fun of me; they'll probably tell me to get lost. "Figure out if the fear is realistic" *(pointing to Step 3)*. Well, it's very realistic. Charlie got the business from them last week, Leroy the month before, and now it's my turn. "Take steps to reduce your fear" *(pointing to Step 4)*. OK, what can I do about this? I could leave, but I want to be at this party. That's why I came. I could make a joke out of it, I guess, but right now it doesn't feel very funny. They're looking at me like they're really angry. But I don't know—I'm not going to roll over on this, I'm going to deal with it head on. I got to move to this skill now, Standing Up for Your Rights *(Skill 27)*. "Pay attention to what's going on in your body" *(pointing to Step 1)*. That's easy. Tight stomach, butterflies, I'm still fearful. But I want to deal with this. "Decide what happened to make you feel dissatisfied" *(pointing to Step 2)*. Well, they're sticking it to me. Just because I don't want to drink the gin, they're sticking it to me. I don't think that's fair. *(Pointing to Step 3)* "Think about ways in which you might stand up for yourself and choose one." I could walk away, or find other folks to hang with, or just tell them where I'm at. That's what I'll do, tell them straight out. *(Pointing to Step 4)* Listen, I hope we can still hang out together. I want to be here. I want to go to the scene that's happening next week, but I don't want to get hooked on that. I'm sorry, I'd like to stay at the party. I'm sorry I just don't want to drink that, and that's the way it is. So let's just hang out together. Be cool.

Vernessa: Well, Arnie . . . OK. I really like you, and if this is how you want to be, fine. I'm going to do my thing, you do yours.

Leader: OK, I want you guys to try this. Difficult refusal situations can be complicated. There certainly are other ways we could do this, with other sequences of two or three or four skills. What would be a situation that each of you has now that's pretty complicated, a refusal situation that's a pretty tough one, where just saying no hasn't worked terribly well? That's the kind of situation we want to role-play. Barbara, how about you?

Barbara: I was in school one day and they were having locker checks for drugs, and my friend had drugs in his locker and he wanted me to hold them for him until the check was over. So he wouldn't take the rap for it.

Leader: And he got pretty angry.

Barbara: Yeah.

Leader: Well, this might be a good situation. Let's try that one. Why don't you guys, Barbara and Ben, come up here. You can stand right over here. Ben, you ask her to hold this for you, and she's going to refuse. You're going to get angry. We want you to get good and angry. Don't hit her, but get good and angry.

Barbara, you said your reaction was fear, and we want to see if you can sort of get into that way of feeling a little bit, and then we'll go through these skills, one, two, three. Let's go at it.

Ben: Barbara, you know about that locker check they're going to have today? Well, I kind of got some of this stuff, and they're going to check my locker, and I've already been in trouble once or twice before. So could you hold this for me until it's over?

Barbara: What is that?

Ben: It's some drugs that I have.

Barbara: No.

Ben: Can you please just hold this for me 'cause I've already been in trouble at least once or twice before. And if they catch up with me again . . . I don't know, I'll probably get expelled for it.

Barbara: I don't want you to get expelled.

Ben: I thought you were a friend, man. I'm going to get expelled from school for these.

Barbara: So will I.

Ben: No you won't. They won't get mad at you.

Leader: He's starting to get angry at you, you're listening, you're doing a good job, you're staying cool, you're not interrupting, you're just listening. Try to understand why he's getting angry.

Barbara: Why are you getting so angry?

Ben: I'm not trying to make you *take* these pills or something. I just want you to hold on to them for me like for two hours or something.

Barbara: No.

Ben: Come on, Barbara!

Barbara: No.

Ben: Hold the pills. Here, I'll put them in your pocket. Just take them and keep them for me until after school, then give them back to me, that's all I'm asking.

Leader: OK, freeze the action. So his anger level seems to be creeping up and up. And from what you described earlier, with the real situation with the other boy, that started to make you fearful. How would you know if you're feeling fearful?

Barbara: Got butterflies.

Leader: OK. Think about what you might be afraid of, what could be happening here? What might he do, or what's going to be the thing to be fearful of here?

Barbara: I'm afraid that I'm going to give in or he's going to hit me or something.

Leader: So the real other person might hit you.

Barbara: Yes.

Leader: That sounds pretty realistic, doesn't it? What could you do to reduce your fear?

Barbara: I can leave. Take them. Or keep refusing.

Leader: OK, let's try the keep refusing in this form, standing up for your rights. You've told us what you're feeling, so we know what that's all about. What happened to make you feel that way is the pressure he's putting on you. How could you stand up for your rights here? What could you do?

Barbara: I could keep refusing, and then that would lead into leaving.

Leader: If he didn't stop, you just split? Let's see what happens.

Ben: Just hold on to these until after school.

Barbara: No.

Ben: You will not be caught with these and if you do, just tell them somebody put them there, or tell them it's your mom's diet pills. I'm going to get expelled, if that's what you want.

Barbara: Ben, if you're that concerned, how come you can't just throw them away?

Ben: 'Cause they're too expensive to throw away. I don't want to lose these. Hold on to them until after school—you will not get in trouble. If you get in trouble, then I'll confess to it.

Barbara: No.

Ben: Come on, I'll just put them in your pocket until after school. *(Reaches out to her pocket.)*

Barbara: No, no. *(Walks out of room.)*

Leader: Let's get some feedback.

Other skill sequences may be suggested. Earlier, Bob used the skill Convincing Others (Skill 14) in a dispute with his mother. He followed the skill steps correctly, but she remained unconvinced. For a successful outcome to be more likely, he may, in addition, need to employ Responding to Failure (Skill 38), Asking a Question (Skill 4), and Negotiating (Skill 25). Benita, in the earlier example, was accused of cheating by her teacher. Her use of Dealing with an Accusation (Skill 40) failed in its goal of resolving the confrontation. Perhaps Benita might have had a better result in her efforts with the teacher had she followed Skill 40 with Apologizing (Skill 13). Finally, Kyle's use of Responding to Teasing (Skill 28) proved insufficient. Perhaps the combination of Dealing with Fear (Skill 20), Standing Up for Your Rights (Skill 27), and Giving Instructions (Skill 11) would be more effective.

Skill Adaptation and Development

As students express concerns and difficulties and as teachers observe problems, new skills can and should be developed. Consider the situation, for example, in which a group of students are continually disruptive when passing from one class to another. The perceptive teacher, recognizing that transitions are difficult for this particular group of students, develops a new skill, titled "Passing to Class." Skill steps might include the following.

Passing to Class

1. When the bell rings, gather your materials.
2. Walk to your locker (put class materials away, get new class materials).
3. Walk to your next class.
4. Say "hi" or wave to students you know or who greet you.
5. When you're in your seat when the bell rings, give yourself a pat on the back.

In a different, fairly common situation, a student regularly completes homework but fails to return the homework. Steps for a new skill to deal with this issue might be as follows.

Handing in Homework

1. Put all completed homework in your Homework Folder.
2. When arriving at your first class, look in your folder. (Look through all your homework to see what to turn in to this teacher.)
3. Take out the homework assignment and put it in the appropriate place (e.g., teacher's desk).
4. Place a checkmark by the class. (At the end of the class, take your folder to the next class.)

In another example, Melisa Genaux, a behavioral expert in the area of autism, developed a specific skill for students with Asperger's syndrome. Because so many of the students with whom she works have behavior difficulty when their routines change, the following skill was developed for instruction:

Changes in Routine/It's Not What I Thought Would Happen Skill

1. Stop.
2. Take a deep breath.
3. Count to five.
4. Say, "OK."
5. Follow the direction.

In some circumstances it may be appropriate to retain a given skill but alter one or more of its behavioral steps. Steps may be simplified as the skills and needs of the students suggest. For example, a child who repeatedly becomes out of control when losing may need a modification of the behavioral steps constituting Skill 33, Being a Good Sport.

---

1. Say to yourself, "Everybody can't win. Maybe I'll win next time."
2. Say congratulations to the other person or team.
3. Walk away and do something else.

Group leaders should use their experience and judgment in adjusting the content of these skills.

CHAPTER 5

Enhancing Skill Generalization

Historically, therapeutic interventions have reflected a core belief in personality change as both the target and outcome of effective intervention; thus, environmental influences on behavior were largely ignored. It has been assumed that the positive changes believed to have taken place within the individual's personality would enable the individual to deal effectively with problematic events wherever and whenever they might occur. That is, transfer and maintenance would occur automatically.

Research on psychotherapy initiated in the 1950s and expanded in the 1960s and 1970s sought to ascertain whether gains at the end of the formal intervention had in fact generalized across settings and/or time. Stokes and Baer (1977) described this time as one in which transfer and maintenance were hoped for and noted if they did occur ("train and hope"). The overwhelming result of these investigations was that, much more often than not, transfer and maintenance of intervention gains did not occur. Treatment and training did not persist automatically, nor did learning necessarily transfer (Goldstein & Kanfer, 1979; Keeley, Shemberg, & Carbonell, 1976). This failure, revealed by evidence accumulated during the train-and-hope phase, led to a third phase—the development, evaluation, and use of procedures explicitly designed to enhance transfer and maintenance of intervention gains.

As the social skills movement in general and Skillstreaming in particular have matured and

evidence regarding effectiveness has accumulated, it has become clear that skill acquisition is a reliable finding across both training methods and populations. However, generalization is another matter. Generalization to both new settings (transfer) and over time (maintenance) has been reported to occur in only a minority of cases. The main concern of any teaching effort is not how students perform in the teaching setting but how well they perform in their real lives. Therefore, generalization is often considered the most important goal in social skills instruction (Gresham, 1998). Approaches to enhance transfer and maintenance are listed in Table 4 and discussed in the following pages.

Beyond these strategies, many concerned with the social development of children and adolescents hypothesize that social skills often fail to generalize due to the presence of stronger, competing problem behaviors. Group members may fail to use a newly learned skill not just because reinforcement in their real lives does not occur or because the Skillstreaming instructor has not attended to the generalization principles adequately during the instruction. As Gresham, Sugai, and Horner (2001) state, "One reason . . . that socially skilled behaviors may fail to generalize is because the newly taught behavior is masked or overpowered by older and stronger competing behaviors" (p. 340). Although failure of generalization is surely to occur if these are not put in place, some students may experience intense emotions such

---

Table 4: Transfer- and Maintenance-Enhancing Procedures

Transfer

Before Instruction

Entrapment (including relevant peers in the instruction)

During Instruction

1. Provision of general principles (general case programming)

2. Overlearning (maximizing response availability)

3. Stimulus variability (training sufficient exemplars, training loosely)

4. Identical elements (programming common stimuli)

After Instruction

5. Instructed generalization

6. Mediated generalization (self-recording, self-reinforcement, self-punishment, self-instruction)

Maintenance

During the Skillstreaming Intervention

1. Thinning reinforcement (increase intermittency, unpredictability)

2. Delaying reinforcement

3. Fading prompts

4. Providing booster sessions

5. Preparing for real-life nonreinforcement

Beyond the Skillstreaming Intervention

6. Programming for reinforcement in the natural environment

7. Using natural reinforcers

---

as anger or anxiety or in other ways have difficulties in self-regulating their emotions or behaviors. For these youth, Skillstreaming efforts must include additional strategies to refine skill use (chapter 4) and reduce problem behaviors (chapter 6).

The Generalization Integrity Checklist, included in Appendix B, guides Skillstreaming instructors in the use of generalization principles and strategies and helps ensure that the fidelity of Skillstreaming generalization is addressed. This tool is for use by group leaders to evaluate how they incorporate generalization into their training before, during, and after carrying out Skillstreaming instructional procedures. The checklist may also be used by Skillstreaming master trainers as they work with and observe novice group leaders.

TRANSFER-ENHANCING PROCEDURES

Efforts to develop means of maximizing transfer and maintenance have resulted in considerable success. A variety of useful techniques have been

developed, evaluated, and put into practice. As suggested by Kame'enui and Simmons (1990), the generalization and maintenance procedures described are generally separated into procedures to implement before, during, and after instruction.

Before Instruction

Entrapment

Peer influences are strong in the interpersonal lives of most young persons ages 12 to 18. Smoke pot? Drink beer? Have sex? Break a school window? Play ball? Hang out here? Hang out there? Steal that car? Raise a hand in class? Buy those pants? Walk like this? Talk like that? The answers to these questions, big and small, are often determined in interactions with peers. For most adolescents, the clique, the group, and the gang are powerful forces. Therefore, skills selected must be socially valid, significant, or important to others, including peers (Schoenfeld, Rutherford, Gable, & Rock, 2008).

Skillstreaming further employs the principle of transfer enhancement by including as group members the same people the youth interacts with on a regular basis outside of the group (McIntosh & MacKay, 2008; Walker, Ramsey, & Gresham, 2004). Including the peer group allows peers to reward the target student for skill use (Maag, 2006). This concept is referred to as entrapment, or providing natural reinforcement by peers for the student's performance of a desirable social behavior (McConnell, 1987). Thus, if possible, in the school setting all members of a Skillstreaming group should be from one class. For the same reason, in residential, agency, or institutional settings, teaching groups are most often constructed to directly parallel the facility's unit, crew, cottage, or ward structure. Participation in the same group affords an excellent opportunity to teach participants positive alternatives for dealing with their real-life difficulties.

Instruction that focuses on the peer group and promoting entrapment (Maag, 2005) is a recent advance in social skills training. Including the peer group in the learning process provides the opportunity for the group member to be rewarded by the people who have the strongest influence on his or her behavior during the adolescent years.

Peer feedback has been shown to have positive effects on prosocial behavior. For example, Moroz and Jones (2002) implemented a positive peer reporting program, which taught students to describe and provide praise to socially isolated classmates during structured sessions. Results showed a decrease in negative behaviors and an increase in positive social interactions in the classroom. Jones, Young, and Friman (2000) also instructed peers in giving positive feedback to delinquent, socially rejected adolescents. This protocol included looking at the learner, smiling, saying a positive thing the learner did or said, and giving verbal praise. Their results indicated improved peer acceptance for the target youth. Younger children have also been successfully taught how to recognize socially appropriate behavior and tell teachers when peers have behaved in socially appropriate ways (to "tootle" versus

"tattle") (Skinner, Cashwell, & Skinner, 2000). Results of these studies suggest that involving peers in the efforts to improve the social behaviors of skill-deficient children and adolescents is likely to enhance effectiveness by positively changing their social lives.

During Instruction

Provision of General Principles

Generalization may be facilitated by providing the student with the general mediating principles that govern satisfactory performance on both the original and transfer task. The student can be given the rules, strategies, or organizing principles that lead to successful performance. The general finding that understanding the principles underlying successful performance can enhance transfer to new tasks and contexts has been reported in a number of domains of psychological research, including studies of labeling, rules, advance organizers, and learning sets. It is a robust finding, with empirical support in both laboratory and psychoeducational settings.

No matter how competently Skillstreaming leaders seek to create in the role-play setting the "feel" of the real-life setting in which the student will need to use the skill and no matter how well the coactor in a given role-play matches the actual qualities the real target person possesses, there will always be differences between role-play and real world. Even when the student has role-played the skill a number of times, the demands of the actual situation will depart in some respects from the demands portrayed in the role-play. And the real parent, real peer, or real teacher is likely to respond at least somewhat differently than the student's role-play partner. When the student has a good grasp of the principles underlying a situation (demands, expected behaviors, norms, purposes, rules) and the principles underlying the skill (why these steps, in this order, toward which ends), successful transfer of skill performance becomes more likely.

Overlearning

Transfer of training is enhanced by procedures that maximize overlearning or response availability: The likelihood that a response will be available is clearly a function of its prior use. We repeat and repeat foreign language phrases we are trying to learn, we insist that our child spend an hour per day in piano practice, and we devote considerable time practicing to make a golf swing smooth and automatic. These are simply expressions of the response-availability notion—that is, the more we have practiced responses (especially correct ones), the easier it will be to use them in other contexts or at later times. It has been well established that, other things being equal, the response emitted most frequently in the past is more likely to be emitted on subsequent occasions. However, it is not sheer practice of attempts at effective behaviors that is of most benefit to transfer but practice of successful attempts. Overlearning involves extending learning over more trials than would be necessary merely to produce initial changes in the individual's behavior. In all too many instances, one or two successes at a given task are taken as evidence to move on to the next task or the next level of the original task. This is an error in terms of transfer via overlearning. To maximize transfer, the guiding rule should not be "practice makes perfect" (implying that one simply practices until one gets it right and then moves on) but "practice of perfect" (implying numerous overlearning trials of correct responses after the initial success).

Some students who have just received good feedback from group members and leaders about their role-play (all steps followed and well portrayed) may object to the request that they role-play the skill a second or third time. Although valid concerns exist about the consequences of boredom when teaching a group of often restless students, the value of skill repetition cannot be overstressed. Often leaders, not students, are most bored by the repetition. To assuage student concerns, leaders can point to the value for professional athletes of warm-ups, shoot-arounds, batting practice, and other repetitive practice. Such practice makes core skills nearly automatic and frees the player to concentrate on strategy.

In many real-life contexts, people and events actually work against the student's use of prosocial behaviors. It is therefore appropriate for a Skillstreaming group to spend two, three, or even more sessions role-playing a single skill. To reduce the possible interference of new learning on previously learned materials, a second skill should be introduced only when a student can recall the steps of the first skill, has had opportunities to role-play it, and has shown some initial transfer outside of the group teaching setting (e.g., has successfully completed a homework assignment).

Stimulus Variability

The previous section addressed enhancement of transfer by means of practice and repetition—that is, by the sheer number of correct skill responses the student makes. Transfer is also enhanced by the variability or range of situations to which the individual responds. Teaching related to even two situations is better than teaching related to one. As Kazdin (1975) comments:

> One way to program response maintenance and transfer of training is to develop the target behavior in a variety of situations and in the presence of several individuals. If the response is associated with a range of settings, individuals, and other cues, it is less likely to be lost when the situations change. (p. 21)

Epps, Thompson, and Lane (1985) discuss stimulus variability for transfer enhancement as it might operate in school contexts under the rubrics "train sufficient examples" and "train loosely." They observe that generalization of new skills or behaviors can also be facilitated by training students under a wide variety of conditions. Manipulating the numbers of leaders, settings, and response classes involved in the intervention promotes generalization by exposing students to a variety of situations. If, for example, students are asked to role-play a given skill correctly three times, each attempt should involve a different co-actor, a different setting, and, especially, a different need for the same skill.

Identical Elements

In perhaps the earliest experimental work dealing with transfer enhancement, Thorndike and Woodworth (1901) concluded that, when one habit had a facilitative effect on another, it was to the degree that the habits shared identical elements. Ellis (1965) and Osgood (1953) later emphasized the importance for transfer of similarity between characteristics of the training and application tasks. As Osgood (1953) noted: "The greater the similarity between practice and test stimuli, the greater the amount of positive transfer" (p. 213).

In Skillstreaming, the principle of identical elements is implemented by procedures that increase the "real-lifeness" of the stimuli (places, people, events, etc.) to which the leader is helping the student learn to respond with effective, satisfying behaviors. Two broad strategies exist for attaining such high levels of correspondence between in-group and extra-group stimuli. The first concerns the place in which Skillstreaming takes place. Typically, groups remain in the school or institution and by use of props and imagination recreate the feel of the real-world context in which the student plans to use the skill. Because skills learned in context are more likely to generalize (Gresham, Sugai, & Horner, 2001), whenever possible, the Skillstreaming group leaves the formal teaching setting and meets in the actual locations in which the problem behaviors occur: "Fight on the playground? Let's have our session there." "Sitting alone at lunch? Let's move to the lunchroom." "Argument with a teacher in the hallway? Today's group will meet out there."

After Instruction

Instructed Generalization

One of the group leaders should be the person with whom the students regularly interact (e.g.,

a classroom teacher). This group leader's experience with group members aids in identifying needed skills and allows for prompting and coaching of student skill use as situations arise during the day (Pelco & Reed-Victor, 2007). As stated by McIntosh & MacKay (2008), "the person teaching the [social skills] lessons should be the person who supervises the generalization setting" (p. 19). The Skillstreaming group leader may additionally imbed instruction within naturally occurring events, such as academic skill classes (Smith & Gilles, 2003). This powerful strategy, termed instructed generalization or capturing teachable moments, greatly enhances both skill learning and generalization.

Mediated Generalization

The one certain commonality present in both teaching and real-life settings is the target student. Mediated generalization—mediated by the student, not by others—is an approach to transfer enhancement that relies on instructing the student in a series of self-regulation competencies (Neilans & Israel, 1981). Operationally, it consists of instructing the student in self-recording, self-reinforcement, self-punishment, and self-instruction. Epps et al. (1985), working in a special education setting, have structured these generalization-mediating steps as follows.

Self-recording

1. The teacher sets up the data collection system—that is, selects a target behavior, defines it in measurable terms, and decides on an appropriate recording technique.

2. The teacher tries out the data collection system.

3. The teacher teaches the student how to use the data collection system.

4. The teacher reinforces the student for taking accurate data.

This technique is helpful for several reasons: First, the group leader can become aware of the student's functioning in all school settings. In other words, implementing self-recording procedures may give the teacher an indication of the frequency with which the student actually attempts the skill. Second, skill performance may not always result in positive reinforcement from others, but having the student record performance lets the student know that the teacher will later reinforce these efforts. Finally, many students are far more motivated to use newly learned skills when they, rather than an outside observer, monitor and record their performance.

Self-reinforcement

Steps in self-reinforcement are summarized by Epps et al. (1985) as follows:

1. The teacher determines how many points a student has earned, and the student simply records these.

2. The teacher tells the student to decide how many points should be awarded for appropriate behavior.

3. The student practices self-reinforcement under teacher supervision.

4. The student employs self-reinforcement without teacher supervision.

Frequently, environmental support is insufficient to maintain newly learned skills. In fact, as mentioned earlier, many real-life environments actually discourage efforts at prosocial behavior. For this reason, teaching of self-reinforcement procedures is especially valuable.

Self-recording forms provide a reinforcing function. Self-reinforcement may also consist of verbal praise, in addition to (and later in lieu of) earning points. For example, if the student follows all the steps of a particular skill especially well, self-reinforcement might take the form of saying something positive (e.g., "Good for me" or "I did a good job"). Teachers can help encourage students by having them rehearse self-rewarding statements following completion of homework assignments or after spontaneous

skill use. Videotaping role-play efforts can also be very reinforcing; in addition, being able to review performance helps students assess their skill proficiency.

Self-punishment

Self-punishment is taught in a manner directly parallel to that just described for self-reinforcement. As described here, self-punishment refers to the student's failure to earn points if he or she does not display a desired behavior.

Self-instruction

According to Epps et al. (1985), self-instruction involves the following steps:

1. The teacher models the appropriate behavior while talking through the task aloud so that the student can hear.

2. The student performs the task with overt instructions from the teacher.

3. The student performs the task while talking aloud the self-instructions (overt instructions).

4. The student performs the task with silent (covert) self-instructions.

Cognitive behavior modification strategies, especially those relying heavily on verbal mediation or self-instructional processes, have grown in popularity. Verbal mediation, discussed in chapter 4 as "thinking aloud," is further emphasized during the modeling and role-play portions of the Skillstreaming groups.

MAINTENANCE-ENHANCING PROCEDURES

Maintenance of behaviors developed through skills training approaches is primarily a matter of reinforcement during the original teaching and in the group member's natural environment. The strategies first discussed can be accomplished during the Skillstreaming intervention; the last two apply to generalization after the intervention is over.

During the Skillstreaming Intervention

Thinning Reinforcement

A rich, continuous reinforcement schedule is optimal for the establishment of new behaviors. Maintenance of learned behaviors will be enhanced if the reinforcement is gradually thinned. Thinning of reinforcement proceeds best by moving from a continuous (every trial) schedule, to some form of intermittent schedule, to the level of sparse and infrequent reinforcement characteristic of the natural environment. In fact, the maintenance-enhancing goal of such a thinning process is to make the reinforcement schedule indistinguishable from that typically found in real-world contexts. For example, a student would initially receive a reward for each time he uses a skill, as recorded on Homework Report 1, then the reinforcement would gradually be thinned and the student would receive the reward (perhaps a larger or more desirable reward) for two or more skill performances.

Delaying Reinforcement

Resistance to extinction is also enhanced by delay of reinforcement. During the early stages of learning a new skill, immediate reinforcement contingent upon display of the behavior or skill is necessary. Once the skill has become a part of the adolescent's behavioral repertoire, reinforcement should be delayed, more closely approximating the reinforcing conditions in the natural environment.

Delay of reinforcement may be implemented by (a) increasing the size or complexity of the responses required before reinforcement is provided; (b) adding a time delay between the response and the delivery of reinforcement; and (c) in token systems, increasing the interval between the receipt of tokens and the opportunity to spend them and/or requiring more tokens in exchange for a given reinforcer (Sulzer-Azaroff & Mayer, 1997). For example, the student may initially receive a reward (e.g., tokens) for performing the skill in real life as soon as the skill is observed, then later receive a token for his or her self-report of skill use at the end of the day.

Fading Prompts

Prompting may involve describing the specific types of situations in the real world in which students should use a given skill (i.e., instructed generalization). Students can be encouraged to use a particular skill or verbally prompted in a variety of real-life settings. Historically, teachers have used this principle of generalization by prompting students during "teachable moments," or times the skill is actually needed. When potential problems arise in the classroom, the teacher can elicit a prosocial response by suggesting a particular skill. For example, Alisha, who often became disruptive in the classroom during math independent practice, was again making negative comments under her breath and fumbling in her purse. Rather than waiting for Alisha to become more disruptive and assessing that Alisha was becoming increasingly frustrated, the teacher suggested that she use Asking for Help (Skill 9). Standing near to her, the teacher was able to respond quickly to Alisha's use of the skill. This proactive approach turns naturally occurring problem situations into realistic learning opportunities, thus providing more opportunities for practice. Furthermore, it helps create a positive environment for learning ways to deal with interpersonal problems.

Another way of prompting skill use is to provide written prompts in the form of leader-created cue cards or cue sheets. Cue cards and sheets list the behavioral steps of a skill, along with a space for the student to check each step, either as each is enacted or after all steps are completed. The card may also include a place for self-evaluation. The student may tape the card to his or her desk, if it is a skill that is to be used in the classroom, or keep it in a pocket or folder if it is for use in another setting (e.g., on the school bus, in the hallways, in another classroom, at home).

Displaying a poster of a given skill will help students remember to practice it. Placed wherever it is most appropriate, the cue poster presents the title of the skill and its behavioral steps. If students have been instructed in the skills of Avoiding Trouble with Others (Skill 29) and Using Self-Control (Skill 26), for example, displaying cue posters for these skills in the area of the school where these problems most often occur (e.g., the hallways, cafeteria, and gym) may remind the students of these particular skills and skill steps.

Maintenance may be enhanced by the gradual removal of such suggestions, reminders, coaching, or instruction. Fading of prompts is a means of moving away from artificial control (the leader's) to more natural self-control of desirable behaviors. As is true for all the enhancement techniques examined here, fading of prompts should be carefully planned and systematically implemented.

Providing Booster Sessions

Periodically, it may be necessary to reinstate instruction for certain prosocial behaviors to continue in the natural environment. Booster sessions between teacher and student (behavioral coaching), either on a preplanned schedule or as needed, have proven valuable (Feindler & Ecton, 1986; Karoly & Steffen, 1980; Walker et al., 2004). When the teacher notices that skills previously taught are not used on a consistent basis, these sessions may also be carried out with the group as a whole. In such cases, the skill is retaught via the same methods as initially presented (modeling, role-playing, performance feedback, and generalization). Because the instruction is a review of the skill, the session will likely move more quickly than initial skill instruction.

Preparing for Real-Life Nonreinforcement

Both teacher and student may take energetic steps to maximize the likelihood that reinforcement for appropriate behaviors will occur in the natural environment. Nevertheless, on a number of occasions, reinforcement will not be forthcoming. Thus, it is important for the student to be prepared for this eventuality. As described previously in this chapter, self-reinforcement is one option when desirable behaviors are performed correctly but are unrewarded by external sources.

Graduated homework assignments

The student may also be prepared for nonreinforcement in the natural environment by completing graduated homework assignments. It may become clear at times as Skillstreaming homework is discussed that the real-life figure is too difficult a target, too harsh, too unresponsive, or simply too unlikely to provide reinforcement. When this is the case, with the newly learned skill still fragile, leaders may redirect the homework assignment toward two or three more benevolent target figures. When the student finally does use the skill correctly with the original target figure and receives no reinforcement, these previously reinforced trials help minimize the likelihood that the behavior will be extinguished.

Group reward plans

Using plans in which all group members work together to achieve a common goal helps to create a cooperative spirit in the classroom and will often result in group members' reminding one another to use the skill when a situation suggests its use. For example, the group may decide on a special activity or privilege they would like to earn (e.g., a special field trip, a group lunch, class period to play board games, ice-cream party). The activity selected for the celebration should be one in which the group members are motivated to work toward and one in which they may practice the prosocial skills they have learned. The type of reinforcement or celebration should be based on the length of time it takes to earn the privilege. The group leader decides on the number of points needed to earn the celebration and how many points the group can earn. For example, if the group members together could earn 50 points, a celebration in school may need 500 points, whereas an off-campus celebration may need 750 points. It is most helpful if a smaller celebration is selected first so the group may earn this more quickly. As students become familiar with the group reinforcement system, a larger celebration may then be planned. Individual students earn the points for the entire group until enough points are earned for the activity.

This strategy emphasizes the use of prosocial skills, reminds students to use selected skills, publicly reinforces skill use, and encourages working together to achieve a goal.

Contingency contracting

Contingency contracting, an additional type of homework, is an agreement between the teacher and student stating a behavioral goal the student will work to achieve and the reward that will be earned for achieving that goal. The goal and reward are negotiated by the teacher and student. Typically, both parties agree to carry out an action—the student to perform a selected behavior or skill (for a given length of time or a predetermined number of times) and the teacher to provide the mutually agreed on reinforcement (e.g., a class popcorn party). Contingency contracting has been found to both enhance generalization of learned skills, in addition to reducing the problematic behavior. For example, Mruzek, Cohen, and Smith (2007) additionally found that contingency contracting, along with Skillstreaming, decreased problem behavior for students on the autism spectrum.

Homme, Csanyi, Gonzales, and Rechs (1969) present several rules to follow when implementing contingency contracts. These include the following:

1. Initial contracts should require a small amount of behavior change.

2. The payoff (reward) should be given immediately after the performance of the task.

3. Frequent rewards should be provided.

4. Contracts should reward accomplishments rather than obedience.

5. The terms should be clearly stated.

6. Contracts should be fair.

7. Contracts should be reviewed regularly.

8. Contracts should be phrased in a positive manner.

9. Contracting should be carried out consistently.

Further, contracts should be in writing, not merely verbal; signed by both teacher and student; have beginning and ending dates; and, if appropriate, specify a reward for a particular behavior or skill performance and a bonus reward for extraordinary performance. (Figure 5, in chapter 2, presents a sample contract.)

Social skills games

A variety of games can be developed and used to enhance skill learning. Group games require students to practice a variety of social skills (e.g., joining in, being a good sport). Types of games that lend themselves well to Skillstreaming include board games and role-play games.

Cartledge and Milburn (1980) make several important points worth considering when using social skills games:

1. The connection between performing a skill in the game setting and in real life needs to be made explicit.

2. The winner (if there is one) should be determined on the basis of performance rather than solely on the basis of chance.

3. If rewards are used, they should be given for appropriate (skilled) participation rather than for winning.

4. Participants should not be "out" in a game without provisions for being allowed to participate again within a short period of time.

5. If teaming is required, skill-deficient adolescents should be included on the same team as those with greater skill competence.

Prosocial skills folders

All students in the Skillstreaming group should keep a prosocial skills folder. This is simply a way of organizing materials—cue cards, homework assignments, skill contracts, awards, self-monitoring forms, lists of appropriate alternative activities for use with particular skills, and the like. Students will then have an easy record of the behavioral steps to the skills they have practiced in the past.

Beyond the Skillstreaming Intervention

The maintenance-enhancing techniques examined thus far are directed toward the student. But maintenance of appropriate behaviors also may be enhanced by efforts directed toward others, especially those in the student's natural environment who function as the main providers of reinforcement.

Programming for Reinforcement in the Natural Environment

The student's larger interpersonal world includes a variety of people—parents, siblings, peers, teachers, neighbors, classmates, and others. By their responsiveness or unresponsiveness to the student's newly learned skills, to a large extent they control the destiny of these behaviors. We all react to what the important people in our lives think or feel about our behavior. What they reward, we are more likely to continue doing. What they are indifferent or hostile to will tend to fall into disuse.

During the past several years, Skillstreaming efforts have included increased involvement of educators, agency and institutional staff, parents, and peers in students' acquisition and maintenance of skills. Our earlier suggestion that support staff be trained as "transfer coaches" is one way we have served this goal (see

chapter 1). Parents have been a second target for procedures designed to enhance the likelihood that prosocial skills, once learned, will be maintained.

Using Natural Reinforcers

An especially valuable approach to maintenance enhancement is the use of reinforcers that occur naturally and readily in the student's real-world environment. Galassi and Galassi (1984) offer the following comment:

> We need to target those behaviors for changes that are most likely to be seen as acceptable, desirable, and positive by others. Ayllon and Azrin (1968) refer to this as the "Relevance of Behavior Rule." "Teach only those behaviors that will continue to be reinforced after training." (p. 10)

Alberto and Troutman (2006) suggest a four-step process to facilitate the use of natural reinforcers:

1. Observe which specific behaviors are regularly reinforced and how they are reinforced in the major settings that constitute the student's natural environment.

2. Instruct the student in a selected number of such naturally reinforced behaviors (e.g., certain social skills, grooming behaviors).

3. Teach the student how to recruit or request reinforcement (e.g., by tactfully asking peers or others for approval or recognition).

4. Teach the student how to recognize reinforcement when it is offered because its presence in certain gestures or facial expressions may be quite subtle for many students.

CHAPTER 6

Managing Behavioral Concerns

Problems can and do occur in the Skillstreaming group. Group members may not wish to attend, or their attendance may be sporadic. They may be unmotivated to participate as requested or may fail to see the relevance of the skill curriculum to the demands of their everyday lives. In a variety of ways, they may actively resist meaningful group involvement. Their resistive behavior may interfere not only with their new skill acquisition but also with the learning of others in the group.

This chapter first describes common types of resistance that youth in Skillstreaming groups display. It next examines responses to group member resistance according to three tiers or levels of intervention: universal strategies (to be used with managing the group as a whole), targeted strategies (for some students exhibiting moderate behavior problems), and individual strategies (for individual students with significant problematic behavior).

GROUP MEMBER RESISTANCE

Though not infinite, the ways participants may seek to thwart, circumvent, object to, or resist participation in the Skillstreaming group are numerous. These are listed in Table 5.

Inactivity

Minimal participation involves group members who seldom volunteer, provide only brief answers, and in general give leaders a feeling that they are "pulling teeth" to keep the group at its various skills training tasks. A more extreme form of minimal participation is *apathy,* in which nearly everything the leaders do to direct, enliven, or activate the group is met with a lack of interest and spontaneity and little if any progress toward group goals.

While it is rare, *falling asleep* does occur from time to time. The sleepers need to be awakened, and the trainers might wisely inquire into the cause of the tiredness. Boredom in the group, lack of sleep, and physical illness are all possible reasons, each requiring a different response.

Hyperactivity

Digression is a repetitive, determined, and strongly motivated movement away from the purposes and procedures of Skillstreaming. Here group members feel some emotion strongly, such as anger or anxiety or despair, and are determined to express it. Or the brief lecture given or the skill portrayed by the leaders or other group members may set off associations with important recent experiences, which the group members feel the need to present and discuss. Digression is also often characterized by "jumping out of role." Rather than merely wandering off track, in digression, the trainees drive the train off its intended course.

Monopolizing involves subtle and not-so-subtle efforts by group members to get more than a fair share of time during a Skillstreaming session. Long monologues, unnecessary requests

---

Table 5: Types of Group Member Resistance

Inactivity

Minimal participation

Apathy

Falling asleep

Hyperactivity

Digression

Monopolizing

Interruption

Excessive restlessness

Active Resistance

Participation but not as instructed

Passive-aggressive isolation

Negativism, refusal

Disruptiveness

Aggression

Sarcasm, put-downs

Bullying, intimidation

Use of threats

Assaultiveness

Cognitive Inadequacies

Inability to pay attention

Inability to understand

Inability to remember

---

to repeat role-plays, elaborate feedback, and other attention-seeking efforts to "remain on stage" are examples of such monopolizing behavior. Similar to monopolizing but more intrusive and insistent, *interruption* is literally breaking into the ongoing flow of a modeling display, role-play, or feedback period with comments, questions, suggestions, observations, or other statements. Interruption may be overly assertive or angry or may take the more pseudobenevolent guise of "help" to the leaders. In either event, such interruptions more often than not detour the group's progress toward its goals.

Excessive restlessness is a more extreme, more physical form of hyperactivity. Participants may fidget while sitting; rock their chairs; get up and pace; or display other nonverbal, verbal, gestural, or postural signs of restlessness. Excessive restlessness will typically be accompanied by digression, monopolizing, or interrupting behavior.

Active Resistance

Group members involved in *participation but not as instructed* are off target. They may be trying

to role-play, serve as coactor, give feedback, or engage in other tasks required in a given Skillstreaming session, but their own personal agendas or misperceptions interfere and they wander off course to irrelevant or semirelevant topics.

Passive-aggressive isolation is not merely apathy, in which group members are simply uninterested in participating. Nor is it participation but not as instructed, in which they actively go off task and raise personal agendas. Passive-aggressive isolation is the purposeful, intentional withholding of appropriate participation, an active shutting down of involvement. It can be thought of as a largely nonverbal "crossing of one's arms" in order to display deliberate nonparticipation.

When displaying *negativism,* participants signal more overtly, by word and deed, the wish to avoid participation in the Skillstreaming group. Open *refusal* may take the form of unwillingness to role-play, listen to instructions, or complete homework assignments. Or members may not come to sessions, come late to sessions, or walk out in the middle of a session.

Disruptiveness encompasses active resistance behaviors more extreme than negativism, such as openly and perhaps energetically ridiculing leaders, other group members, or aspects of the Skillstreaming procedures. Or disruptiveness may be shown by gestures, movements, noises, or other distracting nonverbal behaviors characteristically symbolizing overt criticism and hostility.

Aggression

Sarcasm and put-downs are denigrating trainee comments, made to ridicule the skill enactment or other behaviors of a fellow group member. The intent of such caustic evaluations is to criticize and diminish the appraised worth of such performance.

Bullying and intimidation are especially common problem behaviors because these behaviors are often characteristic of youth selected for Skillstreaming participation. The behaviors in this category are often more severe in both their intent and consequences than sarcasm and put-downs.

Further along on such a continuum, the overt use of *explicit threats* is the next category of Skillstreaming group management problems. One youth may warn another of impending embarrassment, revelation of confidences, or even bodily harm if compliance to one or another demand is not forthcoming.

Finally, on rare occasions, actual *physical assaultiveness* may occur in a Skillstreaming group. This very serious breach of group safety can have particularly harmful consequences for group functioning. For this individual in the group, more intense and individually designed interventions are indicated.

Cognitive Inadequacies

Closely related at times to excessive restlessness, the *inability to pay attention* is often apparently the result of internal or external distractions, daydreaming, or other pressing agendas that command group members' attention. Inability to pay attention except for brief time spans may also be due to one or more forms of cognitive impairment.

Cognitive deficits due to developmental disability, intellectual inadequacy, impoverishment of experience, disease processes, or other sources may result in trainees' *inability to understand* aspects of the Skillstreaming curriculum. Failure to understand can, of course, also result from errors in the clarity and complexity of statements presented by leaders. Material presented in the Skillstreaming group may be both attended to and understood by participants but not remembered.

Inability to remember may result not only in problems of skill transfer but also in group management problems when what is forgotten includes rules and procedures for participation, homework assignments, and so forth.

THREE LEVELS OF INTERVENTION

Which particular means of increasing motivation and reducing behavior problems are best for any given Skillstreaming group will vary according to leader, group member, and setting characteristics. Skillstreaming leaders should begin first with the universal strategies next described and, as necessary, move up the continuum to targeted and individual strategies.

Universal Strategies

Learning Climate

The atmosphere of the Skillstreaming group should be positive. The leader should openly notice group members following group rules and making prosocial choices rather than catching them breaking rules. A benefit of this approach is the fact that when a leader sees a child behaving appropriately and states approval of that behavior publicly, youth engaging in unacceptable behavior are likely to stop that behavior and engage in the behavior that received approval (Kounin, 1970). Such open attempts to "catch them being good" are highly effective in the Skillstreaming group.

Physical structure

The physical environment can structure the learning setting. To minimize potential behavior problems during teaching, the area in which Skillstreaming instruction is carried out needs to be large enough so group members can participate in role-plays without disrupting other participants. Positioning chairs an arm's length away from one another is useful to help create physical distance. To reduce distractions, enticing activities such as games or computers should be moved out of the group's view. Visuals are useful to assist learning; therefore, the group rules or behavioral guidelines should be posted and reviewed prior to each instructional session as a reminder for the entire group to use positive behavior. Allowing space for traffic can minimize disruption of ongoing activities as students move from one area to another. Enhancing the physical structure of the group setting with strategies like those just described can minimize and avert many behavior problems; the structure can then be gradually lessened as group members become more familiar with working together.

Behavioral expectations/rules

Management of the Skillstreaming group begins with collaboration to develop the behavioral rules to follow to create a safe and effective learning environment. A number of effective "rules for use of rules" have emerged in the contingency management literature (Greenwood, Hops, Delquadri, & Guild, 1974; Sarason, Glaser, & Fargo, 1972; Walker, 1979), including the following:

1. Define and communicate rules for behavior in specific behavioral terms. As Walker (1979) notes, it is better (more concrete and behavioral) to say, "Raise your hand before asking a question" than to say, "Be considerate of others." Similarly, "Listen carefully to instructions" or "Pay attention to the feedback procedure" are easier rules to follow than the more ambiguous "Behave in class" or "Do what you are told."

2. It is more effective to tell participants what to do than what not to do. Accentuating the positive finds expression in rules directing group members to take turns, talk over disagreements, and work quietly rather than in rules directing them not to jump in, fight, and speak out.

3. Rules should be made easy to remember. Depending on the age of group members and the difficulty of following the rules, memorization aids may include keeping the rules short and few in number, presenting the rules several times, and posting the rules in written form so everyone can see them.

4. Rule adherence is likely to be greater when group members play a role in rule development, modification, and implementation. This sense of participation may be brought about by discussing rules with the entire group, selecting participants to explain to the group the specific meaning of each rule, and having them role-play the behaviors involved in following the rule.

In addition to these recommendations, further effective rules for rules are that they be developed at the start of the group; that they be fair, reasonable, and within group members' capacity to follow; that all group members understand the rules; and that they be applied equally and fairly to all. Skillstreaming group rules developed in this manner enhance the likelihood that the group will be a safe and productive place for its members.

Supportive Interventions

Adolescents will more readily learn the Skillstreaming curriculum when it is presented in an encouraging and supportive environment. The previous section described considerations related to planning and structuring such a learning environment. The following interventions are designed to support students' desirable behaviors in an unobtrusive manner within the actual teaching sequence. These interventions include group teaching techniques, enhancing motivation, behavioral redirection, and relationship-based techniques.

Group teaching techniques

What do teachers actually do to support positive behaviors in the learning setting? Kounin's (1970) early research is relevant to group instruction in today's schools and other group instructional settings. First, the group leader knows what is going on. Such *with-it-ness* is communicated to the group in a number of ways, including swift and consistent recognition and, when necessary, consequating of low-level behaviors likely to grow into disruptiveness or more serious aggression. Closely connected to such attentiveness is *over-lapping*, the ability to manage simultaneously two or more classroom events, whether instructional or disciplinary. *Smoothness*, the ability to transition from one activity to another without downtime, is a third facilitative group leader behavior. Downtime is a time for students to become bored and act out; avoiding or minimizing downtime significantly deters such behaviors.

Another way to minimize boredom is by instructing with *momentum*, maintaining a steady progress or movement throughout a particular lesson, class, or school day. A *group focus*, the ability to keep the entire class or group involved in Skillstreaming, also diminishes the likelihood of student disruption. Finally, an especially significant contributor to a supportive learning environment is the group leader's communication of *optimistic expectations*. Students live up to (and, unfortunately, also down to) what important people in their lives expect of them. The teacher who expects a child to be a "slow learner" or a "behavior problem" because of his or her past record, a sibling's past poor performance, or the neighborhood the student comes from will likely be rewarded with low performance or behavior problems. By contrast, the teacher who lets the student know he or she can achieve and will have the teacher's help along the way is likely to motivate the student to be more successful and less disruptive. The message is expect the best of the students—you may well get it!

Consistent application of rules and procedures provides clear expectations for student behavior and establishes that the group leader (or teacher) is in charge of the group (or class). Yet such consistency is challenging to maintain over time. Teachers become tired, overworked, and distracted. When this occurs, students are quick to get the message that perhaps "just this once" can become more than once. Then the boundary between what is and is not acceptable is no longer clear. Students of all ages test the limits to reestablish the boundary, and, as this happens, the foundation for a supportive learning environment begins to erode.

Supportive environments are predictable environments. As noted previously, a well thought out and fairly and consistently enforced set of the school rules or guidelines strongly helps establish such predictability. Consistent enforcement means that all staff are aware of and enforce rules in agreed-upon ways. But the demands of fairness and consistency may be contradictory at times. Consistency requires rule enforcement for all applicable occasions; fairness may require taking special circumstances into account and deliberately not enforcing a given rule in some instances.

Enhancing motivation

Motivation is not an easy task. Many of the youth offered the opportunity to learn from Skillstreaming are highly competent in the regular use of antisocial behavior. Furthermore, these behaviors may be frequently encouraged and rewarded by significant people in these students' lives—family, peers, and others. Two types of motivators are at the group leader's disposal: extrinsic and intrinsic. *Extrinsic motivators* are tangible rewards provided contingent upon performance of desired behaviors. Tangible motivators are, in fact, widely used in schools and other institutions serving children and youth. The stars and stickers of the preschool and primary years take the form of points and special privileges and activities in the later grades. Extrinsic rewards appear to be especially useful in eliciting initial involvement in learning unfamiliar skills.

Many teachers of Skillstreaming report that using only external rewards—whether in the form of tangible reinforcers, a token economy, a levels system, or other incentives—is insufficient on a sustained basis. Substantial intrinsic motivators also must be present.

In Skillstreaming, one *intrinsic motivator* resides in the skills themselves, especially those that students select themselves and use successfully in their real-world settings. As discussed in chapter 1, negotiating the skill curriculum is central. Allowing adolescents to select the skills they feel they need is a major step toward participation motivation. When student-selected (or, to perhaps a somewhat lesser degree, teacher-selected) skills yield positive outcomes in interactions with family, peers, or significant others, motivation is further enhanced.

Behavioral redirection

One way to encourage a student's appropriate behavior while preventing the occurrence of negative actions is to employ behavioral redirection. For example, a student who frequently disrupts the Skillstreaming group by making negative comments under his breath, may be asked to assist the group leader in pointing out the skill steps as they are being role-played. Still another student who feels the need to dominate conversation in the group may be asked to write her ideas on the computer. Behavioral redirection allows the teacher to emphasize the student's positive, helping actions without having to ignore the student's negative behaviors or deal with them in a manner disruptive to the learning of others.

Relationship-based techniques

Psychologists and educators have long known that the better the relationship between the helper and client (or teacher and student), the more positive and productive the outcome of their interaction. In fact, it has been demonstrated that a positive relationship is a potent factor in effecting academic achievement (Jones & Jones, 2000), in addition to long-term behavior change. The techniques next described draw primarily on the relationship between teacher and student and can often be combined with other management techniques for maximum effect. Specifically, these include empathic encouragement and threat reduction.

Empathic encouragement is a strategy in which the teacher or group leader first shows understanding of the difficulty the student is experiencing and then urges the student to participate as instructed. Often this additional one-to-one attention will motivate the student to participate and follow the teacher's guidance. In applying this technique, the teacher first listens to the student's explanation of the problem and expresses an understanding of the student's feelings and behavior (e.g., "I know learning something new can be very frustrating"). If appropriate, the teacher responds that the student's view is a valid alternative for dealing with the problem. The teacher then restates his or her own view with supporting reasons and probable outcomes and urges the student to try out the suggestion (e.g., "If you don't try the skill, you won't know if you can do it. I have confidence in you that you can do it.")

Threat reduction is helpful in dealing with students' anxiety. Adolescents who find role-playing or other types of participation threatening may react with inappropriate or disruptive behaviors or withdraw from the learning process. To deal with this problem, the teacher should provide reassurance (e.g., "The group and I will be here to help you and give you as much support as you want.") The group leader should also encourage group members to express support for role-players and others who participate. Other strategies for threat reduction include postponing the student's role-playing until last, first coaching the student through the role-play at another time away from the group, and clarifying and restructuring those aspects of the task that the student experiences as threatening.

Capturing Teachable Moments

Capturing teachable moments employs Skillstreaming itself to better manage the Skillstreaming group. The problem behaviors subsequently discussed in this chapter—minimal participation, disruptiveness, digression, bullying, and so forth—may each be viewed as a behavioral excess. Each behavior may equally well be construed as a behavioral *deficiency* (e.g., too much monopolizing is too little listening to others, too much bullying is too little empathy directed toward others). Thus, an additional means for reducing problem behaviors is to replace them with desirable behaviors. The Skillstreaming curriculum permits teaching the skills as scheduled, as part of regular sessions, or at teachable moments that serve to reduce resistance and open opportunities to learn yet other skills.

Sometimes the planned schedule must be abandoned in favor of dealing with a problem that has just occurred. If the group appears tense and upset due to an issue that just occurred (e.g., an argument in the hallway, a physical altercation on the way to group), continuing the planned agenda will clearly not meet the students' immediate needs. Instead, the group leader should restructure the plan as in the following example.

The two leaders are conducting the session-opening homework report segment of a Skillstreaming meeting. The skill role-played the previous session was Expressing Affection (Skill 19). In role-playing this skill, one group member, Jane, rehearsed with another member skill steps involving approaching a male student to invite him to an upcoming party.

Leader: Jane, how did your homework work out? Did you go to Lee and ask him to go to that Saturday party with you?

Jane: No, I didn't. I didn't say anything to Lee, and I want you to know that I'm really pissed off today.

Leader: Oh? What's going on?

Jane: You said this group was a confidential group, that one of our rules was whatever happens in the group stays in the group. Somebody told Lee that I think he's cute. It really makes me mad as hell and embarrassed as hell. I don't know who told him, but right after the meeting last week I saw Jennifer go over to Lee and say something. I think she told him, and I'm going to smack her in the face right now.

Jane stands up and begins moving toward Jennifer. At this point it is the leader's responsibility to do two things. The first is to make clear that the first group member will not be permitted to physically harm the second and to take immediate steps to make sure such containment occurs. Once safety is assured, the leader captures the teachable moment presented by the confrontation and turns it into an opportunity for learning. The group member, Jane, seeks to resolve her anger by attacking the peer she believes is its source. The chance is to teach Jane an alternative, more prosocially skilled way of handling the same situation. As a bonus, the situation presents the opportunity to teach for the second youth, Jennifer, a complementary skill.

Leader: *(To Jane)* Jane, we are not going to permit you to hit Jennifer, but I know you're really angry. I think there are better ways to express how you feel. Do you remember about three sessions back we learned the skill Standing Up for Your Rights? As I recall, you did a pretty good job role-playing it, but your homework on it with your father was a bit of a problem. Remember? Here's a skill card for it. I'd like you to practice it right now with Jennifer. Rather than hit her, let her know what you think and feel by acting out these steps.

(To Jennifer) Jennifer, you can see that Jane is really angry with you. She's going to say something to you about her suspicion that you spoke to Lee about what happened in here. You may get angry back at her—I don't know—but I want you to try to respond to her with a skill we haven't learned yet. It's called Dealing with an Accusation. Here is the skill card for it. Got it?

Targeted Strategies

For most students, employing universal strategies is effective in supporting students' desirable behaviors in an unobtrusive manner within the instructional setting while, in most cases, allowing instruction to continue. At times, however, for some students, more structured and directive interventions may be necessary. While universal interventions just described will continue to be used with all students in the group, additional targeted interventions are indicated with a smaller number of students.

Understanding Function of Behavior Problems

The first step in managing problem behaviors at the targeted level is for the group leaders to ask themselves "Why at this moment is the student engaging in this particular behavior?" All behavior serves a purpose or a function. To intervene in useful ways, teachers must be able to assess that function.

Typical functions of problem behavior include seeking attention, escaping of a task or expectation, avoiding a person, or self-regulating emotion (e.g., reducing anxiety). The diagnosis, or hypothesis about the function of problem behavior, will often suggest the cure. It is possible to ask group members direct questions to confirm the diagnosis—for example, Could it be that you don't want to participate? Could it be that you want me to leave you alone? Or, could it be that this whole thing seems too complicated? The goal in understanding the function of problem behaviors is straightforward: to maximize the level of youth involvement and on-task time and therefore increase learning, as well as to minimize time spent in distraction, aggression, or other off-task behaviors.

Perhaps the leader's hypothesis is that the group member displays a particular resistive behavior at a particular moment because what is being asked is too complicated (too many steps, too complex a challenge, too demanding a requirement). If this is the case, a good attempt at resistance reduction would be to simplify and decrease demands on the trainee's abilities. Steps group leaders have taken to simplify what is being asked of participants include the following:

1. Reward minimal accomplishment.
2. Shorten the role-play.
3. Have the leader "feed" sentences to the group member.
4. Have the group member read a prepared script portraying the behavioral steps.
5. Have the group member play the coactor role first.

Alternatively, perhaps the leader feels the task is not too complicated: "Helen has handled even more difficult skills in here quite well. Perhaps she's feeling threatened. The feedback given by Charlie and Ed on the last role-play was really tough. Helen had a hard time dealing with it. Maybe Helen fears she's about to become their next target." If threat and intimidation are central in the trainer's diagnosis, threat-reduction steps should be taken immediately. Several possibilities of this type are as follows:

1. Employ additional leader modeling.
2. Postpone group member's role-playing until last in sequence.

3. Provide reassurance.

4. Provide empathic encouragement.

5. Clarify aspects of the task that are experienced as threatening.

6. Restructure aspects of the task that are experienced as threatening.

Targeting and Addressing Aggression

The Skillstreaming leader functions not only as a competent teacher, model, and role-play/feedback guide but also as a protector. In creating a safe learning environment, the leader must immediately correct any efforts to bully, intimidate, dominate, or otherwise treat other group members in an inappropriate, aggressive manner. Vigilance serves not only to protect the attacked but also to provide additional skills training for the attacker. The following excerpt from a Skillstreaming workshop for group leaders illustrates this dual benefit.

Leader: You four pretend you are adolescents in a relatively new Skillstreaming group. Ellen and I have modeled a new skill, and Carolyn has just completed the group's first role-play of it. It is a skill she needs badly in her personal life. Since I privately think she did a fine job in following the skill's steps during her role-play, I'm hoping she gets the kind of positive performance feedback from her peers in this group that will motivate her to really use the skill where and when it will be helpful for her. "Karen," I ask this first trainee, "Could you tell us what Carolyn did to carry out the first skill step and how well you think she did it?" And Karen here says, "It was really nice what she said. When she turned to Barbara [the co-actor] and said, 'I appreciate the invitation a lot, but I can't go,' it was right on target, firm but friendly." "Thanks, Karen," I say, as I think, "Good, this is just the kind of feedback I hoped she'd get." Then I turn to Bill and ask for his feedback to Carolyn on her handling of Step 2, and it, too, is clear and positive. Finally, I ask Jane for her appraisal of the enactment of Step 3, and she responds, "It was so bad I thought I would puke as she did it."

Jane's statement instantly initiates three problems for the group and for the leaders, and they all revolve around this issue of protection. The first concerns Jane. All Jane is doing is showing the very type of aggressive behavior that made her a part of the Skillstreaming group in the first place. Her behavior is threatening to another group member and must be dealt with but dealt with in a manner that is instructive, constructive, and protective not only of Carolyn but also of Jane. The second problem is Bill and Karen. They have not role-played yet, and they are thinking, "Oh, my god, when I get up to role-play, will Jane stick it to me the way she just stuck it to Carolyn?" The third problem is Carolyn. Carolyn is getting the kind of feedback that will discourage rather than encourage her to use the skill. So how does the leader serve as a protector for *all* of these group members?

Leader: One way to do it would be to say to Jane, "Look, Jane, it's good that you could give Carolyn frank feedback, but the way you said it is not going to help her. Can you say it in a more constructive way?" *(behavioral redirection)* If that's not in Jane's repertoire, if she doesn't know how to do that, I would stand Jane up, have her face Carolyn, and I would do what the psychodrama people do, the alter ego technique, where you stand behind her and whisper in her ear: "Jane, I'm going to say certain things to you—you say them to Carolyn."

That teaches Jane a little bit about giving constructive feedback and lets her know that threatening comments are not acceptable. Carolyn gets the feedback, and this helps encourage real-world skill use. Bill and Karen get the message that if Jane sticks it to them, the trainer will come to their aid. In an active manner, we have provided protection plus instruction to all four group members.

Behavior Management Techniques

Both behaviors promoting skill learning and behaviors inhibiting such progress can be managed via competent use of behavior management techniques (i.e., behavior modification). Beyond the repeated demonstration that they work, behavior management techniques are relatively easy to learn and use; may be teacher-, peer-, parent-, and/or self-administered; are generally cost effective; yield typically unambiguous behavior-change results; and have a long history of successful application (with aggressive youth in particular).

A reinforcer is an event that increases the subsequent frequency of any behavior it follows. When the presentation of an event following a behavior increases its frequency, the event is referred to as a *positive reinforcer*. Most leaders of Skillstreaming groups will need to use some type of reinforcement system (e.g., social and token) to positively reinforce rule following. Table 6 lists specific examples of commonly used material, social, activity, and token reinforcers. A more detailed discussion of principles of behavior management techniques—positive and negative reinforcement, time-out, is included as Appendix C in this book.

Individual Strategies

Students who do not increase positive behaviors when provided with universal interventions (consistent structure and routines, along with

supportive interventions) or with targeted procedures may require an individual behavior plan. A student for whom it is frequently necessary to use time-out, for example, will likely benefit from such a plan. Individual plans are more likely to be successful if they are based on consideration of the function of the student's problem behavior. Following is a brief summary of the processes of functional behavioral assessment and the corresponding development of a behavior intervention plan.

Functional Behavioral Assessment

Functional assessment is a method for identifying the variables that reliably predict and maintain problem behavior. The goal of the assessment is to better understand behavior and why the individual acts in this manner. Assessment includes evaluating the antecedents that prompt undesirable behavior to occur, the consequences that maintain the behavior, and the setting events or broad context in which it occurs.

It is important to distinguish between *functional behavior analysis* and *functional behavioral assessment,* or FBA, which is now widely used in schools and other application settings. Originally developed from the field of applied behavior analysis, functional behavior analysis was used in highly controlled settings by manipulating variables to assess their impact on behavior (Horner & Carr, 1997; Gresham, Watson, & Skinner, 2001). It has been employed most frequently to assess the purpose of aberrant behavior, often self-abuse or severe aggression of individuals with developmental disabilities (Ingram, Lewis-Palmer, & Sugai, 2005).

The Individuals with Disabilities Education Act (IDEA, 1997, 2004) includes the requirement that an FBA be conducted in schools when a change to a more restrictive placement due to disciplinary action is considered, when IEP behavioral goals are not sufficient, when a student has been suspended for more than 10 days, and when the student's behavior impedes school functioning or others' ability to learn

Table 6: Commonly Used Reinforcers

Privileges (School)

Listening to CD while working

Locker pass

Early lunch

Computer time

Library pass

Going out for lunch

Listening to iPod while working

Using the school laptop

Privileges (Home)

Having dating privileges

Getting driver's license

Reading

Having an extended curfew

Receiving car privileges

Staying up late

Staying overnight with friends

Having time off from chores

Dating during the week

Having the opportunity to earn money

Selecting television program

Using the family computer

Choosing own bedtime

Participating in activities with friends

Having a part-time job

Having friends over

Rollerblading/skateboarding

Having additional time on the cell phone

Social

Smiles

Hugs

Winks

Verbal praise

Head nods

Thumbs-up sign

Receiving attention when talking

Being asked for opinion

Token (home)

Extra money

Own checking account

Allowance

Gift certificate

Token (school)

Points or coupons to earn privileges as listed above or items such as:

    Tickets to school sporting events

    Food coupons

    School supplies

    Discount coupons for school store

(Cook et al., 2007). This requirement brought FBA technology into the daily lives of teachers, administrators, and support personnel as they worked to transfer the strategy to students in the schools in meaningful ways. FBA is the process recommended most frequently to address severe maladaptive behaviors (Blood & Neel, 2007).

The goal of an FBA is to design meaningful supports for individual students in need of intense interventions and support (Ingram et al., 2005). Outcomes of an FBA include operation-ally defining the problem behavior, identifying the antecedents that predict occurrence and nonoccurrence of the behavior, and identifying the consequences maintaining the behavior (McIntosh, Flannery, Sugai, Braun, & Cochrane, 2008). In other words, questions to be answered through the FBA process include the following (Horner & Carr, 1997):

1. What maintains the problem behavior?

2. What is our prediction of when the problem will occur and when it will not occur?

3. How can we prevent the problem behavior?

4. What do we do when the problem does occur?

FBA is a team-based process involving obtaining information about the student from multiple sources (peers, parents, teachers) and from multiple environments and contexts (e.g., group versus independent; different school settings such as playground, various classrooms, cafeteria; Kulli, 2008). Information is gained through processes such as direct observations, rating scales, and record reviews (Gresham, Watson, & Skinner, 2001). Kern, Hilt, and Gresham (2004) found that, when assessing students with emotional-behavioral disorders and those at risk for these disorders, the most commonly applied methods for FBA in the schools were direct observation and teacher interviews. Once collected, the data are summarized in a way to make decisions regarding useful interventions (Gresham, Watson, & Skinner, 2001) and to describe the relationship among setting events, antecedents, behavior, and consequences (Ingram et al., 2005).

Behavior Intervention Plan

Typically, school behavior plans have been developed based on the disciplinary infraction rather than on individual student needs or the setting in which the challenging behavior occurs (Crone & Horner, 2003). Behavior intervention plans, or BIPs, include both instructional and environmental strategies. Based on the function of the student's problematic behavior (what gains accrue for the student or how the behavior serves to avoid a task, person, or situation), BIPs structure interventions to discourage the student's undesirable behavior, teach acceptable alternative or replacement behaviors, and provide the opportunity and motivation for the student to engage in positive behaviors (Cook et al., 2007). It is important to note here that the focus of both the FBA and following BIP development is not solely to change the student's behavior through teaching skills and changing

consequences but also to change the environment and what adults or peers do to prevent the occurrence of the undesirable behavior (Horner, Sugai, Todd, & Lewis-Palmer, 2000).

Replacement behaviors may be either academic or social and are those that (a) are considered appropriate; (b) serve the same function (e.g., attention, escape); (3) are incompatible with the behavior of concern (e.g., cannot be performed at the same time as the behavior of concern); and (d) are stated positively (Scott, Anderson, & Spaulding, 2008). Further, the replacement behavior should also be meaningful to the student and serve the student's real-life need.

BIPs must also include changing setting events and antecedents to reduce the occurrences of the behavior or concern. As stated by Cook et al. (2007), "Altering the environmental events that precede and follow the problem behavior allows educators to act in a proactive manner to deter student problem behavior" (p. 193). Reducing the problem behavior allows the student to learn an alternative replacement behavior (e.g., a prosocial skill). As clearly stated by Carr and his colleagues (2002), "The best time to intervene on problem behavior is when the behavior is not occurring. Intervention takes place in the absence of problem behavior so that such behavior can be prevented from occurring again" (p. 9). In addition, consequences and crisis management procedures are included in the plan. Following the development of the BIP, decisions must be made regarding who must be trained, who will provide the training, and how outcomes for the student will be measured (Scott et al., 2008).

Matching interventions to the function of the problem behavior improves the effectiveness and efficiency of the selected interventions (LaRue, Weiss, & Ferraioli, 2008). Function-based behavior intervention plans have better reduced the number of problem behaviors (Ingram et al., 2005; Trussell, Lewis, & Stichter, 2008) and increased academic engagement (Carter & Horner, 2009; Crone, Hawken, & Bergstrom, 2007).

Steps in the FBA/BIP Process

The FBA/BIP process follows these general steps:

1. Identify the behavior to be changed. To do this, list the student's problem behaviors in concrete, observable, and measurable terms. Then choose one behavior to decrease in frequency. This may be the behavior that bothers you the most or the one creating the greatest problem for the student.

2. Obtain baseline data to determine how frequently and under what conditions, the undesirable behavior occurs. This process need not be complicated. For example, you may list the undesirable behavior and make a tally mark for each occurrence of the behavior on a given day, generally assessing whether the day has been "typical" for the child. Or you may find an A–B–C format useful (specifying *antecedent* conditions under which the behavior occurred, the specific *behavior* exhibited by the child, and the *consequences* that the child receives as a result of that behavior). The A–B–Cs can be written on a sheet of paper and quickly documented whenever the behavior of concern is observed.

3. On the basis of the preceding assessment and including other assessment data as appropriate, consider what setting events (characteristics of the environment) or antecedents (what happens right before the behavior occurs) seem to precipitate the behavior and what factors seem to maintain the problem behavior. Then hypothesize as to the function or purpose of the child's behavior (i.e., what that behavior achieves for the child). Instead of looking solely at the child's overt behavior (e.g., hitting, refusing, crying), ask what the child is accomplishing from this behavior. The answer to this question is a "best guess" about the function of the child's behavior: to gain attention (e.g., from peers or adults), to escape or avoid (e.g., a task or person), or to gain access to something (e.g., a desired item or activity; Jolivette, Scott, & Nelson, 2000). Is the child's goal to seek attention or to belong? To avoid participation? Perhaps the student is displaying the particular resistive behavior to avoid a task he perceives as too complicated (e.g., one that has too many steps). Another student may be experiencing anxiety as she realizes that her turn to role-play is approaching. Still another child may not be receiving the desired amount of attention from others. Another may engage in undesirable behaviors to belong and gain friends.

4. When you have identified what is motivating the student's behavior (e.g., attention, escape, etc.), identify an alternative or replacement behavior. The replacement behavior serves the same function or purpose as the undesirable behavior. For example, if the undesirable behavior is aggression when the student wants to engage in a prefered task (e.g, using the computer or playing a game), the replacement behavior would be Asking Permission (Skill 22).

5. Teach the replacement behavior.

6. Determine an effective reinforcer and deliver it consistently when the replacement behavior occurs. If the reward is given immediately following the replacement behavior, it is more likely that the behavior will be repeated. Some small reinforcer (e.g., verbal encouragement, a token) should be given immediately following the behavior. A larger reward (e.g., a special privilege) may be given later—for example, when the student has performed the skill multiple times.

7. Once the individual plan has been implemented, monitor behavior change. A chart or graph of the replacement behavior and the initial behavior of concern will show the degree of progress. It is important to evaluate the student's progress. If the replacement

behavior is not increasing (or the problem behavior is not decreasing), the plan must be altered. It could be that the hypothesis about the problem behavior was incorrect, that the replacement behavior selected did not serve the same function for the child as the problem behavior, and so forth. Effective individual interventions are ones that work; as such, monitoring the effectiveness of the plan and making needed changes as indicated by the data are important aspects of behavior change.

Case example

The following example illustrates use of these steps to address aggression, a significant behavioral concern that occurred in a Skillstreaming group.

Jane joined the Skillstreaming group because of her verbal and physical aggression in a variety of school settings. The group leader successfully worked with the group to negotiate the skill curriculum, including Jane's skill needs: Using Self-Control (Skill 26), Understanding the Feelings of Others (Skill 17), Keeping Out of Fights (Skill 30), and Negotiating (Skill 25). Behavioral expectations were generated from the group, and several rules were accepted and clearly defined, including talking to others in a kind way and keeping hands and feet to oneself. During Skillstreaming groups, when Jane became agitated or verbally put down another group member, the group leader either redirected Jane to use a more desirable behavior or coached her through one of the prosocial skills that had previously been instructed (Making a Complaint, Skill 31). Nonetheless, Jane continued to give put-downs and in other ways tried to instigate fights with peers during the group instruction.

The teacher decided to increase the positive reinforcement, delivering more frequent points that could then be exchanged for a variety of classroom privileges. Jane seemed to particu-larly enjoy listening to her iPod while working or inviting a friend for lunch in the classroom and most often exchanged her points for these privileges. Although the fights with peers became less frequent, she continued to instigate peer altercations. When this occurred, the teacher or group leader instructed Jane to leave the group for a five-minute time-out. The teacher thought about the function or purpose of Jane's aggression and didn't have any ready answers. It was difficult to determine the precipitating factors involved in Jane's aggression, so the teacher sought the advice of the school's intervention team.

A functional behavioral assessment was then conducted by the team, including Jane's parents. Through observation, checklists, and interviews with Jane, it was discovered that Jane had similar issues at home when her sister had a friend over and in her classes that were more challenging. She did well in classes where she knew the material and could participate successfully. The antecedent to her aggression seemed to be when Jane was not receiving attention. The setting events seemed to be classes that were more difficult for her and when she wasn't allowed to work with one of her friends. The team hypothesized that, when Jane felt she wasn't receiving attention from her peers or adults, she sought out attention by making a negative comment to a peer or in another way instigating a conflict. The objective of Jane's behavior plan, then, became to help her participate in classes and the Skillstreaming group without making disparaging comments or fighting.

The team designed a BIP for Jane in which a replacement behavior was defined. Because the function of Jane's aggression seemed to be attention, the team wanted to create a way for her to receive peer attention without aggression. It was decided that Jane would be allowed three "conversation cards" per day that she could hand to the teacher during independent practice in the class to have a three-minute conversation with a friend in the hallway. The replacement behavior served the same function as the aggression (i.e., attention). Although one of the classroom teachers was initially reluctant to implement this technique, she agreed to give it a try because she was very frustrated with the disruptions that were now occurring. The time taken for the conversation would be far less than the time it took to deal with a disruption.

Jane received coaching in how and when she could use her conversation cards. Her teachers also met together to clarify how the cards would be used. Several skills were also added to the Skillstreaming group to help Jane learn how to interact more appropriately with peers she didn't know well: Starting a Conversation (Skill 2), Joining In (Skill 10), and Helping Others (Skill 24). As these skills were difficult for her, Jane received coaching in these skills prior to participating in the group instruction so she could be more successful in the group. Because Jane's behaviors of concern (negative comments and fighting) were intense and disrupted the learning of others for a significant period of time, the team suggested additional interventions beyond Skillstreaming. In this case, Jane participated in after-school tutoring in the classes in which she had the most difficulty so she could receive attention for her participation (a modification of setting events). She was also allowed to sit next to a friend in the two classes where her disruptions most often occurred, as well as in the Skillstreaming group (a modification of antecedents). She continued to receive positive reinforcement (verbal praise and points) for prosocial interactions. Jane's parents made her time with friends contingent upon not instigating fights at school. In addition, when Jane's sister had friends over, her parents would spend more one-on-one time with Jane. Consequences for instigating fights included not being allowed to spend time with friends after school or on the weekend and time-out in the office away from adult or peer attention. Jane's plan and data related to aggressive incidents were periodically reviewed by the school's intervention team.

Over time, data suggested that Jane was learning more appropriate ways to gain attention from peers and adults. Incidents of aggression decreased along with the frequency of Jane's using her conversation cards. The team decided to share Jane's progress with her, showing her the graphs of how her aggression had decreased. It was also decided to thin her reinforcement by reducing the frequency of earning points. With Jane's development of more prosocial skills, it was further decided to develop a contract regarding use of the conversation cards. The contract included time either during lunch or after school with a friend and the Skillstreaming teacher twice per week if she had five of six conversation cards unused. Even though Jane's issue with aggression is not totally resolved, her teachers and parents, as well as Jane herself, were pleased with her progress.

CHAPTER 7

Building Positive Relationships with Parents

With very few exceptions, parents genuinely care about their children's academic and social progress as they enter the world of school and beyond. Often, cultural and socioeconomic differences impair the development of a common understanding between parents and teachers. Such misunderstandings are unfortunate and have the potential to put the social and emotional welfare of children and adolescents at risk. Although many teachers indicate that parent involvement is difficult to achieve, especially in the higher grades, Skillstreaming is a productive and often nonemotional way to accomplish parent–school collaboration.

Traditionally, parent contact has taken the form of PTA/PTO meetings, parent–teacher conferences, or, as far too often has been the case with a child prone to behave aggressively or disruptively, the "bad news call." Teachers able to create positive relationships with parents often view and deal with parents quite differently. They demonstrate understanding of cultural and economic differences. They recognize and appreciate parents as the youth's first (and continuing) teachers. They seek contact early and frequently, seeing this as an opportunity to collaborate in supportive, mutually reinforcing ways. Displaying such attitudes helps create the opportunity for the parent, teacher, and student to become a problem-solving team.

The role of parents and the family has gradually changed from being on the periphery to being a central focus in the child's education. It is more widely understood that establishing close working relationships with parents, in the early grades especially (i.e., kindergarten through third grade), can have a positive effect on the child's school adjustment (Adams, Womack, Shatzer, & Caldarella, 2010; Bruder, 2010; Strain & Timm, 2001; Walker, Colvin, & Ramsey, 1995). Many times, parents are not only expected to be involved with their child's education but are expected to participate in their child's learning. Opportunities for the youth to be successful in school, home, and peer group increase with a cooperative working relationship between parents and the school.

Unfortunately, teachers and other professionals may not be sufficiently prepared for such collaboration (Friesen & Stephens, 1998). A model for the development of positive and productive relationships presented by Fialka and Mikus (1999) may be helpful to the teacher or other Skillstreaming leader. This model calls for a partnership between home and school that can be developed through specific phases of parent–teacher interaction.

The first phase of relationship development, which Fialka and Mikus call *colliding and campaigning,* involves fostering understanding and beginning to build trust between parent and teacher. During this initial phase of relationship building, each party typically has difficulty listening to the other. Instead, it is often the goal to state their own perspectives about the child, the problem, or the intervention, with the hope of persuading the other to see the issue from their vantage point and to accept their solution. During initial parent contacts, then, it is important for each party to have the goal of listening for understanding, asking for more information, and being willing to explore different possibilities in resolving concerns. With successful work at the first phase, parents and teachers move to the middle phase, *coordinating, cooperating, and compromising,* in which their interactions are based on more effective listening and cooperation. Being able to suspend their personal agendas to explore a common ground and asking each other to explain ideas will give rise to respect for the other and increased capacity for problem solving. *Collaborating and creative partnering,* the third phase of relationship building, continues to be based on listening and inquiring. During this phase, there is more open sharing of each party's needs, hopes, and fears. Differences of opinion are more easily understood and accepted, and decision making becomes more balanced between the parties. Although these phases are described as discrete, relationships will often move back and forth among the phases as parents and teachers engage in problem solving.

Emotional and behavioral problems affect youth at all ages and in all life situations—home, neighborhood, school, church, and so forth. In addition, families experience significant stress when their child has emotional and behavioral problems. Collaboration between teacher and parent best addresses the youth's behavioral and social needs. Communication with the student's family should, therefore, be one of the most important components of any school program (Quinn et al., 2000).

PARENTING AND YOUTH AGGRESSION

Aggression is a difficult behavior to change. It is primarily a learned behavior, and many adolescents have learned it well. From their early years, they live with family and peers who repeatedly model, reward, and even overtly encourage hurtful actions toward others. In a real sense, aggression becomes for many youth a behavior that "works"—both for them and for the significant people in their lives.

In school, agency, and other institutional settings, many chronically aggressive youth participate in interventions like Skillstreaming, designed to teach prosocial alternatives. They learn to maintain self-control or walk away from confrontations rather than incite, attack, or fight. They then use one of these prosocial alternatives in the presence of a family member or neighborhood peer and, rather than reward the constructive attempt, the other party responds critically. "No son of mine is going to be a punk. You hit him before he hits you!" says the parent. "Are you chicken?" says the peer.

Overall, parents do the best they can with what they know. However, parenting styles and practices significantly affect the school and social adjustment. Considerable research evidence suggests that children exhibiting aggression during the preschool years, for example, often have been exposed to harsh, punitive, rigid, and authoritarian discipline and parents who model aggression (Jewett, 1992). Conversely, parenting practices related to prosocial behavior include appropriate and fair discipline, sufficient supervision, involvement in the child's life (e.g., school and peer contacts), an attitude of support, and the ability to resolve conflicts and handle crises in the family (Walker et al., 1995). Reid, Webster-Stratton, and Hammond (2007) have summarized effective parent training strategies, which include reducing harsh and inconsistent parenting, increasing positive and responsive parenting, promoting parent skills in cognitive stimulation, and increasing home–school bonding.

PARENT INVOLVEMENT IN SKILLSTREAMING

Parents can and should be involved in Skillstreaming for a variety of important reasons. First, parenting practices may be at cross purposes with what is taught in the school (Cart-ledge & Milburn, 1995). A specific skill taught in the Skillstreaming group may not be supported at home, and its use may actually be discouraged. For example, a student's attempt to use the skill Standing Up for Your Rights (Skill 27) may be met with the parent response to "stop talking back." Such contradictions from important people in the youth's life will be confusing and may discourage further use of the skill. When parents understand the goals of Skillstreaming, as well as the specific behaviors included, they are far more likely to be receptive to the youth's skill initiations. Furthermore, because Skillstreaming provides a specific way of teaching "what to do," the opportunity exists to alter how parents deal with the youth's problems in the home and with peers and siblings. For example, when parents learn to reinforce and prompt prosocial skill use—and to change the consequences that maintain aggression (Patterson, 1982)—more positive and supportive parenting will likely result. In this way, parent involvement and cooperation in Skillstreaming have the potential to improve parenting skills. In addition, parents' ratings of their children's self-control and social skills have been shown to improve when parents are trained as coaches and involved in the social skills training (Slim, Whiteside, Dittner, & Mellon, 2006).

Second, many social and behavioral problems originate in the home setting (Walker et al., 1995). Therefore, the more settings in which prosocial skill use is prompted and rewarded, the greater the likelihood that the skills taught will be maintained and will generalize. As discussed in chapter 5, adolescents may easily learn the Skillstreaming skills, but they are unlikely to continue to use skills over time or in a variety of situations and environments unless specific procedures are implemented to facilitate their use. Reinforcement and prompting of skill use in the home setting is a way to enhance continued use of skills.

A third rationale for including parents in Skillstreaming concerns the profound effect of modeling on behavior. When parents and sib-lings model behaviors for dealing with stress and anger, for example, the youth has the opportunity to follow these models.

LEVELS OF PARENT INVOLVEMENT

In a survey of teachers, Brannon (2008) found the most successful ways of involving parents include (a) involving the family in homework through discussion or activity, (b) informing parents what is occurring in class via newsletters or website, (c) informing parents of the class and school expectations so they understand and may be supportive, (d) asking parents to volunteer so they are exposed to behavioral expectations, and (e) holding events (such as breakfast or evening programs) to ease parents into the partnership and share what their children are learning.

Orientation Level

The first level of parent involvement can best be described as an orientation to Skillstreaming skills and procedures. The purpose of this level is to promote parent awareness and understanding. An orientation meeting to describe Skillstreaming objectives and ways parents might help the youth use the prosocial skills at home is very helpful. In such a meeting, leaders may present examples of skills, discuss the goals of Skillstreaming, and explain the learning process (modeling, role-playing, performance feedback, and generalization in the form of homework). Showing *The Skillstreaming Video* (Goldstein & McGinnis, 1988) or conducting a mock group are specific activities that will increase parent understanding. Allowing time for questions and input about skills for instruction will also increase parents' understanding and involvement.

An alternative to an orientation meeting is to send a letter home explaining the goals of Skillstreaming instruction and the activities in which the youth will be participating (i.e., watching leaders act out a skill, trying out the skill steps in the group, giving and receiving feedback about skill performance, and completing skill homework assignments). The Parent Orientation Note is helpful in this regard (see sample in Figure 9). Orienting parents to the types of skills and procedures used is necessary because many of the skill-use situations occur in the family environment. If parents are uninformed about Skillstreaming goals, they may justifiably question the purpose of discussing home-related situations at school.

Other ways to promote parent involvement at the orientation level include the following:

1. Have parents assess the youth's skill strengths and weaknesses by completing all or part of the Parent Checklist (in Appendix A) and talk with them about skills they value in the home. Conversations with parents about needed skills will help identify cultural aspects of the skills and permit better choices of where, when, and with whom individual skills will be most beneficial.

2. Frequently inform parents of the youth's progress in the various skill areas, focusing on positive reports.

3. Videorecord the youth in a role-play situation and share this videotape with the parents during a conference to encourage further understanding of Skillstreaming's goals and procedures.

4. Invite parents to participate in a mock Skillstreaming group in which parents learn a skill through modeling, role-playing, feedback, and generalization

5. Encourage parents to support skill learning by giving the youth positive feedback for practicing skills he or she has successfully role-played in the school or other learning environment.

Support Level

Following successful parent involvement at the orientation level, the teacher or other group leader should seek to involve parents at the support level. The goal at this level is to gain more active parental support. Parent activities at this level are as follows:

1. Support the youth's demonstration of the social skill by helping him or her complete assigned homework in the home environment. Feedback to the teacher will be given via the School–Home Note (see sample in Figure 10).

2. Notice and reward the youth's specific skill use in the home and neighborhood environment and provide ongoing encouragement.

3. Observe a Skillstreaming group in progress and participate as coactors in the group.

4. Help assess the youth's skill progress by judging skill performance at home and in neighborhood settings.

Cooperative Level

At the cooperative level, parents are involved in selecting skills needed in the home and neighborhood setting and regularly give feedback to the teacher or other group leader about the youth's use of skills. Parents will also be involved in prompting use of the skills at home and will provide encouragement and reinforcement for skill performance. At the cooperative level, teachers and parents work together as a team to teach and support the child's skill development. The Parent/Staff Skill Rating Form is helpful in this regard (see sample in Figure 11). Staff in residential or other teaching settings may also use this form.

Family Skillstreaming

Program evaluations have suggested that children's prosocial responses are more likely to be rewarded, supported, and even reciprocated if significant others also participate in Skillstreaming training programs. Some of these joint efforts have involved teaching empathy skills to adolescents and their parents (Guzzetta, 1974), teaching delinquent youths and their families alternatives to aggression (Goldstein et al., 1989), and training adolescents and their peer groups in a variety of social skills (Gibbs, Potter, & Goldstein, 1995; Goldstein et al., 1994). The success of these programs strongly suggests the effectiveness of instruction for both

Date _____ 9/1 _____

Dear Parent or Guardian:

Our class is learning to handle a variety of day-to-day concerns that face adolescents in positive, prosocial ways. Following instructions, understanding the feelings of others, negotiating, dealing with group pressure, and avoiding trouble with others are some of the skills we will be working on. We are all learning and practicing the specific steps to handle these skills in acceptable ways.

The process we are using to learn these skills is called Skillstreaming. First, students watch someone else use the skill. Then each student will try out the skill in a role-play situation and receive feedback about how well he or she performed the skill. Finally, each student will be asked to practice the skill in a real-life situation.

Every two weeks or so, whenever a new skill has been introduced, we will be e-mailing or sending a note to you that describes the skill and its steps. We hope that you will review this note with your student and help with practicing the skill at home.

Please feel free to call or e-mail me should you have questions.

Sincerely,

_____ Teacher/Leader _____

Phone _____ 555-1234 _____

E-mail _____ teacherleader@anyschool.com _____

Figure 10: Sample School-Home Note

Student ___Larry___ Date ___3/5___

DESCRIPTION OF LESSON

Skill name ___Negotiating (#25)___

Skill steps:

1. Decide if you and the other person are having a difference of opinion
2. Tell the other person what you think about the problem.
3. Ask the other person what he/she thinks about the problem.
4. Listen openly to his/her answer.
5. Think about why the other person might feel this way.
6. Suggest a compromise.

Skill purpose, use, value ___Learning to negotiate when there is a problem helps us___

___arrive at a peaceful solution.___

DESCRIPTION OF SKILL HOMEWORK

When a difference of opinion occurs with his sister, Larry has agreed to try the
skill of Negotiating.

REQUEST TO PARENTS

1. Provide skill homework recognition and reward.
2. Respond positively to your child's skill use.
3. Return this note with your comments (on the back) about:

   - Quality of homework done
   - Rewards that work/don't work at home
   - Suggestions or questions regarding this skill, other skills, additional homework assignments, other ways to promote school-home collaboration, and so on

4. Please sign and return this form to ___Mrs. Albrecht___

   by ___3/12___

Signature _____ Date ___3/12___

Figure 11: Sample Parent/Staff Skill Rating Form

Date _____ 11/1 _____

_____ Sue _____ is learning
(participant)

the skill of _____ Listening (#1) _____

The steps involved in this skill are:

1. Look at the person who is talking.
2. Think about what is being said.
3. Wait your turn to talk.
4. Say what you want to say.

1. Did he or she demonstrate this skill in your presence? ☑ yes ☐ no

2. How would you rate his or her skill demonstration? *(check one)*

   ☐ poor ☐ below average ☐ average ☑ above average ☐ excellent

3. How sincere was he or she in performing the skill? *(check one)*

   ☐ not sincere ☐ somewhat sincere ☑ very sincere

Comments:

Often when I explain something to Sue, she doesn't seem to listen — she keeps

doing whatever. This time, she stopped, looked at me, and listened!

_____

Please sign and return this form to _____ Mr. Burrows _____

by _____ 11/5 _____

Signature _____ Date _____ 11/5 _____

skill-deficient youth and the significant people in their lives.

For students and their families, schools are increasingly community resources, offering a range of health-related and social service programming. Expansion of the purposes of schools is likely to continue, and family Skillstreaming, in which children and adolescents participate in Skillstreaming along with their siblings and parents, holds promise as a regular offering in this context, as well as in mental health and other settings.

CHAPTER 8

Skillstreaming in the School Context

Teachers and school administrators continue to report their greatest challenge is to reduce classroom and school disruption, often occurring in the form of student aggression and violence. In a 2004 Gallup poll (Rose & Gallup, 2004) educators cited discipline as the most serious issue in today's schools, second only to the lack of financial support. It is further estimated that between 2 and 7 percent of students have significant emotional or behavior problems, which often include anger and aggression (Kauffman, 2005). This chapter reviews issues surrounding school violence and aggression and suggests how Skillstreaming can play a role in reducing them.

VIOLENCE PREVENTION

Although it may be true that students today come to school with many more significant concerns than in the past, certain factors related to the school itself have been found to contribute to violence. Experts generally advocate a multifaceted or combined program of school safety, including the development of school policies addressing weapons and crisis response, environmental factors such as school facilities and family and community resources, and prevention through education. Educational strategies, school climate, and disciplinary policy and methods play a central role.

Educational Strategies

Educational approaches to preventing violence and aggression include conflict management, social skills instruction, mentoring programs, behavioral programs, intensive academic instruction, drug prevention, student advocacy programs, peer helper programs, student assistance (counseling) programs, prejudice reduction/cultural sensitivity curricula, and community service. An important goal of such schoolwide approaches is "to give everyone involved in the school the same skills, language and terminology for handling stress and conflict—to create an environment that is consistently nonviolent and nurturing" (Ascher, 1994, p. 4).

To be effective in reducing discipline problems, improving school climate, and increasing students' self-esteem and ability to assume responsibility (Walker et al., 1995), such programs should be instituted at an early age and should include many individuals in the youth's environment (teachers, peers, and other school staff, such as custodians and paraprofessionals). Furthermore, teachers and other school personnel will need professional staff development in the areas of conflict resolution, how to respond to violence, and team building.

School Climate

The culture or climate of a school is reflected in the prevailing values and beliefs held by school staff, parents, and students. These values and beliefs define acceptable behavior and determine the manner in which the school should function. As stated by Modro (1995):

The most important factor that needs to be addressed even before policies that will support school safety is the atmosphere, or "feeling tone," in which education takes place. Does our educational system reflect a genuine belief in the essential dignity of each child? Do educators believe in the inherent value of the people they serve? The fear is that many mirror for our children what some of them already see reflected in society. (p. 11)

Johnson (2009) reviewed 25 studies published in 2007–2008 that addressed the relationship between the school environment and school violence and considered both the social and physical environments. Lower rates of school violence were associated with positive relationships with teachers, students' clear understanding of the rules and their perceptions that the rules were fair, students feelings of ownership in their school, positive classrooms and other school environments that focused on student understanding, and safety interventions that increased the perception of physical order.

A positive school climate not only provides an environment for students to learn prosocial skills but also enhances academic achievement and teacher retention (Cohen, Pickeral, & McCloskey, 2009; MacNeil, Prater, & Busch, 2009). To learn, students must believe their school is a safe environment, free from harassment and aggression (Goldstein, Young, & Boyd, 2008). Indeed, half of all students who take a weapon to school say they do so for their own protection (Sprague & Walker, 2000).

Learning environments need to create opportunities for children and adolescents to participate in rule setting and to accept responsibility, and they must be taught the skills necessary for prosocial participation in these activities. Creating a better balance of positive to negative consequences is also necessary to foster a positive school climate. Some youth, in particular those who have well-established patterns of undesirable behavior, are most likely to receive an overabundance of negative consequences. For these individuals, positive feelings about school and learning itself are unlikely. Such individuals need more instruction, not less.

Disciplinary Policy and Methods

Exclusionary practices remain the primary way schools deal with student disruption, aggression, and violence. This fact also applies to students at the preschool level, with those in this age group being three times as likely to be expelled than students in grades K through 12 (Gilliam, 2005). The problem is that such practices fail to work in the long run. Suspension and other forms of traditional punishment do not prevent or deter future misconduct for students with chronic or intense behavior problems (Goldstein, Glick, & Gibbs, 1998). Neither do such policies make schools safer; in fact, the opposite appears to be true (Brownstein, 2010). For example, Nickerson and Martens (2008) explored different approaches to school violence prevention through a survey of over 2,000 school principals. These authors found that a focus on security/enforcement and suspending students actually related to a higher incidence of disruption and crime.

In addition, suspension and other exclusionary practices often exacerbate the very behaviors they are designed to extinguish (Mendler & Curwin, 1999). Because we know that time spent in learning is the best predictor of increased academic achievement (Skiba & Sprague, 2008), suspensions often contribute to a student's academic failure. Such long-term negative outcomes include poor academic achievement, grade retention, negative feelings about school, truancy, and dropping out (Bock, Tapscott, & Savner, 1998; Dupper & Bosch, 1996; Hickman, Batholomew, Mathwig, & Heinrichs, 2008). For example, Hickman et al. (2008) examined the histories of school dropouts and graduates. Students who dropped out showed higher rates of behavior problems in early grades, a history of absenteeism as early as first grade, more often repeated a grade, and showed lower grades and test scores than did graduates. Students themselves have reported that suspensions were "not at all" helpful (Costenbader & Markson, 1998). In addition, issues of equity exist: Minority students are more likely to be suspended than nonminority students and are disciplined more severely for minor disciplinary infractions (Advancement Project/Civil Rights Project, 2000; Applied Research Center, 1999; Brownstein, 2010; Cartledge, 2003; Costenbader & Markson, 1998; Skiba, Peterson, & Williams, 1997).

Furthermore, the positive relationship between school attendance and academic success has been well documented, encouraging the examination of the relationship of school suspension to academic achievement (Andrews, Taylor, Martin, & Slate, 1998; Zins, Bloodworth, Weissberg, & Walberg, 2004). The more students are excluded from school, the more likely they are to fall behind academically. And because it is more acceptable to act bad than it is to act stupid (Brendtro, Brokenleg, & Van Bockern, 2002), students are more likely to act disruptively and aggressively to avoid work that is not understood. It makes sense that students who are not in school will fail to learn what they need to learn.

Mayer (2001) summarizes what schools can do to create an environment that will facilitate the reduction of behavior problems:

1. Reduce punitive methods of control
2. Provide clear rules (expectations) for student conduct
3. Assure support to educators
4. Minimize academic failure experiences
5. Teach critical social skills
6. Use function-based behavior management
7. Respect, value, and understand ethnic and cultural differences
8. Support student involvement and participation

Johns, Carr, and Hoots (1995, p. 2-2) recommend that school discipline be evaluated by asking the following questions:

1. Does the disciplinary process allow students to accept responsibility for their actions?
2. Does the disciplinary process continually place importance on the value of academic participation and achievement?
3. Does the disciplinary action build positive self-image?
4. Does the disciplinary action teach students alternative methods of dealing with problems?

In other words, disciplinary programs in schools today and in the future need to be instructional in nature. Instructional alternatives may include assigning the student to a social skills class (dealing with specific alternatives to the conflict that resulted in suspension and where more desirable behaviors may be learned), requiring the student to complete community service (where he or she will be more likely to be exposed to appropriate models and receive the attention needed to foster a more positive self-image), and having the student complete an in-school intervention focusing on conflict resolution.

Bullying

One form of aggression that deserves closer scrutiny is bullying. Bullying is common in preschool and elementary school classrooms (Beane, 1999; Manning, Heron, & Marshall, 1978; Smith & Levan, 1995). Bullying often begins in preschool and presents significant behavioral issues not only for the young child who is the target but for the bully and observers as well.

It is important to distinguish between bullying and other types of aggression that may occur in the classroom and other settings. The most common form of bullying is teasing; however, occasional teasing does not constitute bullying. Neither is bullying considered rough play or accidentally hurtful events. Instead, in bullying there is a physical or psychological imbalance of power (Newman, Horne, & Bartolomucci, 2000). The most accepted definition of bullying is presented by Olweus (1991), who states, "A person is being bullied or victimized when he or she is exposed, repeatedly and over time, to negative actions on the part of one or more persons" (p. 413).

This type of aggression can be either direct or indirect (Olweus, 1993). Direct, or overt, bullying typically is observable verbal, written, or physical aggression. Direct bullying includes hitting, pushing, kicking, and tripping, as well as the verbal behaviors of yelling, threatening, and cursing (Ahmad & Smith, 1994). Cyberbullying, or posting negative or insulting comments on the Internet, is a particularly insidious form of direct bullying. Indirect bullying includes behaviors such as spreading rumors, backbiting or scapegoating, and convincing others to ignore or isolate the victim. Both types can be very harmful.

Bullying also may be a precursor to more severe and dangerous violence (Greenbaum, Turner, & Stephens, 1989; Hoover & Oliver, 1996; Olweus, 1991). Kauffman, Mostert, Trent, and Hallahan (1998) note that "engaging in aggressive antisocial acts is not good for children; it does not help them develop appropriate behavior, but increases the likelihood of further aggression, maladjustment, and academic and social failure" (p. 14). When ignored, bullying often escalates in intensity and continues in frequency (Goldstein, 1999a).

Children and adolescents often engage in bullying or other aggressive acts to exert their power over others or to control a situation—for example, to get what they want, whether it is a toy, candy, a peer's lunch, or attention from peers. Bullying is often unreported because it typically occurs in places without sufficient adult supervision (e.g., playground, lunchroom, hallways, neighborhood park, to and from school). Many students do not report bullying for fear that they will receive even more aggression from the bully. Based on what adults often teach youth, youth are likely to question whether anything will be done about the provocation. After all, haven't adults reinforced from an early age the belief that children shouldn't tattle? Sometimes the target is even reprimanded by the adult, further rewarding the bully for the aggression.

The goal of Skillstreaming is to teach prosocial alternatives. By experiencing direct teaching of behavioral skill steps, children and adolescents who are targets or observers of bullying can learn assertiveness skills to deal effectively with being teased and with other peer provocation (Standing Up for Your Rights, Skill 27; Responding to Teasing, Skill 28), to problem solve (Deciding What Caused a Problem, Skill 44), and to say no (Dealing with Group Pressure, Skill 42). Other skills from the Skillstreaming curriculum also may be effectively used in bullying contexts.

The bully also deserves our attention and instructional efforts. The bully, although often maintaining a level of social status with peers (Hoover & Oliver, 1996), often feels isolated from others. It is important to expand this youth's repertoire of choices by teaching skills to develop empathy and friendship, such as Understanding the Feelings of Others (Skill 17), Helping Others (Skill 24), Being a Good Sport (Skill 33), and the like. In addition, because the bully seeks power or control, he or she can be given influence in a prosocial, positive way by helping to teach the skills to peers or younger children or in other ways assuming a leadership role in Skillstreaming.

INTEGRATION IN THE CURRICULUM

As we move into the 21st century, schools are paying more attention to students' emotional health and are more likely to integrate Skillstreaming within the general education curricula. Marx (2006), for example, recommends that schools "expand programs in thinking and reasoning skills as well as civic and character education" (p. 45). As stated by the Partnership for 21st Century Skills (2008), "All Americans must be skilled at interacting competently and respectfully with others" (p. 10). In *Connecting Teachers, Students, and Standards: Strategies for Success in Diverse and Inclusive Classrooms,* and citing the work of Mercer and Pullen (2005), Voltz, Sims, and Nelson (2010) call for including social skills strategy instruction into the curriculum. They state:

> [Social skill strategy instruction] . . . is designed to teach students how to interact appropriately with others across a variety of situations and settings. Skills such as resisting pressure, accepting criticism, negotiating, following directions, and asking for help are included. (p. 78)

In addition, it is continuing to become more well-accepted that social skills are essential in achieving needed academic outcomes (Schoenfeld et al., 2008). Indeed, the relationship between problem behavior and low academic skills has been widely investigated (Lassen, Steele, & Sailor, 2006; McIntosh & Mackay, 2008; Rock, Fessler, & Church, 1997; Trzesniewski, Moffit, Caspi, Taylor, & Maughan, 2006). Further, Marzano and Haystead (2008) provide examples for including standards in life skills, such as expectations for participation (asking questions, staying focused, raising hand, and work completion).

It is clear that social skills instruction lends itself to being imbedded within the academic curricula as a central goal for all students and that it can be considered as a prevention as well as intervention strategy.

INCLUSION

Another current initiative in schools today provides for increasing inclusion of youngsters with special needs in regular education classrooms. The Individuals with Disabilities Education Act (IDEA, 1997, 2004) calls for educating students with disabilities within the least restrictive environment. In other words, as much as possible, students with disabilities should be educated with nondisabled peers within the general education setting. It has been accepted in recent years that if academic or social benefit can be attained in the regular classroom setting, then a student with disabilities should receive his or her instruction there. Yet many experts in the field of special education believe social benefits are unlikely to occur unless planned and systematic instruction in social skills also takes place. Outcomes for preschool students with disabilities required by IDEA include that they have positive social-emotional skills, demonstrate acquisition of use of knowledge and skills, and use appropriate behavior to meet their needs (Bruder, 2010). Students without disabilities may also need instruction in accepting students with differences. Skillstreaming is often used to teach the prosocial behaviors that will enhance successful inclusion. In many secondary schools, for example, students with emotional and behavioral disorders receive direct Skillstreaming instruction. All staff who teach and interact with the students are involved in the instruction and prompt skill use throughout the school day. Skillstreaming is also used with students with Asperger's syndrome. This project, Connections Research and Treatment Program, provides services for six hours per day, five days per week, for a period of six weeks. Students receive Skillstreaming for four 20-minute cycles each day. An additional 50 minutes in each cycle is devoted to activities in which children practice the social skills they learned and emotion recognition, and expand on their interests.

In the effort to increase prospective teachers' awareness and understanding of students with disabilities, the preservice teaching program at St. Mary's College in Notre Dame, Indiana, implements a field experience called Campus Friends (Turner, 2003). Once per week, students with disabilities come to the campus to interact with college students. Using Skillstreaming, students are taught a variety of prosocial skills. Students also visit areas of the campus community and are prompted to use the prosocial skills they have been taught. In brief, the trend toward inclusion makes it even more important to teach all students (both with and without disabilities) the social skills they need.

MULTI-TIERED SYSTEMS OF SUPPORT

Many schools and districts are developing systems to address both academic and behavioral interventions to meet the learning needs of all students. Tiered systems of support have been evidenced to address student academic concerns through Response to Intervention (RTI) and behavioral concerns through Positive Behavioral Interventions and Supports (PBIS). Recently, social and behavioral concerns have begun to be addressed through RTI in addition to academics. These tiered supports are often composed of three or four levels and offer schools a systematic way to look at the intensity of intervention need. School teams then develop interventions to address the needs of all and implement academic, behavioral, and social interventions along this continuum. Recognizing that academic needs impact behavior and vice versa, schools and districts are now designing multi-tiered systems of support considering both academic and social-behavioral interventions in such tiered models.

For example, Farmer, Farmer, Estell, and Hutchins (2007) offer a three-level system to address both academic and behavioral need. Such systems often include (a) universal strategies to meet the needs of all students, (b) selective or targeted interventions for students who continue to struggle even after high-quality universal instruction is provided, and (c) individual or intense interventions for students not responding to the first two levels. The goal of such systems is to match the intensity of student need with the intensity of interventions.

Positive Behavior Intervention and Supports

PBIS is rapidly gaining acceptance across the country largely because of its strong research base and procedures for training schools in implementation. Funded by a federal grant, The Center on Positive Behavioral Interventions and Supports (www.pbis.org) provides ongoing training assistance to state departments of education and school districts and is a clearinghouse for updated information and new evidence.

The universal (primary) level of prevention includes the development and instruction of school and classroom routines and behavioral expectations through schoolwide social skills training. Skillstreaming is used at this level to instruct all students in skills such as Asking for Help (Skill 9), Listening (Skill 1), and Following Instructions (Skill 12). How these skills look in each area of the school (e.g., cafeteria, hallway, commons, classroom) is demonstrated, and all students in the school have the opportunity to see the skills modeled and to follow through with group role-plays and feedback. New skills are also created depending on the expectations of each school. For example, skills may be developed to teach school routines, such as Passing from Class to Class, Bringing Needed Materials to Class, or Appropriate Talk in the Lunchroom. A new social skill is developed for whatever problem behaviors are experienced by most students. The goal here is to reduce predictable problems so that more time and effort can be directed toward students needing more interventions at the other levels.

Targeted (secondary) prevention provides a system of behavioral supports for those students, fewer in number, who continue to have behavioral difficulties that may result in a school suspension. While still participating in universal interventions, these students experience additionally targeted instruction in Skillstreaming in small groups. At this level, the selection of skills becomes more prescriptive—that is, the specific skills selected for group instruction are those related to the students' problematic behavior. Skills for targeted instruction often include Concentrating on a Task (Skill 50), Using Self-Control (Skill 26), Answering a Complaint (Skill 32), and Keeping Out of Fights (Skill 30). Other types of targeted interventions may include a staff member's checking in with a group of students to better prepare them for the school day or providing group mentoring activities.

For the few students who remain unresponsive to targeted interventions, individual interventions are designed. Students at this level may experience multiple problems and will therefore need multiple interventions. For example, wraparound supports or a behavior intervention plan (BIP) may be necessary to assist students needing this level of support. At this level, Skillstreaming is a part of the student's overall support program, often implemented to teach the student replacement behaviors (acceptable behaviors that serve the same function and are incompatible with problem behavior), as determined through the functional behavioral assessment (FBA) process. This process is described in more depth in chapter 6, on managing behavioral problems.

Response to Intervention

In part because of dissatisfaction with the discrepancy model for identifying students with learning disabilities, the RTI process is advocated as an alternative method for identifying students who have a learning disability. Used primarily to address academic deficits, it is becoming more common to include behavioral and social deficits within this framework (Sugai, Guardino, & Lathrop, 2007). Most RTI models include these components (Bender, 2009):

- ▶ Universal screening to identify students who are not making adequate progress

- ▶ Increasingly intensive interventions presented in levels or tiers

- ▶ Use of evidence-based strategies at all tiers

- ▶ Monitoring of student progress

- ▶ Making data-based decisions when considering moving a student to another tier

What does RTI look like related to social behaviors, and how is Skillstreaming used within this framework? Universal screening for behavior problems and social skills deficits is conducted. This process is often quite easy; most teachers can readily identify at least the students who are

acting out. Reviewing the data from office discipline and counseling referrals is another method of such screening. Once students have been identified, Tier I (or universal social skills instruction) is provided to all students in a manner similar to the PBIS process. The teacher provides whole-class instruction in the skills needed by most students. While continuing to monitor behavioral data, the teacher checks in with a small group of students 10 minutes before school begins and again at the end of the school day (Tier II). This brief check-in time allows the teacher to review the students' behavioral self-monitoring systems and provide encouragement and reinforcement for use of the Tier I skills. Students not making adequate behavioral progress (e.g., continued office referrals) are also assigned to a skills group during homeroom (Tier II). This group is co-instructed by the teacher and a school counselor or other support staff member and addresses the skills for which those in the group have been sent to the office. Based on progress monitoring data, students still not making adequate behavioral progress receive more intense Skillstreaming instruction in a Tier III after-school alternative to suspension skills group, along with other strategies as determined on an individual student basis (e.g., counseling support, wraparound supports). A student needing Tier III intervention continues to benefit from interventions at Tiers I and II. As this example shows, Skillstreaming can be a valuable part of a student's program at all three tiers.

NEW INTERVENTION COMBINATIONS

Although Skillstreaming is effective in teaching prosocial skills and interpersonal competencies, quite often the skills learned are not performed by the students where and when needed. Chapter 5 examined the bases for generalization failures, as well as means for their remediation. As discussed earlier, some students fail to display newly learned skill behaviors because earlier learned behaviors, such as aggression, have been well practiced and therefore more readily available and frequently used.

For this purpose, Goldstein and colleagues (Goldstein et al., 1986; Goldstein et al., 1998) developed Aggression Replacement Training (ART). Used primarily for aggressive adolescents, ART incorporates both anger control training (Feindler, 1979, 1995) and moral reasoning (Kohlberg, 1969, 1973). Students learn what to do from Skillstreaming and what not to do from anger control training. The final component, moral reasoning, is designed to engage students in discussion of values to increase motivation to choose prosocial skill alternatives. A third edition of this widely used program is available (Glick & Gibbs, 2010). The Prepare Curriculum (Goldstein, 1999b) expands the three components of ART to include such areas as empathy training, situational perception training, and problem solving.

Based on ART, The Peace4Kids and Families Program (centerforsafeschools.org) was developed for use in schools to provide interventions for youth in prekindergarten through grade 12. Based in Broomfield, Colorado, the program includes the four components of social skills training, empathy, anger control, and character education. Peace4Kids provides strategies for all students (universal interventions); targeted strategies for students who are at risk; and intensive, individualized interventions for students who do not show improved behavior through the first two levels of intervention. The goal of the program is to implement an effective prevention program, creating a culture of learning and behaving and is used in schools, community-based programs, day treatment, and residential services. An effective parent empowerment component is also included.

PART 2

Skill Outlines
and Homework Reports

Group 1

Beginning Social Skills

Skills 1–8

Skill 1: Listening

SKILL STEPS

1. **Look at the person who is talking.**

   Face the person; establish eye contact.

2. **Think about what is being said.**

   Show this by nodding your head, saying, "Mm-hmm."

3. **Wait your turn to talk.**

   Don't fidget; don't shuffle your feet.

4. **Say what you want to say.**

   Ask questions; express feelings; express your ideas.

SUGGESTED MODELING DISPLAYS

School or neighborhood: Teacher explains classroom assignment to main actor.

Home: Mother feels sad, and main actor listens.

Peer group: Friend describes interesting movie to main actor.

Job: Your boss tells you how to be safe on the job.

COMMENTS

All of the beginning social skills are basic to the functioning of the group. In starting a Skillstreaming group, it is useful for participants to have a reasonable grasp of these skills before proceeding to other skills.

Like Step 2 for this skill, many of the behavioral steps that make up the skills described in this chapter are *thinking* steps. That is, in actual, real-world use of many skills, certain steps are private and occur only in the thinking of the skill user. When modeling or role-playing such thinking steps in Skillstreaming, it is crucial that the enactment be aloud. Public display of thinking steps significantly aids learning.

From *Skillstreaming the Adolescent: A Guide for Teaching Prosocial Skills* (3rd ed.), © 2012 by E. McGinnis, Champaign, IL: Research Press (www.researchpress.com, 800-519-2707).

Skill 1: Listening

Name _____ Date _____

SKILL STEPS

1. Look at the person who is talking.
2. Think about what is being said.
3. Wait your turn to talk.
4. Say what you want to say.

FILL IN NOW

1. Where will you try the skill? _____

2. With whom will you try the skill? _____

3. When will you try the skill? _____

FILL IN AFTER YOU PRACTICE THE SKILL

1. What happened when you did the homework?

   _____

   _____

2. Which skill steps did you really follow?

   _____

   _____

3. How good a job did you do in using the skill? *(check one)*

   ☐ excellent   ☐ good   ☐ fair   ☐ poor

Skillstreaming

Skill 1: Listening

Name _____ Date _____

SKILL STEPS

1. Look at the person who is talking.
2. Think about what is being said.
3. Wait your turn to talk.
4. Say what you want to say.

FILL IN NOW

1. Where will you try the skill? _____

2. With whom will you try the skill? _____

3. When will you try the skill? _____

4. If you do an excellent job, how will you reward yourself? _____

5. If you do a good job, how will you reward yourself? _____

6. If you do a fair job, how will you reward yourself? _____

FILL IN AFTER YOU PRACTICE THE SKILL

1. What happened when you did the homework?

   _____

   _____

2. Which skill steps did you really follow?

   _____

   _____

3. How good a job did you do in using the skill? *(check one)*

   ☐ excellent   ☐ good   ☐ fair   ☐ poor

4. What do you think your next homework assignment should be?

   _____

From *Skillstreaming the Adolescent: A Guide for Teaching Prosocial Skills* (3rd ed.), © 2012 by E. McGinnis, Champaign, IL: Research Press (www.researchpress.com, 800-519-2707).

Skill 2: Starting a Conversation

SKILL STEPS

1. **Greet the other person.**

   Say, "Hi"; shake hands; choose the right time and place.

2. **Make small talk.**

   Talk about sports, the weather, school events, and so forth.

3. **Decide if the other person is listening.**

   Check if the other person is listening: looking at you, nodding, saying, "Mm-hmm."

4. **Bring up the main topic.**

SUGGESTED MODELING DISPLAYS

School or neighborhood: Main actor starts conversation with secretary in school office.

Home: Main actor discusses allowance and/or privileges with parent.

Peer group: Main actor suggests weekend plans to a friend.

Job: Main actor is taking a break with some co-workers and wants some advice from them about a job.

COMMENTS

This is one of the best skills to teach in the first Skillstreaming session with a new group. Groups typically find the skill useful and engaging, and several role-plays may occur in a brief period of time.

Skillstreaming From *Skillstreaming the Adolescent: A Guide for Teaching Prosocial Skills* (3rd ed.), © 2012 by E. McGinnis, Champaign, IL: Research Press (www.researchpress.com, 800-519-2707).

Skill 2: Starting a Conversation

Name _____ Date _____

SKILL STEPS

1. Greet the other person.
2. Make small talk.
3. Decide if the other person is listening.
4. Bring up the main topic.

FILL IN NOW

1. Where will you try the skill? _____

2. With whom will you try the skill? _____

3. When will you try the skill? _____

FILL IN AFTER YOU PRACTICE THE SKILL

1. What happened when you did the homework?

   _____

   _____

2. Which skill steps did you really follow?

   _____

   _____

3. How good a job did you do in using the skill? *(check one)*

   ☐ excellent   ☐ good   ☐ fair   ☐ poor

Skill 2: Starting a Conversation

Name _____ Date _____

SKILL STEPS

1. Greet the other person.
2. Make small talk.
3. Decide if the other person is listening.
4. Bring up the main topic.

FILL IN NOW

1. Where will you try the skill? _____

2. With whom will you try the skill? _____

3. When will you try the skill? _____

4. If you do an excellent job, how will you reward yourself? _____

5. If you do a good job, how will you reward yourself? _____

6. If you do a fair job, how will you reward yourself? _____

FILL IN AFTER YOU PRACTICE THE SKILL

1. What happened when you did the homework?

   _____

   _____

2. Which skill steps did you really follow?

   _____

   _____

3. How good a job did you do in using the skill? *(check one)*

   ☐ excellent   ☐ good   ☐ fair   ☐ poor

4. What do you think your next homework assignment should be?

   _____

Skillstreaming

From *Skillstreaming the Adolescent: A Guide for Teaching Prosocial Skills* (3rd ed.), © 2012 by E. McGinnis, Champaign, IL: Research Press (www.researchpress.com, 800-519-2707).

Skill 3: Having a Conversation

SKILL STEPS

1. **Say what you want to say.**

2. **Ask the other person what he/she thinks.**

3. **Listen to what the other person says.**

   Review steps for Skill 1 (Listening).

4. **Say what you think.**

   Respond to the other person; add new information; ask questions.

5. **Make a closing remark.**

   Discuss types of closing remarks. Steps 1–4 can be repeated many times before Step 5 is done.

SUGGESTED MODELING DISPLAYS

School or neighborhood: Main actor talks with coach about upcoming game.

Home: Main actor talks with brother or sister about school experiences.

Peer group: Main actor discusses vacation plans with friend.

Job: Main actor talks with co-worker about weekend plans.

COMMENTS

This skill starts where Skill 2 (Starting a Conversation) leaves off. After separate practice of each skill, leaders may want to give group members practice in using these skills successively.

Skill 3: Having a Conversation

Name _____ Date _____

SKILL STEPS

1. Say what you want to say.

2. Ask the other person what he/she thinks.

3. Listen to what the other person says.

4. Say what you think.

5. Make a closing remark.

FILL IN NOW

1. Where will you try the skill? _____

2. With whom will you try the skill? _____

3. When will you try the skill? _____

FILL IN AFTER YOU PRACTICE THE SKILL

1. What happened when you did the homework?

    _____

    _____

2. Which skill steps did you really follow?

    _____

    _____

3. How good a job did you do in using the skill? *(check one)*

    ☐ excellent   ☐ good   ☐ fair   ☐ poor

Skillstreaming

From *Skillstreaming the Adolescent: A Guide for Teaching Prosocial Skills* (3rd ed.), © 2012 by E. McGinnis, Champaign, IL: Research Press (www.researchpress.com, 800-519-2707).

Skill 3: Having a Conversation

Name _____ Date _____

SKILL STEPS

1. Say what you want to say.
2. Ask the other person what he/she thinks.
3. Listen to what the other person says.
4. Say what you think.
5. Make a closing remark.

FILL IN NOW

1. Where will you try the skill? _____

2. With whom will you try the skill? _____

3. When will you try the skill? _____

4. If you do an excellent job, how will you reward yourself? _____

5. If you do a good job, how will you reward yourself? _____

6. If you do a fair job, how will you reward yourself? _____

FILL IN AFTER YOU PRACTICE THE SKILL

1. What happened when you did the homework?

   _____

   _____

2. Which skill steps did you really follow?

   _____

   _____

3. How good a job did you do in using the skill? *(check one)*

   ☐ excellent   ☐ good   ☐ fair   ☐ poor

4. What do you think your next homework assignment should be?

   _____

From *Skillstreaming the Adolescent: A Guide for Teaching Prosocial Skills* (3rd ed.), © 2012 by E. McGinnis, Champaign, IL: Research Press (www.researchpress.com, 800-519-2707).

Skill 4: Asking a Question

SKILL STEPS

1. **Decide what you'd like to know more about.**

   Ask about something you don't understand, something you didn't hear, or something confusing.

2. **Decide whom to ask.**

   Think about who has the best information on a topic; consider asking several people.

3. **Think about different ways to ask your question and pick one way.**

   Think about wording; raise your hand; ask in a nonchallenging way.

4. **Pick the right time and place to ask your question.**

   Wait for a pause; wait for privacy.

5. **Ask your question.**

SUGGESTED MODELING DISPLAYS

School or neighborhood: Main actor asks teacher to explain something he/she finds unclear.

Home: Main actor asks parent permission to go out versus telling parent.

Peer group: Main actor asks a friend how to create a blog.

Job: Main actor asks his/her boss to explain the directions to complete a job.

COMMENTS

Leaders should model only single, answerable questions. In role-plays, group members should be instructed to do likewise.

Skillstreaming From *Skillstreaming the Adolescent: A Guide for Teaching Prosocial Skills* (3rd ed.), © 2012 by E. McGinnis, Champaign, IL: Research Press (www.researchpress.com, 800-519-2707).

Skill 4: Asking a Question

Name _____ Date _____

SKILL STEPS

1. Decide what you'd like to know more about.
2. Decide whom to ask.
3. Think about different ways to ask your question and pick one way.
4. Pick the right time and place to ask your question.
5. Ask your question.

FILL IN NOW

1. Where will you try the skill? _____

2. With whom will you try the skill? _____

3. When will you try the skill? _____

FILL IN AFTER YOU PRACTICE THE SKILL

1. What happened when you did the homework?

   _____

   _____

2. Which skill steps did you really follow?

   _____

   _____

3. How good a job did you do in using the skill? *(check one)*

   ☐ excellent   ☐ good   ☐ fair   ☐ poor

From *Skillstreaming the Adolescent: A Guide for Teaching Prosocial Skills* (3rd ed.), © 2012 by E. McGinnis, Champaign, IL: Research Press (www.researchpress.com, 800-519-2707).

Skill 4: Asking a Question

Name _____ Date _____

SKILL STEPS

1. Decide what you'd like to know more about.
2. Decide whom to ask.
3. Think about different ways to ask your question and pick one way.
4. Pick the right time and place to ask your question.
5. Ask your question.

FILL IN NOW

1. Where will you try the skill? _____

2. With whom will you try the skill? _____

3. When will you try the skill? _____

4. If you do an excellent job, how will you reward yourself? _____

5. If you do a good job, how will you reward yourself? _____

6. If you do a fair job, how will you reward yourself? _____

FILL IN AFTER YOU PRACTICE THE SKILL

1. What happened when you did the homework?

    _____

    _____

2. Which skill steps did you really follow?

    _____

    _____

3. How good a job did you do in using the skill? *(check one)*

    ☐ excellent   ☐ good   ☐ fair   ☐ poor

4. What do you think your next homework assignment should be?

    _____

Skillstreaming
From *Skillstreaming the Adolescent: A Guide for Teaching Prosocial Skills* (3rd ed.), © 2012 by E. McGinnis, Champaign, IL: Research Press (www.researchpress.com, 800-519-2707).

Skill 5: Saying Thank You

SKILL STEPS

1. **Decide if the other person said or did something that you want to thank him/her for.**

   It may be a compliment, favor, or gift.

2. **Choose a good time and place to thank the other person.**

   This is a quiet time, a private place, or other time and place where you are sure you will have the other person's attention.

3. **Thank the other person in a friendly way.**

   Express thanks with words, a gift, a letter, or do a return favor.

4. **Tell the other person why you are thanking him/her.**

SUGGESTED MODELING DISPLAYS

School or neighborhood: Main actor thanks teacher for help on a project.

Home: Main actor thanks mother for fixing shirt.

Peer group: Main actor thanks friend for advice.

Job: Main actor thanks co-worker for helping him/her.

From *Skillstreaming the Adolescent: A Guide for Teaching Prosocial Skills* (3rd ed.), © 2012 by E. McGinnis, Champaign, IL: Research Press (www.researchpress.com, 800-519-2707).

Skill 5: Saying Thank You

Name _____ Date _____

SKILL STEPS

1. Decide if the other person said or did something that you want to thank him/her for.
2. Choose a good time and place to thank the other person.
3. Thank the other person in a friendly way.
4. Tell the other person why you are thanking him/her.

FILL IN NOW

1. Where will you try the skill? _____

2. With whom will you try the skill? _____

3. When will you try the skill? _____

FILL IN AFTER YOU PRACTICE THE SKILL

1. What happened when you did the homework?

   _____

   _____

2. Which skill steps did you really follow?

   _____

   _____

3. How good a job did you do in using the skill? *(check one)*

   ☐ excellent   ☐ good   ☐ fair   ☐ poor

Skillstreaming
From *Skillstreaming the Adolescent: A Guide for Teaching Prosocial Skills* (3rd ed.), © 2012 by E. McGinnis, Champaign, IL: Research Press (www.researchpress.com, 800-519-2707).

Skill 5: Saying Thank You

Name _____ Date _____

SKILL STEPS

1. Decide if the other person said or did something that you want to thank him/her for.
2. Choose a good time and place to thank the other person.
3. Thank the other person in a friendly way.
4. Tell the other person why you are thanking him/her.

FILL IN NOW

1. Where will you try the skill? _____

2. With whom will you try the skill? _____

3. When will you try the skill? _____

4. If you do an excellent job, how will you reward yourself? _____

5. If you do a good job, how will you reward yourself? _____

6. If you do a fair job, how will you reward yourself? _____

FILL IN AFTER YOU PRACTICE THE SKILL

1. What happened when you did the homework?

   _____

   _____

2. Which skill steps did you really follow?

   _____

   _____

3. How good a job did you do in using the skill? *(check one)*

   ☐ excellent   ☐ good   ☐ fair   ☐ poor

4. What do you think your next homework assignment should be?

   _____

From *Skillstreaming the Adolescent: A Guide for Teaching Prosocial Skills* (3rd ed.), © 2012 by E. McGinnis, Champaign, IL: Research Press (www.researchpress.com, 800-519-2707).

Skill 6: Introducing Yourself

SKILL STEPS

1. **Choose the right time and place to introduce yourself.**

2. **Greet the other person and tell your name.**

   Shake hands, if appropriate.

3. **Ask the other person his/her name if you need to.**

4. **Tell or ask the other person something to help start your conversation.**

   Tell something about yourself; comment on something you both have in common; ask a question.

SUGGESTED MODELING DISPLAYS

School or neighborhood: Main actor introduces self to a new neighbor.

Home: Main actor introduces self to friend of parents.

Peer group: Main actor introduces self to several classmates at start of school year.

Job: Main actor introduces self to co-workers.

COMMENTS

This skill and Skill 7 (Introducing Other People) are extremely important in a youth's efforts to establish social contacts. They are not intended as lessons in "etiquette." Leaders should be attuned to choosing language appropriate to the particular interpersonal situation.

Skillstreaming

From *Skillstreaming the Adolescent: A Guide for Teaching Prosocial Skills* (3rd ed.), © 2012 by E. McGinnis, Champaign, IL: Research Press (www.researchpress.com, 800-519-2707).

Skill 6: Introducing Yourself

Name _____ Date _____

SKILL STEPS

1. Choose the right time and place to introduce yourself.

2. Greet the other person and tell your name.

3. Ask the other person his/her name if you need to.

4. Tell or ask the other person something to help start your conversation.

FILL IN NOW

1. Where will you try the skill? _____

2. With whom will you try the skill? _____

3. When will you try the skill? _____

FILL IN AFTER YOU PRACTICE THE SKILL

1. What happened when you did the homework?

    _____

    _____

2. Which skill steps did you really follow?

    _____

    _____

3. How good a job did you do in using the skill? *(check one)*

    ☐ excellent   ☐ good   ☐ fair   ☐ poor

Skillstreaming
From *Skillstreaming the Adolescent: A Guide for Teaching Prosocial Skills* (3rd ed.), © 2012 by E. McGinnis, Champaign, IL: Research Press (www.researchpress.com, 800-519-2707).

Skill 6: Introducing Yourself

Name _____ Date _____

SKILL STEPS

1. Choose the right time and place to introduce yourself.
2. Greet the other person and tell your name.
3. Ask the other person his/her name if you need to.
4. Tell or ask the other person something to help start your conversation.

FILL IN NOW

1. Where will you try the skill? _____

2. With whom will you try the skill? _____

3. When will you try the skill? _____

4. If you do an excellent job, how will you reward yourself? _____

5. If you do a good job, how will you reward yourself? _____

6. If you do a fair job, how will you reward yourself? _____

FILL IN AFTER YOU PRACTICE THE SKILL

1. What happened when you did the homework?

   _____

   _____

2. Which skill steps did you really follow?

   _____

   _____

3. How good a job did you do in using the skill? *(check one)*

   ☐ excellent   ☐ good   ☐ fair   ☐ poor

4. What do you think your next homework assignment should be?

   _____

Skillstreaming

Skill 7: Introducing Other People

SKILL STEPS

1. **Name the first person and tell him/her the name of the second person.**

   Speak clearly and loudly enough so that the names are heard by both people.

2. **Name the second person and tell him/her the name of the first person.**

3. **Say something that helps the two people get to know each other.**

   Mention something they have in common; invite them to talk or do something with you; say how you know each of them.

SUGGESTED MODELING DISPLAYS

School or neighborhood: Main actor introduces parent to guidance counselor or teacher.

Home: Main actor introduces new friend to parent.

Peer group: Main actor introduces new neighbor to friends.

Job: Main actor introduces new co-worker to another.

Skill 7: Introducing Other People

Name _____ Date _____

SKILL STEPS

1. Name the first person and tell him/her the name of the second person.
2. Name the second person and tell him/her the name of the first person.
3. Say something that helps the two people get to know each other.

FILL IN NOW

1. Where will you try the skill? _____

2. With whom will you try the skill? _____

3. When will you try the skill? _____

FILL IN AFTER YOU PRACTICE THE SKILL

1. What happened when you did the homework?

   _____

   _____

2. Which skill steps did you really follow?

   _____

   _____

3. How good a job did you do in using the skill? *(check one)*

   ☐ excellent   ☐ good   ☐ fair   ☐ poor

Skillstreaming

From *Skillstreaming the Adolescent: A Guide for Teaching Prosocial Skills* (3rd ed.), © 2012 by E. McGinnis, Champaign, IL: Research Press (www.researchpress.com, 800-519-2707).

Skill 7: Introducing Other People

Name _____ Date _____

SKILL STEPS

1. Name the first person and tell him/her the name of the second person.
2. Name the second person and tell him/her the name of the first person.
3. Say something that helps the two people get to know each other.

FILL IN NOW

1. Where will you try the skill? _____

2. With whom will you try the skill? _____

3. When will you try the skill? _____

4. If you do an excellent job, how will you reward yourself? _____

5. If you do a good job, how will you reward yourself? _____

6. If you do a fair job, how will you reward yourself? _____

FILL IN AFTER YOU PRACTICE THE SKILL

1. What happened when you did the homework?

   _____

   _____

2. Which skill steps did you really follow?

   _____

   _____

3. How good a job did you do in using the skill? *(check one)*

   ☐ excellent   ☐ good   ☐ fair   ☐ poor

4. What do you think your next homework assignment should be?

   _____

Skill 8: Giving a Compliment

SKILL STEPS

1. **Decide what you want to compliment about the other person.**

   It may be the person's appearance, behavior, or an accomplishment.

2. **Decide how to give the compliment.**

   Consider the wording and ways to keep the other person and yourself from feeling embarrassed.

3. **Choose the right time and place to say it.**

   It may be a private place or a time when the other person is unoccupied.

4. **Give the compliment.**

   Be friendly and sincere.

SUGGESTED MODELING DISPLAYS

School or neighborhood: Main actor compliments neighbor on new car or classmate on an assignment done well.

Home: Main actor compliments parent on good dinner or how the parent solved a problem.

Peer group: Main actor compliments friend for avoiding fight.

Job: Main actor compliments co-worker for doing a nice job.

Skill 8: Giving a Compliment

Name _____ Date _____

SKILL STEPS

1. Decide what you want to compliment about the other person.
2. Decide how to give the compliment.
3. Choose the right time and place to say it.
4. Give the compliment.

FILL IN NOW

1. Where will you try the skill? _____

2. With whom will you try the skill? _____

3. When will you try the skill? _____

FILL IN AFTER YOU PRACTICE THE SKILL

1. What happened when you did the homework?

   _____

   _____

2. Which skill steps did you really follow?

   _____

   _____

3. How good a job did you do in using the skill? *(check one)*

   ☐ excellent   ☐ good   ☐ fair   ☐ poor

From *Skillstreaming the Adolescent: A Guide for Teaching Prosocial Skills* (3rd ed.), © 2012 by E. McGinnis, Champaign, IL: Research Press (www.researchpress.com, 800-519-2707).

Skill 8: Giving a Compliment

Name _____ Date _____

SKILL STEPS

1. Decide what you want to compliment about the other person.
2. Decide how to give the compliment.
3. Choose the right time and place to say it.
4. Give the compliment.

FILL IN NOW

1. Where will you try the skill? _____

2. With whom will you try the skill? _____

3. When will you try the skill? _____

4. If you do an excellent job, how will you reward yourself? _____

5. If you do a good job, how will you reward yourself? _____

6. If you do a fair job, how will you reward yourself? _____

FILL IN AFTER YOU PRACTICE THE SKILL

1. What happened when you did the homework?

   _____

   _____

2. Which skill steps did you really follow?

   _____

   _____

3. How good a job did you do in using the skill? *(check one)*

   ☐ excellent   ☐ good   ☐ fair   ☐ poor

4. What do you think your next homework assignment should be?

   _____

Skillstreaming From *Skillstreaming the Adolescent: A Guide for Teaching Prosocial Skills* (3rd ed.), © 2012 by E. McGinnis, Champaign, IL: Research Press (www.researchpress.com, 800-519-2707).

Group II

Advanced Social Skills

Skills 9–14

Skill 9: Asking for Help

SKILL STEPS

1. **Decide what the problem is.**

   Be specific: Who and what are contributing to the problem; what is its effect on you?

2. **Decide if you want help for the problem.**

   Figure out if you can solve the problem alone.

3. **Think about different people who might help you and pick one.**

   Consider all possible helpers and choose the best one.

4. **Tell the person about the problem and ask that person to help you.**

   If the person wants to help you but is unable to do so at the moment, ask the person when a good time would be.

SUGGESTED MODELING DISPLAYS

School or neighborhood: Main actor asks teacher for help with difficult homework problem.

Home: Main actor asks parent for help with personal problem.

Peer group: Main actor asks friend for advice with dating.

Job: Main actor asks supervisor to clarify what he/she is to do.

COMMENTS

The definition of *problem,* as used in this skill, is anything one needs help with, varying from problems with other people to school and other informational problems.

Skill 9: Asking for Help

Name _____ Date _____

SKILL STEPS

1. Decide what the problem is.
2. Decide if you want help for the problem.
3. Think about different people who might help you and pick one.
4. Tell the person about the problem and ask that person to help you.

FILL IN NOW

1. Where will you try the skill? _____

2. With whom will you try the skill? _____

3. When will you try the skill? _____

FILL IN AFTER YOU PRACTICE THE SKILL

1. What happened when you did the homework?

   _____

   _____

2. Which skill steps did you really follow?

   _____

   _____

3. How good a job did you do in using the skill? *(check one)*

   ☐ excellent   ☐ good   ☐ fair   ☐ poor

Skillstreaming From *Skillstreaming the Adolescent: A Guide for Teaching Prosocial Skills* (3rd ed.), © 2012 by E. McGinnis, Champaign, IL: Research Press (www.researchpress.com, 800-519-2707).

Skill 9: Asking for Help

Name _____ Date _____

SKILL STEPS

1. Decide what the problem is.
2. Decide if you want help for the problem.
3. Think about different people who might help you and pick one.
4. Tell the person about the problem and ask that person to help you.

FILL IN NOW

1. Where will you try the skill? _____

2. With whom will you try the skill? _____

3. When will you try the skill? _____

4. If you do an excellent job, how will you reward yourself? _____

5. If you do a good job, how will you reward yourself? _____

6. If you do a fair job, how will you reward yourself? _____

FILL IN AFTER YOU PRACTICE THE SKILL

1. What happened when you did the homework?

   _____

   _____

2. Which skill steps did you really follow?

   _____

   _____

3. How good a job did you do in using the skill? *(check one)*

   ☐ excellent   ☐ good   ☐ fair   ☐ poor

4. What do you think your next homework assignment should be?

   _____

Skillstreaming   From *Skillstreaming the Adolescent: A Guide for Teaching Prosocial Skills* (3rd ed.), © 2012
by E. McGinnis, Champaign, IL: Research Press (www.researchpress.com, 800-519-2707).   **137**

Skill 10: Joining In

SKILL STEPS

1. **Decide if you want to join in an activity others are doing.**

   Check the advantages and disadvantages. Be sure you want to participate in and not disrupt what others are doing.

2. **Decide the best way to join in.**

   You might ask, apply, start a conversation, or introduce yourself.

3. **Choose the best time to join in.**

   Good times are usually during a break in the activity or before the activity gets started.

4. **Join in the activity.**

SUGGESTED MODELING DISPLAYS

School or neighborhood: Main actor signs up for neighborhood sports team.

Home: Main actor joins family in recreational activity.

Peer group: Main actor joins peers in ongoing game, recreational activity, or conversation or joins friends in an online conversation.

Job: Main actor joins group of co-workers at break.

From *Skillstreaming the Adolescent: A Guide for Teaching Prosocial Skills* (3rd ed.), © 2012 by E. McGinnis, Champaign, IL: Research Press (www.researchpress.com, 800-519-2707).

Skill 10: Joining In

Name _____ Date _____

SKILL STEPS

1. Decide if you want to join in an activity others are doing.
2. Decide the best way to join in.
3. Choose the best time to join in.
4. Join in the activity.

FILL IN NOW

1. Where will you try the skill? _____

2. With whom will you try the skill? _____

3. When will you try the skill? _____

FILL IN AFTER YOU PRACTICE THE SKILL

1. What happened when you did the homework?

   _____

   _____

2. Which skill steps did you really follow?

   _____

   _____

3. How good a job did you do in using the skill? *(check one)*

   ☐ excellent   ☐ good   ☐ fair   ☐ poor

Skill 10: Joining In

Name _____ Date _____

SKILL STEPS

1. Decide if you want to join in an activity others are doing.
2. Decide the best way to join in.
3. Choose the best time to join in.
4. Join in the activity.

FILL IN NOW

1. Where will you try the skill? _____

2. With whom will you try the skill? _____

3. When will you try the skill? _____

4. If you do an excellent job, how will you reward yourself? _____

5. If you do a good job, how will you reward yourself? _____

6. If you do a fair job, how will you reward yourself? _____

FILL IN AFTER YOU PRACTICE THE SKILL

1. What happened when you did the homework?

   _____

   _____

2. Which skill steps did you really follow?

   _____

   _____

3. How good a job did you do in using the skill? *(check one)*

   ☐ excellent   ☐ good   ☐ fair   ☐ poor

4. What do you think your next homework assignment should be?

   _____

Skillstreaming

From *Skillstreaming the Adolescent: A Guide for Teaching Prosocial Skills* (3rd ed.), © 2012 by E. McGinnis, Champaign, IL: Research Press (www.researchpress.com, 800-519-2707).

Skill 11: Giving Instructions

SKILL STEPS

1. **Decide what needs to be done.**

   It might be a chore or a favor.

2. **Think about the different people who could do it and choose one.**

3. **Ask that person to do what you want done.**

   Tell the person how to do it when the task is complex.

4. **Ask the other person if he/she understands what to do.**

5. **Change or repeat your instructions if you need to.**

   This step is optional.

SUGGESTED MODELING DISPLAYS

School or neighborhood: Main actor divides chores for decorating gym for school party.

Home: Main actor tells younger brother how to refuse drugs if offered to him or helps a parent use a new cell phone.

Peer group: Main actor instructs friends on how to access a website, download songs, or play a video game.

Job: Main actor gives instructions to co-worker to finish a job.

COMMENTS

This skill often refers to the enlistment of others to carry out a task and thus requires youth to think about division of responsibility, as well as how to obtain support from others.

From *Skillstreaming the Adolescent: A Guide for Teaching Prosocial Skills* (3rd ed.), © 2012 by E. McGinnis, Champaign, IL: Research Press (www.researchpress.com, 800-519-2707).

Skill 11: Giving Instructions

Name _____ Date _____

SKILL STEPS

1. Decide what needs to be done.
2. Think about the different people who could do it and choose one.
3. Ask that person to do what you want done.
4. Ask the other person if he/she understands what to do.
5. Change or repeat your instructions if you need to.

FILL IN NOW

1. Where will you try the skill? _____

2. With whom will you try the skill? _____

3. When will you try the skill? _____

FILL IN AFTER YOU PRACTICE THE SKILL

1. What happened when you did the homework?

   _____

   _____

2. Which skill steps did you really follow?

   _____

   _____

3. How good a job did you do in using the skill? *(check one)*

   ☐ excellent   ☐ good   ☐ fair   ☐ poor

Skillstreaming From *Skillstreaming the Adolescent: A Guide for Teaching Prosocial Skills* (3rd ed.), © 2012 by E. McGinnis, Champaign, IL: Research Press (www.researchpress.com, 800-519-2707).

Skill 11: Giving Instructions

Name _____ Date _____

SKILL STEPS

1. Decide what needs to be done.
2. Think about the different people who could do it and choose one.
3. Ask that person to do what you want done.
4. Ask the other person if he/she understands what to do.
5. Change or repeat your instructions if you need to.

FILL IN NOW

1. Where will you try the skill? _____

2. With whom will you try the skill? _____

3. When will you try the skill? _____

4. If you do an excellent job, how will you reward yourself? _____

5. If you do a good job, how will you reward yourself? _____

6. If you do a fair job, how will you reward yourself? _____

FILL IN AFTER YOU PRACTICE THE SKILL

1. What happened when you did the homework?

   _____

   _____

2. Which skill steps did you really follow?

   _____

   _____

3. How good a job did you do in using the skill? *(check one)*

   ☐ excellent   ☐ good   ☐ fair   ☐ poor

4. What do you think your next homework assignment should be?

   _____

Skill 12: Following Instructions

SKILL STEPS

1. **Listen carefully while you are being told what to do.**

   Take notes if necessary; nod your head; say, "Mm-hmm."

2. **Ask questions about anything you don't understand.**

   The goal is making instructions more specific, more clear.

3. **Decide if you want to follow the instructions and let the other person know your decision.**

   Think about the positive and negative consequences of following the instructions.

4. **Repeat the instructions to yourself.**

   Do this in your own words.

5. **Do what you have been asked to do.**

SUGGESTED MODELING DISPLAYS

School or neighborhood: Main actor follows classroom instructions given by teacher or cafeteria supervisor.

Home: Main actor follows parent's instructions on operating home appliance or cooking with a recipe.

Peer group: Main actor follows friend's instructions on how to save pictures on a computer, how to sign up for a website, or how to transfer songs to an iPod player.

Job: Main actor follows supervisor's directions in doing a job.

COMMENTS

This skill concerns complying with the requests of another person. If the task seems unreasonable, it may be an instance in which another skill is needed (e.g., Negotiating, Making a Complaint).

Skillstreaming

From *Skillstreaming the Adolescent: A Guide for Teaching Prosocial Skills* (3rd ed.), © 2012 by E. McGinnis, Champaign, IL: Research Press (www.researchpress.com, 800-519-2707).

Skill 12: Following Instructions

Name _____ Date _____

SKILL STEPS

1. Listen carefully while you are being told what to do.
2. Ask questions about anything you don't understand.
3. Decide if you want to follow the instructions and let the other person know your decision.
4. Repeat the instructions to yourself.
5. Do what you have been asked to do.

FILL IN NOW

1. Where will you try the skill? _____

2. With whom will you try the skill? _____

3. When will you try the skill? _____

FILL IN AFTER YOU PRACTICE THE SKILL

1. What happened when you did the homework?

   _____

   _____

2. Which skill steps did you really follow?

   _____

   _____

3. How good a job did you do in using the skill? *(check one)*

   ☐ excellent   ☐ good   ☐ fair   ☐ poor

From *Skillstreaming the Adolescent: A Guide for Teaching Prosocial Skills* (3rd ed.), © 2012 by E. McGinnis, Champaign, IL: Research Press (www.researchpress.com, 800-519-2707).

Skill 12: Following Instructions

Name _____ Date _____

SKILL STEPS

1. Listen carefully while you are being told what to do.
2. Ask questions about anything you don't understand.
3. Decide if you want to follow the instructions and let the other person know your decision.
4. Repeat the instructions to yourself.
5. Do what you have been asked to do.

FILL IN NOW

1. Where will you try the skill? _____

2. With whom will you try the skill? _____

3. When will you try the skill? _____

4. If you do an excellent job, how will you reward yourself? _____

5. If you do a good job, how will you reward yourself? _____

6. If you do a fair job, how will you reward yourself? _____

FILL IN AFTER YOU PRACTICE THE SKILL

1. What happened when you did the homework?

   _____

   _____

2. Which skill steps did you really follow?

   _____

   _____

3. How good a job did you do in using the skill? *(check one)*

   ☐ excellent   ☐ good   ☐ fair   ☐ poor

4. What do you think your next homework assignment should be?

   _____

Skillstreaming   From *Skillstreaming the Adolescent: A Guide for Teaching Prosocial Skills* (3rd ed.), © 2012 by E. McGinnis, Champaign, IL: Research Press (www.researchpress.com, 800-519-2707).

Skill 13: Apologizing

SKILL STEPS

1. **Decide if it would be best for you to apologize for something you did.**

   You might apologize for breaking something, making an error, interrupting someone, or hurting someone's feelings.

2. **Think of the different ways you could apologize.**

   Say something; do something; write something.

3. **Choose the best time and place to apologize.**

   Do it privately and as quickly as possible after creating the problem.

4. **Make your apology.**

   This might include an offer to make up for what happened.

SUGGESTED MODELING DISPLAYS

School or neighborhood: Main actor apologizes to neighbor for broken window.

Home: Main actor apologizes to younger sister for picking on her.

Peer group: Main actor apologizes to friend for betraying a confidence.

Job: Main actor apologizes to supervisor for being late from school to the job.

From *Skillstreaming the Adolescent: A Guide for Teaching Prosocial Skills* (3rd ed.), © 2012 by E. McGinnis, Champaign, IL: Research Press (www.researchpress.com, 800-519-2707).

Skill 13: Apologizing

Name _____ Date _____

SKILL STEPS

1. Decide if it would be best for you to apologize for something you did.
2. Think of the different ways you could apologize.
3. Choose the best time and place to apologize.
4. Make your apology.

FILL IN NOW

1. Where will you try the skill? _____

2. With whom will you try the skill? _____

3. When will you try the skill? _____

FILL IN AFTER YOU PRACTICE THE SKILL

1. What happened when you did the homework?

   _____

   _____

2. Which skill steps did you really follow?

   _____

   _____

3. How good a job did you do in using the skill? *(check one)*

   ☐ excellent   ☐ good   ☐ fair   ☐ poor

Skillstreaming

From *Skillstreaming the Adolescent: A Guide for Teaching Prosocial Skills* (3rd ed.), © 2012 by E. McGinnis, Champaign, IL: Research Press (www.researchpress.com, 800-519-2707).

Skill 13: Apologizing

Name _____ Date _____

SKILL STEPS

1. Decide if it would be best for you to apologize for something you did.
2. Think of the different ways you could apologize.
3. Choose the best time and place to apologize.
4. Make your apology.

FILL IN NOW

1. Where will you try the skill? _____

2. With whom will you try the skill? _____

3. When will you try the skill? _____

4. If you do an excellent job, how will you reward yourself? _____

5. If you do a good job, how will you reward yourself? _____

6. If you do a fair job, how will you reward yourself? _____

FILL IN AFTER YOU PRACTICE THE SKILL

1. What happened when you did the homework?

   _____

   _____

2. Which skill steps did you really follow?

   _____

   _____

3. How good a job did you do in using the skill? *(check one)*

   ☐ excellent   ☐ good   ☐ fair   ☐ poor

4. What do you think your next homework assignment should be?

   _____

Skillstreaming   From *Skillstreaming the Adolescent: A Guide for Teaching Prosocial Skills* (3rd ed.), © 2012 by E. McGinnis, Champaign, IL: Research Press (www.researchpress.com, 800-519-2707).   **149**

Skill 14: Convincing Others

SKILL STEPS

1. **Decide if you want to convince someone about something.**

   It might be doing something your way, going someplace, interpreting events, or evaluating ideas.

2. **Tell the other person your idea.**

   Focus on both content of ideas and feelings about point of view.

3. **Ask the other person what he/she thinks about it.**

   This requires use of Listening (Skill 1).

4. **Tell why you think your idea is a good one.**

   Try your best to be fair; "get into the other person's shoes."

5. **Ask the other person to think about what you said before making up his/her mind.**

   Check on the other person's decision at a later point in time.

SUGGESTED MODELING DISPLAYS

School or neighborhood: Main actor convinces teacher to allow extra time on an assignment.

Home: Main actor convinces parent that he/she is responsible enough to stay out late.

Peer group: Main actor convinces friend to include new person in game or social activity.

Job: Main actor convinces store manager that he/she deserves the job.

COMMENTS

In persuading someone of something, a person needs to understand both sides of the argument. Use of this skill assumes that if the other person is asked about his or her position and there is no difference of opinion, the role-play should end at Step 3.

.Skillstreaming

From *Skillstreaming the Adolescent: A Guide for Teaching Prosocial Skills* (3rd ed.), © 2012 by E. McGinnis, Champaign, IL: Research Press (www.researchpress.com, 800-519-2707).

Skill 14: Convincing Others

Name _____ Date _____

SKILL STEPS

1. Decide if you want to convince someone about something.

2. Tell the other person your idea.

3. Ask the other person what he/she thinks about it.

4. Tell why you think your idea is a good one.

5. Ask the other person to think about what you said before making up his/her mind.

FILL IN NOW

1. Where will you try the skill? _____

2. With whom will you try the skill? _____

3. When will you try the skill? _____

FILL IN AFTER YOU PRACTICE THE SKILL

1. What happened when you did the homework?

   _____

   _____

2. Which skill steps did you really follow?

   _____

   _____

3. How good a job did you do in using the skill? *(check one)*

   ☐ excellent   ☐ good   ☐ fair   ☐ poor

From *Skillstreaming the Adolescent: A Guide for Teaching Prosocial Skills* (3rd ed.), © 2012 by E. McGinnis, Champaign, IL: Research Press (www.researchpress.com, 800-519-2707).

Skill 14: Convincing Others

Name _____ Date _____

SKILL STEPS

1. Decide if you want to convince someone about something.
2. Tell the other person your idea.
3. Ask the other person what he/she thinks about it.
4. Tell why you think your idea is a good one.
5. Ask the other person to think about what you said before making up his/her mind.

FILL IN NOW

1. Where will you try the skill? _____

2. With whom will you try the skill? _____

3. When will you try the skill? _____

4. If you do an excellent job, how will you reward yourself? _____

5. If you do a good job, how will you reward yourself? _____

6. If you do a fair job, how will you reward yourself? _____

FILL IN AFTER YOU PRACTICE THE SKILL

1. What happened when you did the homework?

   _____

   _____

2. Which skill steps did you really follow?

   _____

   _____

3. How good a job did you do in using the skill? *(check one)*

   ☐ excellent   ☐ good   ☐ fair   ☐ poor

4. What do you think your next homework assignment should be?

   _____

Skillstreaming

Group III

Skills for Dealing with Feelings

Skills 15–21

Skill 15: Knowing Your Feelings

SKILL STEPS

1. **Tune in to what is going on in your body that helps you know what you are feeling.**

   Some cues are blushing, butterflies in your stomach, tight muscles, and so on.

2. **Decide what happened to make you feel that way.**

   Focus on outside events such as a fight, a surprise, and so forth.

3. **Decide what you could call the feeling.**

   Possibilities are anger, fear, embarrassment, joy, happiness, sadness, disappointment, frustration, excitement, anxiety, and so on. (Leader should create a list of feelings and encourage group members to contribute additional suggestions.)

SUGGESTED MODELING DISPLAYS

School or neighborhood: Main actor gives the wrong answer in class when called on and peers laugh or main actor must give presentation in front of the class.

Home: Main actor is unjustly accused at home.

Peer group: Main actor receives a text or e-mail saying negative things about him/her.

Job: Main actor is corrected by supervisor in front of co-workers or has to tell the boss he/she left part of work uniform at home.

COMMENTS

This has been included as a separate skill for adolescents to learn prior to practicing the expression of feelings to another person. Frequently, feelings can be confused with one another, resulting in rather vague but strong emotions. Once the feeling can be labeled accurately, the group member can go on to the next skill, which involves prosocial modes of expressing the feeling.

Step 1, involving "tuning in" to body feelings, is often a new experience for many participants. Spend as much time as needed in discussing, giving examples, and practicing this step before going on to subsequent steps. Pay particular attention to the physical characteristics the feeling evokes (e.g., feeling hot, heart racing, clenching teeth, etc.).

Skill 15: Knowing Your Feelings

Name _____ Date _____

SKILL STEPS

1. Tune in to what is going on in your body that helps you know what you are feeling.
2. Decide what happened to make you feel that way.
3. Decide what you could call the feeling.

FILL IN NOW

1. Where will you try the skill? _____

2. With whom will you try the skill? _____

3. When will you try the skill? _____

FILL IN AFTER YOU PRACTICE THE SKILL

1. What happened when you did the homework?

   _____

   _____

2. Which skill steps did you really follow?

   _____

   _____

3. How good a job did you do in using the skill? *(check one)*

   ☐ excellent   ☐ good   ☐ fair   ☐ poor

Skillstreaming
■ ■ ■ ■ ■ ■ ■ ■ ■ ■ ■ ■ ■

From *Skillstreaming the Adolescent: A Guide for Teaching Prosocial Skills* (3rd ed.), © 2012 by E. McGinnis, Champaign, IL: Research Press (www.researchpress.com, 800-519-2707).

Skill 15: Knowing Your Feelings

Name _____ Date _____

SKILL STEPS

1. Tune in to what is going on in your body that helps you know what you are feeling.

2. Decide what happened to make you feel that way.

3. Decide what you could call the feeling.

FILL IN NOW

1. Where will you try the skill? _____

2. With whom will you try the skill? _____

3. When will you try the skill? _____

4. If you do an excellent job, how will you reward yourself? _____

5. If you do a good job, how will you reward yourself? _____

6. If you do a fair job, how will you reward yourself? _____

FILL IN AFTER YOU PRACTICE THE SKILL

1. What happened when you did the homework?

   _____

   _____

2. Which skill steps did you really follow?

   _____

   _____

3. How good a job did you do in using the skill? *(check one)*

   ☐ excellent   ☐ good   ☐ fair   ☐ poor

4. What do you think your next homework assignment should be?

   _____

Skill 16: Expressing Your Feelings

SKILL STEPS

1. Tune in to what is going on in your body.

2. Decide what happened to make you feel that way.

3. Decide what you are feeling.

   Possibilities are happy, sad, in a bad mood, nervous, worried, scared, embarrassed, disappointed, frustrated, and so forth. (Leader and group members should develop a list of feelings.)

4. Think about the different ways to express your feeling and pick one.

   Consider prosocial alternatives, such as talking about a feeling, doing a physical activity, telling the object of the feeling about the feeling, walking away from emotional situations, or delaying action. Consider how, when, where, and to whom the feeling could be expressed.

5. Express your feeling.

SUGGESTED MODELING DISPLAYS

School or neighborhood: Main actor tells teacher about feeling nervous before test or is frustrated when a vending machine doesn't work and money is lost.

Home: Main actor tells parent about feeling embarrassed when treated like a child.

Peer group: Main actor hugs friend when learning of friend's success or becomes angry about a friend's changing plans they made together.

Job: Main actor fails at job task and is angry with himself/herself.

.Skillstreaming

From *Skillstreaming the Adolescent: A Guide for Teaching Prosocial Skills* (3rd ed.), © 2012 by E. McGinnis, Champaign, IL: Research Press (www.researchpress.com, 800-519-2707).

Skill 16: Expressing Your Feelings

Name _____ Date _____

SKILL STEPS

1. Tune in to what is going on in your body.

2. Decide what happened to make you feel that way.

3. Decide what you are feeling.

4. Think about the different ways to express your feeling and pick one.

5. Express your feeling.

FILL IN NOW

1. Where will you try the skill? _____

2. With whom will you try the skill? _____

3. When will you try the skill? _____

FILL IN AFTER YOU PRACTICE THE SKILL

1. What happened when you did the homework?

   _____

   _____

2. Which skill steps did you really follow?

   _____

   _____

3. How good a job did you do in using the skill? *(check one)*

   ☐ excellent   ☐ good   ☐ fair   ☐ poor

From *Skillstreaming the Adolescent: A Guide for Teaching Prosocial Skills* (3rd ed.), © 2012 by E. McGinnis, Champaign, IL: Research Press (www.researchpress.com, 800-519-2707).

Skill 16: Expressing Your Feelings

Name _____ Date _____

SKILL STEPS

1. Tune in to what is going on in your body.
2. Decide what happened to make you feel that way.
3. Decide what you are feeling.
4. Think about the different ways to express your feeling and pick one.
5. Express your feeling.

FILL IN NOW

1. Where will you try the skill? _____

2. With whom will you try the skill? _____

3. When will you try the skill? _____

4. If you do an excellent job, how will you reward yourself? _____

5. If you do a good job, how will you reward yourself? _____

6. If you do a fair job, how will you reward yourself? _____

FILL IN AFTER YOU PRACTICE THE SKILL

1. What happened when you did the homework?

   _____

   _____

2. Which skill steps did you really follow?

   _____

   _____

3. How good a job did you do in using the skill? *(check one)*

   ☐ excellent   ☐ good   ☐ fair   ☐ poor

4. What do you think your next homework assignment should be?

   _____

.Skillstreaming

From *Skillstreaming the Adolescent: A Guide for Teaching Prosocial Skills* (3rd ed.), © 2012 by E. McGinnis, Champaign, IL: Research Press (www.researchpress.com, 800-519-2707).

Skill 17: Understanding the Feelings of Others

SKILL STEPS

1. **Watch the other person.**

   Notice tone of voice, posture, and facial expression.

2. **Listen to what the other person is saying.**

   Try to understand the content.

3. **Figure out what the person might be feeling.**

   He/she may be angry, sad, anxious, and so on.

4. **Think about ways to show you understand what he/she is feeling.**

   You might tell him/her, touch him/her, or leave the person alone.

5. **Decide on the best way and do it.**

SUGGESTED MODELING DISPLAYS

School or neighborhood: Main actor brings gift to neighbor whose spouse has been ill.

Home: Main actor recognizes parent is preoccupied with financial concerns and decides to leave parent alone.

Peer group: Main actor lets friend know he/she understands friend's discomfort on meeting new people.

Job: Main actor supports co-worker who is in trouble with the boss.

COMMENTS

This skill is well known by the term *empathy*. Although difficult to teach, it is critical for group members to add it to their repertoire of skills.

Skill 17: Understanding the Feelings of Others

Name _____ Date _____

SKILL STEPS

1. Watch the other person.

2. Listen to what the other person is saying.

3. Figure out what the person might be feeling.

4. Think about ways to show you understand what he/she is feeling.

5. Decide on the best way and do it.

FILL IN NOW

1. Where will you try the skill? _____

2. With whom will you try the skill? _____

3. When will you try the skill? _____

FILL IN AFTER YOU PRACTICE THE SKILL

1. What happened when you did the homework?

   _____

   _____

2. Which skill steps did you really follow?

   _____

   _____

3. How good a job did you do in using the skill? *(check one)*

   ☐ excellent   ☐ good   ☐ fair   ☐ poor

Skillstreaming

From *Skillstreaming the Adolescent: A Guide for Teaching Prosocial Skills* (3rd ed.), © 2012 by E. McGinnis, Champaign, IL: Research Press (www.researchpress.com, 800-519-2707).

Skill 17: Understanding the Feelings of Others

Name _____ Date _____

SKILL STEPS

1. Watch the other person.
2. Listen to what the other person is saying.
3. Figure out what the person might be feeling.
4. Think about ways to show you understand what he/she is feeling.
5. Decide on the best way and do it.

FILL IN NOW

1. Where will you try the skill? _____

2. With whom will you try the skill? _____

3. When will you try the skill? _____

4. If you do an excellent job, how will you reward yourself? _____

5. If you do a good job, how will you reward yourself? _____

6. If you do a fair job, how will you reward yourself? _____

FILL IN AFTER YOU PRACTICE THE SKILL

1. What happened when you did the homework?

   _____

   _____

2. Which skill steps did you really follow?

   _____

   _____

3. How good a job did you do in using the skill? *(check one)*

   ☐ excellent   ☐ good   ☐ fair   ☐ poor

4. What do you think your next homework assignment should be?

   _____

Skillstreaming From *Skillstreaming the Adolescent: A Guide for Teaching Prosocial Skills* (3rd ed.), © 2012
by E. McGinnis, Champaign, IL: Research Press (www.researchpress.com, 800-519-2707). **163**

Skill 18: Dealing with Someone Else's Anger

SKILL STEPS

1. **Listen to the person who is angry.**

   Don't interrupt; stay calm.

2. **Try to understand what the angry person is saying and feeling.**

   Ask questions to get explanations of what you don't understand; restate them to yourself.

3. **Decide if you can say or do something to deal with the situation.**

   Think about ways of dealing with the problem. This may include just listening, being empathic, doing something to correct the problem, ignoring it, or being assertive.

4. **If you can, deal with the other person's anger.**

SUGGESTED MODELING DISPLAYS

School or neighborhood: Main actor responds to teacher who is angry about disruptive behavior in class by agreeing to cooperate and pay attention.

Home: Main actor responds to parent who is angry about messy house by agreeing to do a fair share of work.

Peer group: Main actor responds to admired older sibling's anger when main actor refuses to go out drinking.

Job: Main actor responds to supervisor's general anger and frustration.

COMMENTS

This skill refers to anger directed at the group member. As such, it usually requires the group member to take some action to deal with the situation. Leaders should have the main actor make use of the steps for Skill 1 (Listening) when enacting the first step of this skill.

From *Skillstreaming the Adolescent: A Guide for Teaching Prosocial Skills* (3rd ed.), © 2012 by E. McGinnis, Champaign, IL: Research Press (www.researchpress.com, 800-519-2707).

Skill 18: Dealing with Someone Else's Anger

Name _____ Date _____

SKILL STEPS

1. Listen to the person who is angry.
2. Try to understand what the angry person is saying and feeling.
3. Decide if you can say or do something to deal with the situation.
4. If you can, deal with the other person's anger.

FILL IN NOW

1. Where will you try the skill? _____

2. With whom will you try the skill? _____

3. When will you try the skill? _____

FILL IN AFTER YOU PRACTICE THE SKILL

1. What happened when you did the homework?

   _____

   _____

2. Which skill steps did you really follow?

   _____

   _____

3. How good a job did you do in using the skill? *(check one)*

   ☐ excellent   ☐ good   ☐ fair   ☐ poor

From *Skillstreaming the Adolescent: A Guide for Teaching Prosocial Skills* (3rd ed.), © 2012 by E. McGinnis, Champaign, IL: Research Press (www.researchpress.com, 800-519-2707).

Skill 18: Dealing with Someone Else's Anger

Name _____ Date _____

SKILL STEPS

1. Listen to the person who is angry.
2. Try to understand what the angry person is saying and feeling.
3. Decide if you can say or do something to deal with the situation.
4. If you can, deal with the other person's anger.

FILL IN NOW

1. Where will you try the skill? _____

2. With whom will you try the skill? _____

3. When will you try the skill? _____

4. If you do an excellent job, how will you reward yourself? _____

5. If you do a good job, how will you reward yourself? _____

6. If you do a fair job, how will you reward yourself? _____

FILL IN AFTER YOU PRACTICE THE SKILL

1. What happened when you did the homework?

   _____

   _____

2. Which skill steps did you really follow?

   _____

   _____

3. How good a job did you do in using the skill? *(check one)*

   ☐ excellent   ☐ good   ☐ fair   ☐ poor

4. What do you think your next homework assignment should be?

   _____

Skillstreaming

From *Skillstreaming the Adolescent: A Guide for Teaching Prosocial Skills* (3rd ed.), © 2012 by E. McGinnis, Champaign, IL: Research Press (www.researchpress.com, 800-519-2707).

Skill 19: Expressing Affection

SKILL STEPS

1. **Decide if you have good feelings about the other person.**

2. **Decide if the other person would like to know about your feelings.**

   Consider the possible consequences (e.g., happiness, misinterpretation, embarrassment, encouragement of friendship).

3. **Choose the best way to express your feelings.**

   Do something, say something, give gift, send card, telephone, offer invitation.

4. **Choose the best time and place to express your feelings.**

   Minimize distractions and possible interruptions.

5. **Express your feelings in a friendly way.**

SUGGESTED MODELING DISPLAYS

School or neighborhood: Main actor expresses positive feelings toward guidance counselor after sharing personal problem.

Home: Main actor brings small gift to parent as token of affection.

Peer group: Main actor expresses friendly feelings toward new acquaintance.

Job: Main actor expresses appreciation to co-worker for helping him/her.

COMMENTS

Although participants initially will associate this skill with romantic relationships, they will soon grasp the notion that affection and caring can be expressed toward a wide variety of persons.

Skill 19: Expressing Affection

Name _____ Date _____

SKILL STEPS

1. Decide if you have good feelings about the other person.
2. Decide if the other person would like to know about your feelings.
3. Choose the best way to express your feelings.
4. Choose the best time and place to express your feelings.
5. Express your feelings in a friendly way.

FILL IN NOW

1. Where will you try the skill? _____

2. With whom will you try the skill? _____

3. When will you try the skill? _____

FILL IN AFTER YOU PRACTICE THE SKILL

1. What happened when you did the homework?

   _____

   _____

2. Which skill steps did you really follow?

   _____

   _____

3. How good a job did you do in using the skill? *(check one)*

   ☐ excellent　　☐ good　　☐ fair　　☐ poor

Skillstreaming

From *Skillstreaming the Adolescent: A Guide for Teaching Prosocial Skills* (3rd ed.), © 2012 by E. McGinnis, Champaign, IL: Research Press (www.researchpress.com, 800-519-2707).

Skill 19: Expressing Affection

Name _____ Date _____

SKILL STEPS

1. Decide if you have good feelings about the other person.
2. Decide if the other person would like to know about your feelings.
3. Choose the best way to express your feelings.
4. Choose the best time and place to express your feelings.
5. Express your feelings in a friendly way.

FILL IN NOW

1. Where will you try the skill? _____

2. With whom will you try the skill? _____

3. When will you try the skill? _____

4. If you do an excellent job, how will you reward yourself? _____

5. If you do a good job, how will you reward yourself? _____

6. If you do a fair job, how will you reward yourself? _____

FILL IN AFTER YOU PRACTICE THE SKILL

1. What happened when you did the homework?

   _____

   _____

2. Which skill steps did you really follow?

   _____

   _____

3. How good a job did you do in using the skill? *(check one)*

   ☐ excellent   ☐ good   ☐ fair   ☐ poor

4. What do you think your next homework assignment should be?

   _____

From *Skillstreaming the Adolescent: A Guide for Teaching Prosocial Skills* (3rd ed.), © 2012 by E. McGinnis, Champaign, IL: Research Press (www.researchpress.com, 800-519-2707).

Skill 20: Dealing with Fear

SKILL STEPS

1. **Decide if you are feeling afraid.**

   Use Skill 15 (Knowing Your Feelings).

2. **Think about what you might be afraid of.**

   Think about alternative possibilities and choose the most likely one.

3. **Figure out if the fear is realistic.**

   Is the feared object really a threat? You may need to check this out with another person or need more information.

4. **Take steps to reduce your fear.**

   You might talk with someone, leave the scene, or gradually approach the frightening situation.

SUGGESTED MODELING DISPLAYS

School or neighborhood: Main actor is fearful of repercussions after breaking neighbor's window and discusses fear with parent.

Home: Main actor is afraid of being home alone and arranges to have friend visit.

Peer group: After being teased by older neighborhood youth, main actor is fearful of being beaten up and takes steps to avoid confrontation.

Job: After messing up a job, main actor is afraid of being called out.

COMMENTS

Group discussion can be quite useful in examining how realistic particular fears are. Leaders should be sensitive to the fact that group members may be reluctant to reveal their fears to peers. Modeling of frightening situations may help them overcome this reluctance.

Skillstreaming

From *Skillstreaming the Adolescent: A Guide for Teaching Prosocial Skills* (3rd ed.), © 2012 by E. McGinnis, Champaign, IL: Research Press (www.researchpress.com, 800-519-2707).

Skill 20: Dealing with Fear

Name _____ Date _____

SKILL STEPS

1. Decide if you are feeling afraid.
2. Think about what you might be afraid of.
3. Figure out if the fear is realistic.
4. Take steps to reduce your fear.

FILL IN NOW

1. Where will you try the skill? _____

2. With whom will you try the skill? _____

3. When will you try the skill? _____

FILL IN AFTER YOU PRACTICE THE SKILL

1. What happened when you did the homework?

   _____

   _____

2. Which skill steps did you really follow?

   _____

   _____

3. How good a job did you do in using the skill? *(check one)*

   ☐ excellent   ☐ good   ☐ fair   ☐ poor

Skill 20: Dealing with Fear

Name _____ Date _____

SKILL STEPS

1. Decide if you are feeling afraid.
2. Think about what you might be afraid of.
3. Figure out if the fear is realistic.
4. Take steps to reduce your fear.

FILL IN NOW

1. Where will you try the skill? _____

2. With whom will you try the skill? _____

3. When will you try the skill? _____

4. If you do an excellent job, how will you reward yourself? _____

5. If you do a good job, how will you reward yourself? _____

6. If you do a fair job, how will you reward yourself? ___   _____

FILL IN AFTER YOU PRACTICE THE SKILL

1. What happened when you did the homework?

   _____

   _____

2. Which skill steps did you really follow?

   _____

   _____

3. How good a job did you do in using the skill? *(check one)*

   ☐ excellent   ☐ good   ☐ fair   ☐ poor

4. What do you think your next homework assignment should be?

   _____

Skillstreaming

From *Skillstreaming the Adolescent: A Guide for Teaching Prosocial Skills* (3rd ed.), © 2012 by E. McGinnis, Champaign, IL: Research Press (www.researchpress.com, 800-519-2707).

Skill 21: Rewarding Yourself

SKILL STEPS

1. **Decide if you have done something that deserves a reward.**

   It might be something you have succeeded at or some area of progress.

2. **Decide what you could say to reward yourself.**

   Use praise, approval, or encouragement.

3. **Decide what you could do to reward yourself.**

   You might buy something, go someplace, or increase or decrease an activity.

4. **Reward yourself.**

   Say and do it.

SUGGESTED MODELING DISPLAYS

School or neighborhood: Main actor rewards self after studying hard and doing well on exam by going to movie after school.

Home: Main actor rewards self with positive self-statement after avoiding fight with older sibling.

Peer group: Main actor rewards self by playing video games at the arcade after convincing peers to stay out of a fight.

Job: Main actor rewards self with positive self-statement after receiving a compliment on job performance by supervisor.

COMMENTS

Have participants apply the following rules, all of which increase the effectiveness of self-reward:

Reward yourself as soon as possible after successful performance.

Reward yourself only after successful performance, not before.

The better your performance, the better your self-reward.

See chapter 5 for further discussion of self-reward.

Skill 21: Rewarding Yourself

Name _____ Date _____

SKILL STEPS

1. Decide if you have done something that deserves a reward.
2. Decide what you could say to reward yourself.
3. Decide what you could do to reward yourself.
4. Reward yourself.

FILL IN NOW

1. Where will you try the skill? _____

2. With whom will you try the skill? _____

3. When will you try the skill? _____

FILL IN AFTER YOU PRACTICE THE SKILL

1. What happened when you did the homework?

   _____

   _____

2. Which skill steps did you really follow?

   _____

   _____

3. How good a job did you do in using the skill? *(check one)*

   ☐ excellent   ☐ good   ☐ fair   ☐ poor

Skillstreaming

From *Skillstreaming the Adolescent: A Guide for Teaching Prosocial Skills* (3rd ed.), © 2012 by E. McGinnis, Champaign, IL: Research Press (www.researchpress.com, 800-519-2707).

Skill 21: Rewarding Yourself

Name _____ Date _____

SKILL STEPS

1. Decide if you have done something that deserves a reward.
2. Decide what you could say to reward yourself.
3. Decide what you could do to reward yourself.
4. Reward yourself.

FILL IN NOW

1. Where will you try the skill? _____

2. With whom will you try the skill? _____

3. When will you try the skill? _____

4. If you do an excellent job, how will you reward yourself? _____

5. If you do a good job, how will you reward yourself? _____

6. If you do a fair job, how will you reward yourself? _____

FILL IN AFTER YOU PRACTICE THE SKILL

1. What happened when you did the homework?

   _____

   _____

2. Which skill steps did you really follow?

   _____

   _____

3. How good a job did you do in using the skill? *(check one)*

   ☐ excellent   ☐ good   ☐ fair   ☐ poor

4. What do you think your next homework assignment should be?

   _____

From *Skillstreaming the Adolescent: A Guide for Teaching Prosocial Skills* (3rd ed.), © 2012 by E. McGinnis, Champaign, IL: Research Press (www.researchpress.com, 800-519-2707).

Group IV

Skill Alternatives to Aggression

Skills 22–30

Skill 22: Asking Permission

SKILL STEPS

1. **Decide what you would like to do for which you need permission.**

   Ask if you want to borrow something or request a special privilege.

2. **Decide whom you have to ask for permission.**

   Ask the owner, manager, or teacher.

3. **Decide how to ask for permission.**

   Ask out loud; ask privately; ask in writing.

4. **Pick the right time and place.**

5. **Ask for permission.**

SUGGESTED MODELING DISPLAYS

School or neighborhood: Main actor asks shop teacher for permission to use new power tool.

Home: Main actor asks parent for permission to stay out past curfew or to use parent's new cell phone.

Peer group: Main actor asks friend for permission to borrow sporting equipment or video game.

Job: Main actor asks supervisor to come in late in order to study for a test at school.

COMMENTS

Prior to practicing this skill, it is frequently useful to discuss situations that require permission. Some adolescents tend to ask permission for things that could be done independently (without permission), whereas others neglect to ask permission in situations that require doing so.

From *Skillstreaming the Adolescent: A Guide for Teaching Prosocial Skills* (3rd ed.), © 2012 by E. McGinnis, Champaign, IL: Research Press (www.researchpress.com, 800-519-2707).

Skill 22: Asking Permission

Name _____ Date _____

SKILL STEPS

1. Decide what you would like to do for which you need permission.
2. Decide whom you have to ask for permission.
3. Decide how to ask for permission.
4. Pick the right time and place.
5. Ask for permission.

FILL IN NOW

1. Where will you try the skill? _____

2. With whom will you try the skill? _____

3. When will you try the skill? _____

FILL IN AFTER YOU PRACTICE THE SKILL

1. What happened when you did the homework?

   _____

   _____

2. Which skill steps did you really follow?

   _____

   _____

3. How good a job did you do in using the skill? *(check one)*

   ☐ excellent   ☐ good   ☐ fair   ☐ poor

Skillstreaming From *Skillstreaming the Adolescent: A Guide for Teaching Prosocial Skills* (3rd ed.), © 2012 by E. McGinnis, Champaign, IL: Research Press (www.researchpress.com, 800-519-2707).

Skill 22: Asking Permission

Name _____ Date _____

SKILL STEPS

1. Decide what you would like to do for which you need permission.
2. Decide whom you have to ask for permission.
3. Decide how to ask for permission.
4. Pick the right time and place.
5. Ask for permission.

FILL IN NOW

1. Where will you try the skill? _____

2. With whom will you try the skill? _____

3. When will you try the skill? _____

4. If you do an excellent job, how will you reward yourself? _____

5. If you do a good job, how will you reward yourself? _____

6. If you do a fair job, how will you reward yourself? _____

FILL IN AFTER YOU PRACTICE THE SKILL

1. What happened when you did the homework?

   _____

   _____

2. Which skill steps did you really follow?

   _____

   _____

3. How good a job did you do in using the skill? *(check one)*

   ☐ excellent   ☐ good   ☐ fair   ☐ poor

4. What do you think your next homework assignment should be?

   _____

From *Skillstreaming the Adolescent: A Guide for Teaching Prosocial Skills* (3rd ed.), © 2012 by E. McGinnis, Champaign, IL: Research Press (www.researchpress.com, 800-519-2707).

Skill 23: Sharing Something

SKILL STEPS

1. **Decide if you might like to share some of what you have.**

   Divide the item between yourself and the other person or allow the other to use the item.

2. **Think about how the other person might feel about your sharing.**

   He/she might feel pleased, indifferent, suspicious, or insulted.

3. **Offer to share in a direct and friendly way.**

   Make the offer sincere, allowing the other to decline if he/she wishes.

SUGGESTED MODELING DISPLAYS

School or neighborhood: Main actor offers to share books with classmate who has forgotten his/her book.

Home: Main actor offers to share candy with sibling.

Peer group: Main actor invites friend to try his new video game.

Job: Main actor invites co-worker to share food at a break.

From *Skillstreaming the Adolescent: A Guide for Teaching Prosocial Skills* (3rd ed.), © 2012 by E. McGinnis, Champaign, IL: Research Press (www.researchpress.com, 800-519-2707).

Skill 23: Sharing Something

Name _____ Date _____

SKILL STEPS

1. Decide if you might like to share some of what you have.
2. Think about how the other person might feel about your sharing.
3. Offer to share in a direct and friendly way.

FILL IN NOW

1. Where will you try the skill? _____

2. With whom will you try the skill? _____

3. When will you try the skill? _____

FILL IN AFTER YOU PRACTICE THE SKILL

1. What happened when you did the homework?

   _____

   _____

2. Which skill steps did you really follow?

   _____

   _____

3. How good a job did you do in using the skill? *(check one)*

   ☐ excellent   ☐ good   ☐ fair   ☐ poor

Skill 23: Sharing Something

Name _____ Date _____

SKILL STEPS

1. Decide if you might like to share some of what you have.
2. Think about how the other person might feel about your sharing.
3. Offer to share in a direct and friendly way.

FILL IN NOW

1. Where will you try the skill? _____

2. With whom will you try the skill? _____

3. When will you try the skill? _____

4. If you do an excellent job, how will you reward yourself? _____

5. If you do a good job, how will you reward yourself? _____

6. If you do a fair job, how will you reward yourself? _____

FILL IN AFTER YOU PRACTICE THE SKILL

1. What happened when you did the homework?

   _____

   _____

2. Which skill steps did you really follow?

   _____

   _____

3. How good a job did you do in using the skill? *(check one)*

   ☐ excellent   ☐ good   ☐ fair   ☐ poor

4. What do you think your next homework assignment should be?

   _____

Skillstreaming From *Skillstreaming the Adolescent: A Guide for Teaching Prosocial Skills* (3rd ed.), © 2012 by E. McGinnis, Champaign, IL: Research Press (www.researchpress.com, 800-519-2707).

Skill 24: Helping Others

SKILL STEPS

1. **Decide if the other person might need and want your help.**

   Think about the needs of the other person; observe.

2. **Think of the ways you could be helpful.**

3. **Ask the other person if he/she needs and wants your help.**

   Make the offer sincere, allowing the other to decline if he/she wishes.

4. **Help the other person.**

SUGGESTED MODELING DISPLAYS

School or neighborhood: Main actor offers to help teacher arrange chairs in classroom.

Home: Main actor offers to help prepare dinner.

Peer group: Main actor offers to bring class assignments home for sick friend.

Job: When finished with own job, main actor offers to help co-worker to finish.

 From *Skillstreaming the Adolescent: A Guide for Teaching Prosocial Skills* (3rd ed.), © 2012 by E. McGinnis, Champaign, IL: Research Press (www.researchpress.com, 800-519-2707).

Skill 24: Helping Others

Name _____ Date _____

SKILL STEPS

1. Decide if the other person might need and want your help.
2. Think of the ways you could be helpful.
3. Ask the other person if he/she needs and wants your help.
4. Help the other person.

FILL IN NOW

1. Where will you try the skill? _____

2. With whom will you try the skill? _____

3. When will you try the skill? _____

FILL IN AFTER YOU PRACTICE THE SKILL

1. What happened when you did the homework?

   _____

   _____

2. Which skill steps did you really follow?

   _____

   _____

3. How good a job did you do in using the skill? *(check one)*

   ☐ excellent   ☐ good   ☐ fair   ☐ poor

Skillstreaming

From *Skillstreaming the Adolescent: A Guide for Teaching Prosocial Skills* (3rd ed.), © 2012 by E. McGinnis, Champaign, IL: Research Press (www.researchpress.com, 800-519-2707).

Skill 24: Helping Others

Name _____ Date _____

SKILL STEPS

1. Decide if the other person might need and want your help.

2. Think of the ways you could be helpful.

3. Ask the other person if he/she needs and wants your help.

4. Help the other person.

FILL IN NOW

1. Where will you try the skill? _____

2. With whom will you try the skill? _____

3. When will you try the skill? _____

4. If you do an excellent job, how will you reward yourself? _____

5. If you do a good job, how will you reward yourself? _____

6. If you do a fair job, how will you reward yourself? _____

FILL IN AFTER YOU PRACTICE THE SKILL

1. What happened when you did the homework?

   _____

   _____

2. Which skill steps did you really follow?

   _____

   _____

3. How good a job did you do in using the skill? *(check one)*

   ☐ excellent   ☐ good   ☐ fair   ☐ poor

4. What do you think your next homework assignment should be?

   _____

Skillstreaming   From *Skillstreaming the Adolescent: A Guide for Teaching Prosocial Skills* (3rd ed.), © 2012
by E. McGinnis, Champaign, IL: Research Press (www.researchpress.com, 800-519-2707).   **187**

Skill 25: Negotiating

SKILL STEPS

1. **Decide if you and the other person are having a difference of opinion.**

   Are you getting tense or arguing?

2. **Tell the other person what you think about the problem.**

   State your own position and your perception of the other's position.

3. **Ask the other person what he/she thinks about the problem.**

4. **Listen openly to his/her answer.**

5. **Think about why the other person might feel this way.**

6. **Suggest a compromise.**

   Be sure the proposed compromise takes into account the opinions and feelings of both persons.

SUGGESTED MODELING DISPLAYS

School or neighborhood: Main actor negotiates with neighbor a fee for after-school chores.

Home: Main actor negotiates with parent about curfew or chores.

Peer group: Main actor negotiates with friend about recreational activity in which to participate.

Job: Main actor negotiates with co-worker to change work hours.

COMMENTS

Negotiating is a skill that presupposes mastery of Understanding the Feelings of Others (Skill 17). We suggest that Skill 17 be reviewed prior to teaching Negotiating. Negotiating is also similar in some respects to Skill 14 (Convincing Others). Negotiating, however, introduces the concept of compromise, a concept often worth discussing before role-playing this skill.

Skillstreaming
From *Skillstreaming the Adolescent: A Guide for Teaching Prosocial Skills* (3rd ed.), © 2012 by E. McGinnis, Champaign, IL: Research Press (www.researchpress.com, 800-519-2707).

Skill 25: Negotiating

Name _____ Date _____

SKILL STEPS

1. Decide if you and the other person are having a difference of opinion.
2. Tell the other person what you think about the problem.
3. Ask the other person what he/she thinks about the problem.
4. Listen openly to his/her answer.
5. Think about why the other person might feel this way.
6. Suggest a compromise.

FILL IN NOW

1. Where will you try the skill? _____

2. With whom will you try the skill? _____

3. When will you try the skill? _____

FILL IN AFTER YOU PRACTICE THE SKILL

1. What happened when you did the homework?

   _____

   _____

2. Which skill steps did you really follow?

   _____

   _____

3. How good a job did you do in using the skill? *(check one)*

   ☐ excellent   ☐ good   ☐ fair   ☐ poor

From *Skillstreaming the Adolescent: A Guide for Teaching Prosocial Skills* (3rd ed.), © 2012 by E. McGinnis, Champaign, IL: Research Press (www.researchpress.com, 800-519-2707).

Skill 25: Negotiating

Name _____ Date _____

SKILL STEPS

1. Decide if you and the other person are having a difference of opinion.
2. Tell the other person what you think about the problem.
3. Ask the other person what he/she thinks about the problem.
4. Listen openly to his/her answer.
5. Think about why the other person might feel this way.
6. Suggest a compromise.

FILL IN NOW

1. Where will you try the skill? _____

2. With whom will you try the skill? _____

3. When will you try the skill? _____

4. If you do an excellent job, how will you reward yourself? _____

5. If you do a good job, how will you reward yourself? _____

6. If you do a fair job, how will you reward yourself? _____

FILL IN AFTER YOU PRACTICE THE SKILL

1. What happened when you did the homework?

   _____

   _____

2. Which skill steps did you really follow?

   _____

   _____

3. How good a job did you do in using the skill? *(check one)*

   ☐ excellent   ☐ good   ☐ fair   ☐ poor

4. What do you think your next homework assignment should be?

   _____

Skillstreaming
From *Skillstreaming the Adolescent: A Guide for Teaching Prosocial Skills* (3rd ed.), © 2012 by E. McGinnis, Champaign, IL: Research Press (www.researchpress.com, 800-519-2707).

Skill 26: Using Self-Control

SKILL STEPS

1. **Tune in to what it is going on in your body that helps you know you are about to lose control of yourself.**

   Are you getting tense, angry, hot, fidgety?

2. **Decide what happened to make you feel this way.**

   Consider both outside events and "internal" events (thoughts).

3. **Think about ways in which you might control yourself.**

   Slow down; count to 10; breathe deeply; assert yourself; leave; do something else.

4. **Choose the best way to control yourself and do it.**

SUGGESTED MODELING DISPLAYS

School or neighborhood: Main actor keeps from yelling at teacher when teacher gives harsh criticism.

Home: Main actor controls self when parent forbids desired activity.

Peer group: Main actor controls self when friend takes something without asking permission.

Job: Main actor keeps from yelling at his/her supervisor when corrected on work.

COMMENTS

It is often helpful to discuss various ways of controlling oneself before role-playing the skill. A list of self-control techniques can be written on the whiteboard or easel pad and used to generate alternative tactics to use in a variety of situations.

Skill 26: Using Self-Control

Name _____ Date _____

SKILL STEPS

1. Tune in to what it is going on in your body that helps you know you are about to lose control of yourself.
2. Decide what happened to make you feel this way.
3. Think about ways in which you might control yourself.
4. Choose the best way to control yourself and do it.

FILL IN NOW

1. Where will you try the skill? _____

2. With whom will you try the skill? _____

3. When will you try the skill? _____

FILL IN AFTER YOU PRACTICE THE SKILL

1. What happened when you did the homework?

   _____

   _____

2. Which skill steps did you really follow?

   _____

   _____

3. How good a job did you do in using the skill? *(check one)*

   ☐ excellent   ☐ good   ☐ fair   ☐ poor

Skillstreaming

From *Skillstreaming the Adolescent: A Guide for Teaching Prosocial Skills* (3rd ed.), © 2012 by E. McGinnis, Champaign, IL: Research Press (www.researchpress.com, 800-519-2707).

Skill 26: Using Self-Control

Name _____ Date _____

SKILL STEPS

1. Tune in to what it is going on in your body that helps you know you are about to lose control of yourself.
2. Decide what happened to make you feel this way.
3. Think about ways in which you might control yourself.
4. Choose the best way to control yourself and do it.

FILL IN NOW

1. Where will you try the skill? _____

2. With whom will you try the skill? _____

3. When will you try the skill? _____

4. If you do an excellent job, how will you reward yourself? _____

5. If you do a good job, how will you reward yourself? _____

6. If you do a fair job, how will you reward yourself? _____

FILL IN AFTER YOU PRACTICE THE SKILL

1. What happened when you did the homework?

   _____

   _____

2. Which skill steps did you really follow?

   _____

   _____

3. How good a job did you do in using the skill? *(check one)*

   ☐ excellent   ☐ good   ☐ fair   ☐ poor

4. What do you think your next homework assignment should be?

   _____

From *Skillstreaming the Adolescent: A Guide for Teaching Prosocial Skills* (3rd ed.), © 2012 by E. McGinnis, Champaign, IL: Research Press (www.researchpress.com, 800-519-2707).

Skill 27: Standing Up for Your Rights

SKILL STEPS

1. **Pay attention to what is going on in your body that helps you know that you are dissatisfied and would like to stand up for yourself.**

   Some cues are tight muscles, butterflies in your stomach, and so forth.

2. **Decide what happened to make you feel dissatisfied.**

   Are you being taken advantage of, ignored, mistreated, or teased?

3. **Think about ways in which you might stand up for yourself and choose one.**

   Seek help; say what is on your mind; get a majority opinion; choose the right time and place.

4. **Stand up for yourself in a direct and reasonable way.**

SUGGESTED MODELING DISPLAYS

School or neighborhood: Main actor approaches teacher after being disciplined unfairly.

Home: Main actor talks with parent about need for more privacy.

Peer group: Main actor talks with peer after not being chosen for the club (team).

Job: Main actor talks with supervisor about work hours assigned.

COMMENTS

Also known as assertiveness, this skill is particularly important for withdrawn or shy group members, as well as for those whose typical responses are inappropriately aggressive.

Skillstreaming   From *Skillstreaming the Adolescent: A Guide for Teaching Prosocial Skills* (3rd ed.), © 2012 by E. McGinnis, Champaign, IL: Research Press (www.researchpress.com, 800-519-2707).

Skill 27: Standing Up for Your Rights

Name _____ Date _____

SKILL STEPS

1. Pay attention to what is going on in your body that helps you know that you are dissatisfied and would like to stand up for yourself.

2. Decide what happened to make you feel dissatisfied.

3. Think about ways in which you might stand up for yourself and choose one.

4. Stand up for yourself in a direct and reasonable way.

FILL IN NOW

1. Where will you try the skill? _____

2. With whom will you try the skill? _____

3. When will you try the skill? _____

FILL IN AFTER YOU PRACTICE THE SKILL

1. What happened when you did the homework?

   _____

   _____

2. Which skill steps did you really follow?

   _____

   _____

3. How good a job did you do in using the skill? *(check one)*

   ☐ excellent ☐ good ☐ fair ☐ poor

Skillstreaming   From *Skillstreaming the Adolescent: A Guide for Teaching Prosocial Skills* (3rd ed.), © 2012
by E. McGinnis, Champaign, IL: Research Press (www.researchpress.com, 800-519-2707).

Skill 27: Standing Up for Your Rights

Name _____ Date _____

SKILL STEPS

1. Pay attention to what is going on in your body that helps you know that you are dissatisfied and would like to stand up for yourself.

2. Decide what happened to make you feel dissatisfied.

3. Think about ways in which you might stand up for yourself and choose one.

4. Stand up for yourself in a direct and reasonable way.

FILL IN NOW

1. Where will you try the skill? _____

2. With whom will you try the skill? _____

3. When will you try the skill? _____

4. If you do an excellent job, how will you reward yourself? _____

5. If you do a good job, how will you reward yourself? _____

6. If you do a fair job, how will you reward yourself? _____

FILL IN AFTER YOU PRACTICE THE SKILL

1. What happened when you did the homework?

   _____

   _____

2. Which skill steps did you really follow?

   _____

   _____

3. How good a job did you do in using the skill? *(check one)*

   ☐ excellent   ☐ good   ☐ fair   ☐ poor

4. What do you think your next homework assignment should be?

   _____

Skillstreaming

From *Skillstreaming the Adolescent: A Guide for Teaching Prosocial Skills* (3rd ed.), © 2012 by E. McGinnis, Champaign, IL: Research Press (www.researchpress.com, 800-519-2707).

Skill 28: Responding to Teasing

SKILL STEPS

1. **Decide if you are being teased.**

   Are others making jokes or whispering?

2. **Think about ways to deal with the teasing.**

   Gracefully accept it; make a joke of it; ignore it.

3. **Choose the best way and do it.**

   When possible, avoid alternatives that foster aggression, malicious counterteasing, and withdrawal.

SUGGESTED MODELING DISPLAYS

School or neighborhood: Main actor ignores classmate's comments when volunteering to help teacher after class.

Home: Main actor tells sibling to stop teasing about new haircut.

Peer group: Main actor deals with peer's teasing about a girlfriend or boyfriend by making a joke of it.

Job: Main actor deals with co-worker's teasing about liking another co-worker.

From *Skillstreaming the Adolescent: A Guide for Teaching Prosocial Skills* (3rd ed.), © 2012 by E. McGinnis, Champaign, IL: Research Press (www.researchpress.com, 800-519-2707).

Skill 28: Responding to Teasing

Name _____ Date _____

SKILL STEPS

1. Decide if you are being teased.

2. Think about ways to deal with the teasing.

3. Choose the best way and do it.

FILL IN NOW

1. Where will you try the skill? _____

2. With whom will you try the skill? _____

3. When will you try the skill? _____

FILL IN AFTER YOU PRACTICE THE SKILL

1. What happened when you did the homework?

   _____

   _____

2. Which skill steps did you really follow?

   _____

   _____

3. How good a job did you do in using the skill? *(check one)*

   ☐ excellent   ☐ good   ☐ fair   ☐ poor

Skillstreaming From *Skillstreaming the Adolescent: A Guide for Teaching Prosocial Skills* (3rd ed.), © 2012 by E. McGinnis, Champaign, IL: Research Press (www.researchpress.com, 800-519-2707).

Skill 28: Responding to Teasing

Name _____ Date _____

SKILL STEPS

1. Decide if you are being teased.
2. Think about ways to deal with the teasing.
3. Choose the best way and do it.

FILL IN NOW

1. Where will you try the skill? _____

2. With whom will you try the skill? _____

3. When will you try the skill? _____

4. If you do an excellent job, how will you reward yourself? _____

5. If you do a good job, how will you reward yourself? _____

6. If you do a fair job, how will you reward yourself? _____

FILL IN AFTER YOU PRACTICE THE SKILL

1. What happened when you did the homework?

   _____

   _____

2. Which skill steps did you really follow?

   _____

   _____

3. How good a job did you do in using the skill? *(check one)*

   ☐ excellent ☐ good ☐ fair ☐ poor

4. What do you think your next homework assignment should be?

   _____

Skill 29: Avoiding Trouble with Others

SKILL STEPS

1. **Decide if you are in a situation that might get you into trouble.**

   Examine immediate and long-range consequences.

2. **Decide if you want to get out of the situation.**

   Consider risks versus gains.

3. **Tell the other people what you decided and why.**

4. **Suggest other things you might do.**

   Consider prosocial alternatives.

5. **Do what you think is best for you.**

SUGGESTED MODELING DISPLAYS

School or neighborhood: Main actor tells classmates he/she will not cut class with them.

Home: Main actor refuses to take family car without permission.

Peer group: Main actor decides not to join peers in shoplifting.

Job: Main actor refuses to take part in co-workers' plan to steal from employer.

COMMENTS

In Step 3, the reasons for decisions may vary according to the group member's level of moral reasoning (e.g., fear of punishment, social conformity, concern for others).

From *Skillstreaming the Adolescent: A Guide for Teaching Prosocial Skills* (3rd ed.), © 2012 by E. McGinnis, Champaign, IL: Research Press (www.researchpress.com, 800-519-2707).

Skill 29: Avoiding Trouble with Others

Name _____ Date _____

SKILL STEPS

1. Decide if you are in a situation that might get you into trouble.
2. Decide if you want to get out of the situation.
3. Tell the other people what you decided and why.
4. Suggest other things you might do.
5. Do what you think is best for you.

FILL IN NOW

1. Where will you try the skill? _____

2. With whom will you try the skill? _____

3. When will you try the skill? _____

FILL IN AFTER YOU PRACTICE THE SKILL

1. What happened when you did the homework?

   _____

   _____

2. Which skill steps did you really follow?

   _____

   _____

3. How good a job did you do in using the skill? *(check one)*

   ☐ excellent   ☐ good   ☐ fair   ☐ poor

From *Skillstreaming the Adolescent: A Guide for Teaching Prosocial Skills* (3rd ed.), © 2012 by E. McGinnis, Champaign, IL: Research Press (www.researchpress.com, 800-519-2707).   **201**

Skill 29: Avoiding Trouble with Others

Name _____ Date _____

SKILL STEPS

1. Decide if you are in a situation that might get you into trouble.
2. Decide if you want to get out of the situation.
3. Tell the other people what you decided and why.
4. Suggest other things you might do.
5. Do what you think is best for you.

FILL IN NOW

1. Where will you try the skill? _____

2. With whom will you try the skill? _____

3. When will you try the skill? _____

4. If you do an excellent job, how will you reward yourself? _____

5. If you do a good job, how will you reward yourself? _____

6. If you do a fair job, how will you reward yourself? _____

FILL IN AFTER YOU PRACTICE THE SKILL

1. What happened when you did the homework?

   _____

   _____

2. Which skill steps did you really follow?

   _____

   _____

3. How good a job did you do in using the skill? *(check one)*

   ☐ excellent   ☐ good   ☐ fair   ☐ poor

4. What do you think your next homework assignment should be?

   _____

Skillstreaming

From *Skillstreaming the Adolescent: A Guide for Teaching Prosocial Skills* (3rd ed.), © 2012 by E. McGinnis, Champaign, IL: Research Press (www.researchpress.com, 800-519-2707).

Skill 30: Keeping Out of Fights

SKILL STEPS

1. **Stop and think about why you want to fight.**

2. **Decide what you want to happen in the long run.**

    What is the long-range outcome?

3. **Think about other ways to handle the situation besides fighting.**

    You might negotiate, stand up for your rights, ask for help, or pacify the person.

4. **Decide on the best way to handle the situation and do it.**

SUGGESTED MODELING DISPLAYS

School or neighborhood: Main actor tells classmate that he/she wants to talk out their differences instead of being pressured to fight.

Home: Main actor resolves potential fight with older sibling by asking parent to intervene.

Peer group: Main actor goes for help when he/she sees peers fighting on school steps.

Job: Main actor avoids a fight when co-worker makes the accusation that he/she is trying to schmooze the boss.

COMMENTS

Prior to teaching this skill, it is often useful to review Skill 26 (Using Self-Control).

Skill 30: Keeping Out of Fights

Name _____ Date _____

SKILL STEPS

1. Stop and think about why you want to fight.
2. Decide what you want to happen in the long run.
3. Think about other ways to handle the situation besides fighting.
4. Decide on the best way to handle the situation and do it.

FILL IN NOW

1. Where will you try the skill? _____

2. With whom will you try the skill? _____

3. When will you try the skill? _____

FILL IN AFTER YOU PRACTICE THE SKILL

1. What happened when you did the homework?

   _____

   _____

2. Which skill steps did you really follow?

   _____

   _____

3. How good a job did you do in using the skill? *(check one)*

   ☐ excellent   ☐ good   ☐ fair   ☐ poor

Skillstreaming

Skill 30: Keeping Out of Fights

Name _____ Date _____

SKILL STEPS

1. Stop and think about why you want to fight.
2. Decide what you want to happen in the long run.
3. Think about other ways to handle the situation besides fighting.
4. Decide on the best way to handle the situation and do it.

FILL IN NOW

1. Where will you try the skill? _____

2. With whom will you try the skill? _____

3. When will you try the skill? _____

4. If you do an excellent job, how will you reward yourself? _____

5. If you do a good job, how will you reward yourself? _____

6. If you do a fair job, how will you reward yourself? _____

FILL IN AFTER YOU PRACTICE THE SKILL

1. What happened when you did the homework?

   _____

   _____

2. Which skill steps did you really follow?

   _____

   _____

3. How good a job did you do in using the skill? *(check one)*

   ☐ excellent   ☐ good   ☐ fair   ☐ poor

4. What do you think your next homework assignment should be?

   _____

From *Skillstreaming the Adolescent: A Guide for Teaching Prosocial Skills* (3rd ed.), © 2012 by E. McGinnis, Champaign, IL: Research Press (www.researchpress.com, 800-519-2707).

Group V

Skills for Dealing with Stress

Skills 31–42

Skill 31: Making a Complaint

SKILL STEPS

1. **Decide what your complaint is.**

   What is the problem?

2. **Decide whom to complain to.**

   Who can resolve it?

3. **Tell that person your complaint.**

   Consider alternative ways to complain (e.g., politely, assertively, privately).

4. **Tell that person what you would like done about the problem.**

   Offer a helpful suggestion about resolving the problem.

5. **Ask how he/she feels about what you've said.**

SUGGESTED MODELING DISPLAYS

School or neighborhood: Main actor complains to guidance counselor about being assigned to class that is too difficult.

Home: Main actor complains to sibling about unfair division of chores.

Peer group: Main actor complains to friend about spreading a rumor or doing the same thing every Friday night.

Job: Main actor complains to supervisor about working too many or too few hours.

Skill 31: Making a Complaint

Name _____ Date _____

SKILL STEPS

1. Decide what your complaint is.
2. Decide whom to complain to.
3. Tell that person your complaint.
4. Tell that person what you would like done about the problem.
5. Ask how he/she feels about what you've said.

FILL IN NOW

1. Where will you try the skill? _____

2. With whom will you try the skill? _____

3. When will you try the skill? _____

FILL IN AFTER YOU PRACTICE THE SKILL

1. What happened when you did the homework?

   _____

   _____

2. Which skill steps did you really follow?

   _____

   _____

3. How good a job did you do in using the skill? *(check one)*

   ☐ excellent ☐ good ☐ fair ☐ poor

Skillstreaming

From *Skillstreaming the Adolescent: A Guide for Teaching Prosocial Skills* (3rd ed.), © 2012 by E. McGinnis, Champaign, IL: Research Press (www.researchpress.com, 800-519-2707).

Skill 31: Making a Complaint

Name _____ Date _____

SKILL STEPS

1. Decide what your complaint is.
2. Decide whom to complain to.
3. Tell that person your complaint.
4. Tell that person what you would like done about the problem.
5. Ask how he/she feels about what you've said.

FILL IN NOW

1. Where will you try the skill? _____

2. With whom will you try the skill? _____

3. When will you try the skill? _____

4. If you do an excellent job, how will you reward yourself? _____

5. If you do a good job, how will you reward yourself? _____

6. If you do a fair job, how will you reward yourself? _____

FILL IN AFTER YOU PRACTICE THE SKILL

1. What happened when you did the homework?

    _____

    _____

2. Which skill steps did you really follow?

    _____

    _____

3. How good a job did you do in using the skill? *(check one)*

    ☐ excellent   ☐ good   ☐ fair   ☐ poor

4. What do you think your next homework assignment should be?

    _____

Skill 32: Answering a Complaint

SKILL STEPS

1. **Listen to the complaint.**

   Listen openly.

2. **Ask the person to explain anything you don't understand.**

3. **Tell the person that you understand the complaint.**

   Rephrase; acknowledge the content and feeling.

4. **State your ideas about the complaint, accepting the blame if appropriate.**

5. **Suggest what each of you could do about the complaint.**

   You might compromise, defend your position, or apologize.

SUGGESTED MODELING DISPLAYS

School or neighborhood: Main actor responds to neighbor's complaint about noisy party or classmate complains main actor isn't helping with group project.

Home: Main actor responds to parent's complaint about selection of friends.

Peer group: Main actor responds to friend's complaint about returning sporting equipment in poor condition or not chipping in for gas.

Job: Main actor responds to co-worker about a complaint about not doing his/her fair-share of the work.

Skillstreaming

From *Skillstreaming the Adolescent: A Guide for Teaching Prosocial Skills* (3rd ed.), © 2012 by E. McGinnis, Champaign, IL: Research Press (www.researchpress.com, 800-519-2707).

Skill 32: Answering a Complaint

Name _____ Date _____

SKILL STEPS

1. Listen to the complaint.
2. Ask the person to explain anything you don't understand.
3. Tell the person that you understand the complaint.
4. State your ideas about the complaint, accepting the blame if appropriate.
5. Suggest what each of you could do about the complaint.

FILL IN NOW

1. Where will you try the skill? _____

2. With whom will you try the skill? _____

3. When will you try the skill? _____

FILL IN AFTER YOU PRACTICE THE SKILL

1. What happened when you did the homework?

   _____

   _____

2. Which skill steps did you really follow?

   _____

   _____

3. How good a job did you do in using the skill? *(check one)*

   ☐ excellent   ☐ good   ☐ fair   ☐ poor

From *Skillstreaming the Adolescent: A Guide for Teaching Prosocial Skills* (3rd ed.), © 2012 by E. McGinnis, Champaign, IL: Research Press (www.researchpress.com, 800-519-2707).

Skill 32: Answering a Complaint

Name _____ Date _____

SKILL STEPS

1. Listen to the complaint.
2. Ask the person to explain anything you don't understand.
3. Tell the person that you understand the complaint.
4. State your ideas about the complaint, accepting the blame if appropriate.
5. Suggest what each of you could do about the complaint.

FILL IN NOW

1. Where will you try the skill? _____

2. With whom will you try the skill? _____

3. When will you try the skill? _____

4. If you do an excellent job, how will you reward yourself? _____

5. If you do a good job, how will you reward yourself? _____

6. If you do a fair job, how will you reward yourself? _____

FILL IN AFTER YOU PRACTICE THE SKILL

1. What happened when you did the homework?

   _____

   _____

2. Which skill steps did you really follow?

   _____

   _____

3. How good a job did you do in using the skill? *(check one)*

   ☐ excellent   ☐ good   ☐ fair   ☐ poor

4. What do you think your next homework assignment should be?

   _____

.Skillstreaming
From *Skillstreaming the Adolescent: A Guide for Teaching Prosocial Skills* (3rd ed.), © 2012 by E. McGinnis, Champaign, IL: Research Press (www.researchpress.com, 800-519-2707).

Skill 33: Being a Good Sport

SKILL STEPS

1. Think about how you did and how the other person did in the game you played.

2. Think of a true compliment you could give the other person about his/her game.

   Say "Good try," "Congratulations," or "Getting better."

3. Think about his/her reactions to what you might say.

   The reaction might be pleasure, anger, or embarrassment.

4. Choose the compliment you think is best and say it.

SUGGESTED MODELING DISPLAYS

School or neighborhood: Main actor talks to classmate who has made starting team.

Home: Main actor wins at a computer game with younger sibling.

Peer group: New acquaintance does well in pickup game.

Job: Main actor compliments co-worker who has just received a compliment from a supervisor for a job done well.

Skill 33: Being a Good Sport

Name _____ Date _____

SKILL STEPS

1. Think about how you did and how the other person did in the game you played.

2. Think of a true compliment you could give the other person about his/her game.

3. Think about his/her reactions to what you might say.

4. Choose the compliment you think is best and say it.

FILL IN NOW

1. Where will you try the skill? _____

2. With whom will you try the skill? _____

3. When will you try the skill? _____

FILL IN AFTER YOU PRACTICE THE SKILL

1. What happened when you did the homework?

   _____

   _____

2. Which skill steps did you really follow?

   _____

   _____

3. How good a job did you do in using the skill? *(check one)*

   ☐ excellent   ☐ good   ☐ fair   ☐ poor

Skillstreaming From *Skillstreaming the Adolescent: A Guide for Teaching Prosocial Skills* (3rd ed.), © 2012 by E. McGinnis, Champaign, IL: Research Press (www.researchpress.com, 800-519-2707).

Skill 33: Being a Good Sport

Name _____ Date _____

SKILL STEPS

1. Think about how you did and how the other person did in the game you played.

2. Think of a true compliment you could give the other person about his/her game.

3. Think about his/her reactions to what you might say.

4. Choose the compliment you think is best and say it.

FILL IN NOW

1. Where will you try the skill? _____

2. With whom will you try the skill? _____

3. When will you try the skill? _____

4. If you do an excellent job, how will you reward yourself? _____

5. If you do a good job, how will you reward yourself? _____

6. If you do a fair job, how will you reward yourself? _____

FILL IN AFTER YOU PRACTICE THE SKILL

1. What happened when you did the homework?

   _____

   _____

2. Which skill steps did you really follow?

   _____

   _____

3. How good a job did you do in using the skill? *(check one)*

   ☐ excellent   ☐ good   ☐ fair   ☐ poor

4. What do you think your next homework assignment should be?

   _____

From *Skillstreaming the Adolescent: A Guide for Teaching Prosocial Skills* (3rd ed.), © 2012 by E. McGinnis, Champaign, IL: Research Press (www.researchpress.com, 800-519-2707).

Skill 34: Dealing with Embarrassment

SKILL STEPS

1. Decide if you are feeling embarrassed.

2. Decide what happened to make you feel embarrassed.

3. Decide on what will help you feel less embarrassed and do it.

    Correct the cause; minimize it; ignore it; distract others; use humor; reassure yourself.

SUGGESTED MODELING DISPLAYS

School or neighborhood: Main actor deals with embarrassment the day after refusing pressure from peers to use drugs.

Home: Mother catches main actor necking with boyfriend or girlfriend or shares stories of main actor when he/she was younger in front of a date.

Peer group: Main actor is embarrassed by being overheard when discussing a private matter.

Job: Main actor feels embarrassed when a supervisor calls him/her out in front of co-workers.

COMMENTS

Prior to teaching this skill, it is often useful to review Skill 15 (Knowing Your Feelings).

From *Skillstreaming the Adolescent: A Guide for Teaching Prosocial Skills* (3rd ed.), © 2012 by E. McGinnis, Champaign, IL: Research Press (www.researchpress.com, 800-519-2707).

Skill 34: Dealing with Embarrassment

Name _____ Date _____

SKILL STEPS

1. Decide if you are feeling embarrassed.
2. Decide what happened to make you feel embarrassed.
3. Decide on what will help you feel less embarrassed and do it.

FILL IN NOW

1. Where will you try the skill? _____

2. With whom will you try the skill? _____

3. When will you try the skill? _____

FILL IN AFTER YOU PRACTICE THE SKILL

1. What happened when you did the homework?

   _____

   _____

2. Which skill steps did you really follow?

   _____

   _____

3. How good a job did you do in using the skill? *(check one)*

   ☐ excellent   ☐ good   ☐ fair   ☐ poor

Skillstreaming From *Skillstreaming the Adolescent: A Guide for Teaching Prosocial Skills* (3rd ed.), © 2012 by E. McGinnis, Champaign, IL: Research Press (www.researchpress.com, 800-519-2707).

Skill 34: Dealing with Embarrassment

Name _____ Date _____

SKILL STEPS

1. Decide if you are feeling embarrassed.
2. Decide what happened to make you feel embarrassed.
3. Decide on what will help you feel less embarrassed and do it.

FILL IN NOW

1. Where will you try the skill? _____

2. With whom will you try the skill? _____

3. When will you try the skill? _____

4. If you do an excellent job, how will you reward yourself? _____

5. If you do a good job, how will you reward yourself? _____

6. If you do a fair job, how will you reward yourself? _____

FILL IN AFTER YOU PRACTICE THE SKILL

1. What happened when you did the homework?

   _____

   _____

2. Which skill steps did you really follow?

   _____

   _____

3. How good a job did you do in using the skill? *(check one)*

   ☐ excellent   ☐ good   ☐ fair   ☐ poor

4. What do you think your next homework assignment should be?

   _____

Skillstreaming
From *Skillstreaming the Adolescent: A Guide for Teaching Prosocial Skills* (3rd ed.), © 2012 by E. McGinnis, Champaign, IL: Research Press (www.researchpress.com, 800-519-2707).

Skill 35: Dealing with Being Left Out

SKILL STEPS

1. **Decide if you are being left out.**

   Are you being ignored or rejected?

2. **Think about why the other people might be leaving you out of something.**

3. **Decide how you could deal with the problem.**

   You might wait, leave, tell the other people how their behavior affects you, or ask to be included.

4. **Choose the best way and do it.**

SUGGESTED MODELING DISPLAYS

School or neighborhood: Main actor tells teacher about disappointment after not being picked for committee.

Home: Main actor asks sibling to include him/her in planned activity with other friends.

Peer group: Main actor is left out of plans for party.

Job: Main actor is left out by co-workers who are getting together after work.

Skill 35: Dealing with Being Left Out

Name _____ Date _____

SKILL STEPS

1. Decide if you are being left out.
2. Think about why the other people might be leaving you out of something.
3. Decide how you could deal with the problem.
4. Choose the best way and do it.

FILL IN NOW

1. Where will you try the skill? _____

2. With whom will you try the skill? _____

3. When will you try the skill? _____

FILL IN AFTER YOU PRACTICE THE SKILL

1. What happened when you did the homework?

   _____

   _____

2. Which skill steps did you really follow?

   _____

   _____

3. How good a job did you do in using the skill? *(check one)*

   ☐ excellent   ☐ good   ☐ fair   ☐ poor

Skillstreaming

From *Skillstreaming the Adolescent: A Guide for Teaching Prosocial Skills* (3rd ed.), © 2012 by E. McGinnis, Champaign, IL: Research Press (www.researchpress.com, 800-519-2707).

Skill 35: Dealing with Being Left Out

Name _____ Date _____

SKILL STEPS

1. Decide if you are being left out.
2. Think about why the other people might be leaving you out of something.
3. Decide how you could deal with the problem.
4. Choose the best way and do it.

FILL IN NOW

1. Where will you try the skill? _____

2. With whom will you try the skill? _____

3. When will you try the skill? _____

4. If you do an excellent job, how will you reward yourself? _____

5. If you do a good job, how will you reward yourself? _____

6. If you do a fair job, how will you reward yourself? _____

FILL IN AFTER YOU PRACTICE THE SKILL

1. What happened when you did the homework?

   _____

   _____

2. Which skill steps did you really follow?

   _____

   _____

3. How good a job did you do in using the skill? *(check one)*

   ☐ excellent   ☐ good   ☐ fair   ☐ poor

4. What do you think your next homework assignment should be?

   _____

Skillstreaming From *Skillstreaming the Adolescent: A Guide for Teaching Prosocial Skills* (3rd ed.), © 2012 by E. McGinnis, Champaign, IL: Research Press (www.researchpress.com, 800-519-2707).

Skill 36: Standing Up for a Friend

SKILL STEPS

1. **Decide if your friend has not been treated fairly by others.**

   Has your friend been criticized, teased, or taken advantage of?

2. **Decide if your friend wants you to stand up for him/her.**

3. **Decide how to stand up for your friend.**

   You might assert his/her rights, explain, or apologize.

4. **Stand up for your friend.**

SUGGESTED MODELING DISPLAYS

School or neighborhood: Main actor explains to teacher that friend has been accused unjustly.

Home: Main actor defends friend's reputation when parent is critical.

Peer group: Main actor defends friend when peers are teasing.

Job: Main actor responds to co-worker when another accuses him/her of not working hard enough.

Skillstreaming From *Skillstreaming the Adolescent: A Guide for Teaching Prosocial Skills* (3rd ed.), © 2012 by E. McGinnis, Champaign, IL: Research Press (www.researchpress.com, 800-519-2707).

Skill 36: Standing Up for a Friend

Name _____ Date _____

SKILL STEPS

1. Decide if your friend has not been treated fairly by others.
2. Decide if your friend wants you to stand up for him/her.
3. Decide how to stand up for your friend.
4. Stand up for your friend.

FILL IN NOW

1. Where will you try the skill? _____

2. With whom will you try the skill? _____

3. When will you try the skill? _____

FILL IN AFTER YOU PRACTICE THE SKILL

1. What happened when you did the homework?

   _____

   _____

2. Which skill steps did you really follow?

   _____

   _____

3. How good a job did you do in using the skill? *(check one)*

   ☐ excellent   ☐ good   ☐ fair   ☐ poor

From *Skillstreaming the Adolescent: A Guide for Teaching Prosocial Skills* (3rd ed.), © 2012 by E. McGinnis, Champaign, IL: Research Press (www.researchpress.com, 800-519-2707).

225

Skill 36: Standing Up for a Friend

Name _____ Date _____

SKILL STEPS

1. Decide if your friend has not been treated fairly by others.
2. Decide if your friend wants you to stand up for him/her.
3. Decide how to stand up for your friend.
4. Stand up for your friend.

FILL IN NOW

1. Where will you try the skill? _____

2. With whom will you try the skill? _____

3. When will you try the skill? _____

4. If you do an excellent job, how will you reward yourself? _____

5. If you do a good job, how will you reward yourself? _____

6. If you do a fair job, how will you reward yourself? _____

FILL IN AFTER YOU PRACTICE THE SKILL

1. What happened when you did the homework?

   _____

   _____

2. Which skill steps did you really follow?

   _____

   _____

3. How good a job did you do in using the skill? *(check one)*

   ☐ excellent   ☐ good   ☐ fair   ☐ poor

4. What do you think your next homework assignment should be?

   _____

Skill 37: Responding to Persuasion

SKILL STEPS

1. **Listen to the other person's ideas on the topic.**

   Listen openly; try to see the topic from the other person's viewpoint.

2. **Decide what you think about the topic.**

   Distinguish your own ideas from the ideas of others.

3. **Compare what he/she said with what you think.**

   Agree; disagree; modify; postpone a decision.

4. **Decide which idea you like better and tell the other person about it.**

SUGGESTED MODELING DISPLAYS

School or neighborhood: Main actor deals with high-pressure sales pitch.

Home: Main actor deals with parental pressure to dress in a particular way for a party or a job interview.

Peer group: Main actor deals with friend's persuasive argument to try drugs.

Job: Main actor responds to co-workers who want to complain to the supervisor about another's job performance.

Skill 37: Responding to Persuasion

Name _____ Date _____

SKILL STEPS

1. Listen to the other person's ideas on the topic.
2. Decide what you think about the topic.
3. Compare what he/she said with what you think.
4. Decide which idea you like better and tell the other person about it.

FILL IN NOW

1. Where will you try the skill? _____

2. With whom will you try the skill? _____

3. When will you try the skill? _____

FILL IN AFTER YOU PRACTICE THE SKILL

1. What happened when you did the homework?

   _____

   _____

2. Which skill steps did you really follow?

   _____

   _____

3. How good a job did you do in using the skill? *(check one)*

   ☐ excellent   ☐ good   ☐ fair   ☐ poor

Skillstreaming

From *Skillstreaming the Adolescent: A Guide for Teaching Prosocial Skills* (3rd ed.), © 2012 by E. McGinnis, Champaign, IL: Research Press (www.researchpress.com, 800-519-2707).

Skill 37: Responding to Persuasion

Name _____ Date _____

SKILL STEPS

1. Listen to the other person's ideas on the topic.
2. Decide what you think about the topic.
3. Compare what he/she said with what you think.
4. Decide which idea you like better and tell the other person about it.

FILL IN NOW

1. Where will you try the skill? _____

2. With whom will you try the skill? _____

3. When will you try the skill? _____

4. If you do an excellent job, how will you reward yourself? _____

5. If you do a good job, how will you reward yourself? _____

6. If you do a fair job, how will you reward yourself? _____

FILL IN AFTER YOU PRACTICE THE SKILL

1. What happened when you did the homework?

   _____

   _____

2. Which skill steps did you really follow?

   _____

   _____

3. How good a job did you do in using the skill? *(check one)*

   ☐ excellent   ☐ good   ☐ fair   ☐ poor

4. What do you think your next homework assignment should be?

   _____

From *Skillstreaming the Adolescent: A Guide for Teaching Prosocial Skills* (3rd ed.), © 2012 by E. McGinnis, Champaign, IL: Research Press (www.researchpress.com, 800-519-2707).

Skill 38: Responding to Failure

SKILL STEPS

1. **Decide if you have failed at something.**

   The failure may be interpersonal, academic, or athletic.

2. **Think about why you failed.**

   It could be due to skill, motivation, or luck. Include personal reasons and circumstances.

3. **Think about what you could do to keep from failing another time.**

   Evaluate what is under your control to change: If a skill problem, practice; if motivation, increase effort; if circumstances, think of ways to change them.

4. **Decide if you want to try again.**

5. **Try again using your new idea.**

SUGGESTED MODELING DISPLAYS

School or neighborhood: Main actor deals with failing grade on exam.

Home: Main actor fails at attempt to help younger sibling with a project.

Peer group: Main actor deals with being turned down for date.

Job: Main actor deals with not being selected for a special job by his/her supervisor.

Skillstreaming

From *Skillstreaming the Adolescent: A Guide for Teaching Prosocial Skills* (3rd ed.), © 2012 by E. McGinnis, Champaign, IL: Research Press (www.researchpress.com, 800-519-2707).

Skill 38: Responding to Failure

Name _____ Date _____

SKILL STEPS

1. Decide if you have failed at something.
2. Think about why you failed.
3. Think about what you could do to keep from failing another time.
4. Decide if you want to try again.
5. Try again using your new idea.

FILL IN NOW

1. Where will you try the skill? _____

2. With whom will you try the skill? _____

3. When will you try the skill? _____

FILL IN AFTER YOU PRACTICE THE SKILL

1. What happened when you did the homework?

   _____

   _____

2. Which skill steps did you really follow?

   _____

   _____

3. How good a job did you do in using the skill? *(check one)*

   ☐ excellent   ☐ good   ☐ fair   ☐ poor

From *Skillstreaming the Adolescent: A Guide for Teaching Prosocial Skills* (3rd ed.), © 2012
by E. McGinnis, Champaign, IL: Research Press (www.researchpress.com, 800-519-2707).

Skill 38: Responding to Failure

Name _____ Date _____

SKILL STEPS

1. Decide if you have failed at something.
2. Think about why you failed.
3. Think about what you could do to keep from failing another time.
4. Decide if you want to try again.
5. Try again using your new idea.

FILL IN NOW

1. Where will you try the skill? _____

2. With whom will you try the skill? _____

3. When will you try the skill? _____

4. If you do an excellent job, how will you reward yourself? _____

5. If you do a good job, how will you reward yourself? _____

6. If you do a fair job, how will you reward yourself? _____

FILL IN AFTER YOU PRACTICE THE SKILL

1. What happened when you did the homework?

   _____

   _____

2. Which skill steps did you really follow?

   _____

   _____

3. How good a job did you do in using the skill? *(check one)*

   ☐ excellent   ☐ good   ☐ fair   ☐ poor

4. What do you think your next homework assignment should be?

   _____

Skillstreaming

From *Skillstreaming the Adolescent: A Guide for Teaching Prosocial Skills* (3rd ed.), © 2012 by E. McGinnis, Champaign, IL: Research Press (www.researchpress.com, 800-519-2707).

Skill 39: Dealing with Contradictory Messages

SKILL STEPS

1. **Decide if someone is telling you two opposite things at the same time.**

   This could be in words, in nonverbal behavior, or in saying one thing and doing another.

2. **Think of ways to tell the other person that you don't understand what he/she means.**

   Confront the person; ask.

3. **Choose the best way to tell the person and do it.**

SUGGESTED MODELING DISPLAYS

School or neighborhood: Main actor deals with teacher who verbalizes approval but scowls at same time.

Home: Main actor confronts parent who verbalizes trust but refuses to grant privileges.

Peer group: Main actor deals with friend who makes general invitation but never really includes main actor in plans.

Job: Main actor is confused by co-worker who acts like he/she wants to be a friend but then excludes main actor.

COMMENTS

In teaching this skill, it is important to encourage youth to observe the behaviors of others around them closely. See if they can think about a person who says yes but at the same time shakes his or her head to mean no. See if they can think about a person who says, "Take your time" but at the same time makes them hurry up. That is, be sure to include situations in which the person is told two conflicting things, as well as those involving a person saying one thing and doing the opposite.

In Step 1, this deciphering of the message is essential; otherwise, the group member will be unable to proceed to Steps 2 and 3.

From *Skillstreaming the Adolescent: A Guide for Teaching Prosocial Skills* (3rd ed.), © 2012 by E. McGinnis, Champaign, IL: Research Press (www.researchpress.com, 800-519-2707).

Skill 39: Dealing with Contradictory Messages

Name _____ Date _____

SKILL STEPS

1. Decide if someone is telling you two opposite things at the same time.
2. Think of ways to tell the other person that you don't understand what he/she means.
3. Choose the best way to tell the person and do it.

FILL IN NOW

1. Where will you try the skill? _____

2. With whom will you try the skill? _____

3. When will you try the skill? _____

FILL IN AFTER YOU PRACTICE THE SKILL

1. What happened when you did the homework?

   _____

   _____

2. Which skill steps did you really follow?

   _____

   _____

3. How good a job did you do in using the skill? *(check one)*

   ☐ excellent   ☐ good   ☐ fair   ☐ poor

Skillstreaming
From *Skillstreaming the Adolescent: A Guide for Teaching Prosocial Skills* (3rd ed.), © 2012 by E. McGinnis, Champaign, IL: Research Press (www.researchpress.com, 800-519-2707).

Skill 39: Dealing with Contradictory Messages

Name _____ Date _____

SKILL STEPS

1. Decide if someone is telling you two opposite things at the same time.

2. Think of ways to tell the other person that you don't understand what he/she means.

3. Choose the best way to tell the person and do it.

FILL IN NOW

1. Where will you try the skill? _____

2. With whom will you try the skill? _____

3. When will you try the skill? _____

4. If you do an excellent job, how will you reward yourself? _____

5. If you do a good job, how will you reward yourself? _____

6. If you do a fair job, how will you reward yourself? _____

FILL IN AFTER YOU PRACTICE THE SKILL

1. What happened when you did the homework?

   _____

   _____

2. Which skill steps did you really follow?

   _____

   _____

3. How good a job did you do in using the skill? *(check one)*

   ☐ excellent   ☐ good   ☐ fair   ☐ poor

4. What do you think your next homework assignment should be?

   _____

Skillstreaming From *Skillstreaming the Adolescent: A Guide for Teaching Prosocial Skills* (3rd ed.), © 2012 by E. McGinnis, Champaign, IL: Research Press (www.researchpress.com, 800-519-2707).

Skill 40: Dealing with an Accusation

SKILL STEPS

1. **Think about what the other person has accused you of.**

   Is the accusation accurate or inaccurate?

2. **Think about why the person might have accused you.**

   Have you infringed on his/her rights or property? Has a rumor been started by someone else?

3. **Think about ways to answer the person's accusation.**

   Deny it; explain your own behavior; correct the other person's perceptions; assert yourself; apologize; offer to make up for what happened.

4. **Choose the best way and do it.**

SUGGESTED MODELING DISPLAYS

School or neighborhood: Main actor is accused of breaking neighbor's window.

Home: Parent accuses main actor of hurting sibling's feelings.

Peer group: Friend accuses main actor of lying.

Job: Main actor is accused of not working hard enough by co-worker.

Skillstreaming From *Skillstreaming the Adolescent: A Guide for Teaching Prosocial Skills* (3rd ed.), © 2012 by E. McGinnis, Champaign, IL: Research Press (www.researchpress.com, 800-519-2707).

Skill 40: Dealing with an Accusation

Name _____ Date _____

SKILL STEPS

1. Think about what the other person has accused you of.
2. Think about why the person might have accused you.
3. Think about ways to answer the person's accusation.
4. Choose the best way and do it.

FILL IN NOW

1. Where will you try the skill? _____

2. With whom will you try the skill? _____

3. When will you try the skill? _____

FILL IN AFTER YOU PRACTICE THE SKILL

1. What happened when you did the homework?

   _____

   _____

2. Which skill steps did you really follow?

   _____

   _____

3. How good a job did you do in using the skill? *(check one)*

   ☐ excellent   ☐ good   ☐ fair   ☐ poor

Skillstreaming

From *Skillstreaming the Adolescent: A Guide for Teaching Prosocial Skills* (3rd ed.), © 2012
by E. McGinnis, Champaign, IL: Research Press (www.researchpress.com, 800-519-2707).

Skill 40: Dealing with an Accusation

Name _____ Date _____

SKILL STEPS

1. Think about what the other person has accused you of.
2. Think about why the person might have accused you.
3. Think about ways to answer the person's accusation.
4. Choose the best way and do it.

FILL IN NOW

1. Where will you try the skill? _____

2. With whom will you try the skill? _____

3. When will you try the skill? _____

4. If you do an excellent job, how will you reward yourself? _____

5. If you do a good job, how will you reward yourself? _____

6. If you do a fair job, how will you reward yourself? _____

FILL IN AFTER YOU PRACTICE THE SKILL

1. What happened when you did the homework?

   _____

   _____

2. Which skill steps did you really follow?

   _____

   _____

3. How good a job did you do in using the skill? *(check one)*

   ☐ excellent ☐ good ☐ fair ☐ poor

4. What do you think your next homework assignment should be?

   _____

Skillstreaming

From *Skillstreaming the Adolescent: A Guide for Teaching Prosocial Skills* (3rd ed.), © 2012 by E. McGinnis, Champaign, IL: Research Press (www.researchpress.com, 800-519-2707).

Skill 41: Getting Ready for a Difficult Conversation

SKILL STEPS

1. **Think about how you will feel during the conversation.**

   You might be tense, anxious, or impatient.

2. **Think about how the other person will feel.**

   He/she may feel anxious, bored, or angry.

3. **Think about different ways you could say what you want to say.**

4. **Think about what the other person might say back to you.**

5. **Think about any other things that might happen during the conversation.**

   Repeat Steps 1–5 at least twice, using different approaches to the situation.

6. **Choose the best approach you can think of and try it.**

SUGGESTED MODELING DISPLAYS

School or neighborhood: Main actor prepares to talk with teacher about dropping subject.

Home: Main actor prepares to tell parent about school failure.

Peer group: Main actor prepares to ask for first date.

Job: Main actor prepares to talk with co-worker about an accusation the co-worker made regarding work performance.

COMMENTS

In preparing for difficult or stressful conversations, it is useful for group members to see that the way they approach the situation can influence the final outcome. This skill involves rehearsing a variety of approaches and then reflecting on which approach produces the best results. Feedback from other group members on the effectiveness of each approach can be particularly useful.

Skill 41: Getting Ready for a Difficult Conversation

Name _____ Date _____

SKILL STEPS

1. Think about how you will feel during the conversation.

2. Think about how the other person will feel.

3. Think about different ways you could say what you want to say.

4. Think about what the other person might say back to you.

5. Think about any other things that might happen during the conversation.

6. Choose the best approach you can think of and try it.

FILL IN NOW

1. Where will you try the skill? _____

2. With whom will you try the skill? _____

3. When will you try the skill? _____

FILL IN AFTER YOU PRACTICE THE SKILL

1. What happened when you did the homework?

   _____

   _____

2. Which skill steps did you really follow?

   _____

   _____

3. How good a job did you do in using the skill? *(check one)*

   ☐ excellent   ☐ good   ☐ fair   ☐ poor

Skillstreaming From *Skillstreaming the Adolescent: A Guide for Teaching Prosocial Skills* (3rd ed.), © 2012 by E. McGinnis, Champaign, IL: Research Press (www.researchpress.com, 800-519-2707).

Skill 41: Getting Ready for a Difficult Conversation

Name _____ Date _____

SKILL STEPS

1. Think about how you will feel during the conversation.
2. Think about how the other person will feel.
3. Think about different ways you could say what you want to say.
4. Think about what the other person might say back to you.
5. Think about any other things that might happen during the conversation.
6. Choose the best approach you can think of and try it.

FILL IN NOW

1. Where will you try the skill? _____

2. With whom will you try the skill? _____

3. When will you try the skill? _____

4. If you do an excellent job, how will you reward yourself? _____

5. If you do a good job, how will you reward yourself? _____

6. If you do a fair job, how will you reward yourself? _____

FILL IN AFTER YOU PRACTICE THE SKILL

1. What happened when you did the homework?

   _____

   _____

2. Which skill steps did you really follow?

   _____

   _____

3. How good a job did you do in using the skill? *(check one)*

   ☐ excellent   ☐ good   ☐ fair   ☐ poor

4. What do you think your next homework assignment should be?

   _____

Skill 42: Dealing with Group Pressure

SKILL STEPS

1. **Think about what the group wants you to do and why.**

   Listen to other people; decide what the real meaning is; try to understand what is being said.

2. **Decide what you want to do.**

   Yield; resist; delay; negotiate.

3. **Decide how to tell the group what you want to do.**

   Give reasons; talk to one person only; delay; assert yourself.

4. **Tell the group what you have decided.**

SUGGESTED MODELING DISPLAYS

School or neighborhood: Main actor deals with group pressure to vandalize neighborhood.

Home: Main actor deals with family pressure to break up friendship.

Peer group: Main actor deals with pressure to fight.

Job: Main actor deals with pressure to complain about co-worker.

Skillstreaming

From *Skillstreaming the Adolescent: A Guide for Teaching Prosocial Skills* (3rd ed.), © 2012 by E. McGinnis, Champaign, IL: Research Press (www.researchpress.com, 800-519-2707).

Skill 42: Dealing with Group Pressure

Name _____ Date _____

SKILL STEPS

1. Think about what the group wants you to do and why.
2. Decide what you want to do.
3. Decide how to tell the group what you want to do.
4. Tell the group what you have decided.

FILL IN NOW

1. Where will you try the skill? _____

2. With whom will you try the skill? _____

3. When will you try the skill? _____

FILL IN AFTER YOU PRACTICE THE SKILL

1. What happened when you did the homework?

   _____

   _____

2. Which skill steps did you really follow?

   _____

   _____

3. How good a job did you do in using the skill? *(check one)*

   ☐ excellent   ☐ good   ☐ fair   ☐ poor

Skill 42: Dealing with Group Pressure

Name _____ Date _____

SKILL STEPS

1. Think about what the group wants you to do and why.
2. Decide what you want to do.
3. Decide how to tell the group what you want to do.
4. Tell the group what you have decided.

FILL IN NOW

1. Where will you try the skill? _____

2. With whom will you try the skill? _____

3. When will you try the skill? _____

4. If you do an excellent job, how will you reward yourself? _____

5. If you do a good job, how will you reward yourself? _____

6. If you do a fair job, how will you reward yourself? _____

FILL IN AFTER YOU PRACTICE THE SKILL

1. What happened when you did the homework?

   _____

   _____

2. Which skill steps did you really follow?

   _____

   _____

3. How good a job did you do in using the skill? *(check one)*

   ☐ excellent   ☐ good   ☐ fair   ☐ poor

4. What do you think your next homework assignment should be?

   _____

Skillstreaming

From *Skillstreaming the Adolescent: A Guide for Teaching Prosocial Skills* (3rd ed.), © 2012 by E. McGinnis, Champaign, IL: Research Press (www.researchpress.com, 800-519-2707).

Group VI

Planning Skills

Skills 43–50

Skill 43: Deciding on Something to Do

SKILL STEPS

1. **Decide whether you are feeling bored or dissatisfied with what you are doing.**

   Are you not concentrating, getting fidgety, disrupting others who are involved in an activity?

2. **Think of things you have enjoyed doing in the past.**

3. **Decide which one you might be able to do now.**

   Focus on prosocial alternatives; include others if appropriate.

4. **Start the activity.**

SUGGESTED MODELING DISPLAYS

School or neighborhood: Main actor chooses after-school activity in which to participate.

Home: Main actor thinks up activity that will earn him/her money.

Peer group: Main actor suggests that friends play basketball instead of hanging around.

Job: Main actor suggests an activity with co-workers after work.

Skill 43: Deciding on Something to Do

Name _____ Date _____

SKILL STEPS

1. Decide whether you are feeling bored or dissatisfied with what you are doing.
2. Think of things you have enjoyed doing in the past.
3. Decide which one you might be able to do now.
4. Start the activity.

FILL IN NOW

1. Where will you try the skill? _____

2. With whom will you try the skill? _____

3. When will you try the skill? _____

FILL IN AFTER YOU PRACTICE THE SKILL

1. What happened when you did the homework?

   _____

   _____

2. Which skill steps did you really follow?

   _____

   _____

3. How good a job did you do in using the skill? *(check one)*

   ☐ excellent   ☐ good   ☐ fair   ☐ poor

.Skillstreaming From *Skillstreaming the Adolescent: A Guide for Teaching Prosocial Skills* (3rd ed.), © 2012 by E. McGinnis, Champaign, IL: Research Press (www.researchpress.com, 800-519-2707).

Skill 43: Deciding on Something to Do

Name _____ Date _____

SKILL STEPS

1. Decide whether you are feeling bored or dissatisfied with what you are doing.
2. Think of things you have enjoyed doing in the past.
3. Decide which one you might be able to do now.
4. Start the activity.

FILL IN NOW

1. Where will you try the skill? _____

2. With whom will you try the skill? _____

3. When will you try the skill? _____

4. If you do an excellent job, how will you reward yourself? _____

5. If you do a good job, how will you reward yourself? _____

6. If you do a fair job, how will you reward yourself? _____

FILL IN AFTER YOU PRACTICE THE SKILL

1. What happened when you did the homework?

   _____

   _____

2. Which skill steps did you really follow?

   _____

   _____

3. How good a job did you do in using the skill? *(check one)*

   ☐ excellent   ☐ good   ☐ fair   ☐ poor

4. What do you think your next homework assignment should be?

   _____

Skill 44: Deciding What Caused a Problem

SKILL STEPS

1. Define what the problem is.

2. Think about possible causes of the problem.

   Was it yourself, others, or events; intentional, accidental, or both?

3. Decide which are the most likely causes of the problem.

4. Check out what really caused the problem.

   Ask others; observe the situation again.

SUGGESTED MODELING DISPLAYS

School or neighborhood: Main actor evaluates reasons for teacher's abruptness.

Home: Main actor evaluates likely causes of parents' having an argument.

Peer group: Main actor evaluates why he/she feels nervous with particular friend.

Job: Main actor evaluates how to deal with co-worker who doesn't seem to like him/her.

COMMENTS

This skill is intended to help group members determine the degree to which they are responsible for a particular problem and the degree to which the causes of the problem are outside of their control.

.Skillstreaming

From *Skillstreaming the Adolescent: A Guide for Teaching Prosocial Skills* (3rd ed.), © 2012 by E. McGinnis, Champaign, IL: Research Press (www.researchpress.com, 800-519-2707).

Skill 44: Deciding What Caused a Problem

Name _____ Date _____

SKILL STEPS

1. Define what the problem is.
2. Think about possible causes of the problem.
3. Decide which are the most likely causes of the problem.
4. Check out what really caused the problem.

FILL IN NOW

1. Where will you try the skill? _____

2. With whom will you try the skill? _____

3. When will you try the skill? _____

FILL IN AFTER YOU PRACTICE THE SKILL

1. What happened when you did the homework?

   _____

   _____

2. Which skill steps did you really follow?

   _____

   _____

3. How good a job did you do in using the skill? *(check one)*

   ☐ excellent   ☐ good   ☐ fair   ☐ poor

Skill 44: Deciding What Caused a Problem

Name _____ Date _____

SKILL STEPS

1. Define what the problem is.
2. Think about possible causes of the problem.
3. Decide which are the most likely causes of the problem.
4. Check out what really caused the problem.

FILL IN NOW

1. Where will you try the skill? _____

2. With whom will you try the skill? _____

3. When will you try the skill? _____

4. If you do an excellent job, how will you reward yourself? _____

5. If you do a good job, how will you reward yourself? _____

6. If you do a fair job, how will you reward yourself? _____

FILL IN AFTER YOU PRACTICE THE SKILL

1. What happened when you did the homework?

   _____

   _____

2. Which skill steps did you really follow?

   _____

   _____

3. How good a job did you do in using the skill? *(check one)*

   ☐ excellent ☐ good ☐ fair ☐ poor

4. What do you think your next homework assignment should be?

   _____

Skillstreaming

From *Skillstreaming the Adolescent: A Guide for Teaching Prosocial Skills* (3rd ed.), © 2012 by E. McGinnis, Champaign, IL: Research Press (www.researchpress.com, 800-519-2707).

Skill 45: Setting a Goal

SKILL STEPS

1. **Figure out what goal you want to reach.**

2. **Find out all the information you can about how to reach your goal.**

   Talk with friends; read; observe others; ask authorities.

3. **Think about the steps you will need to take to reach your goal.**

   Consider your abilities, materials, help from others, and skills needed.

4. **Take the first step toward your goal.**

SUGGESTED MODELING DISPLAYS

School or neighborhood: Main actor decides to improve a grade in a class.

Home: Main actor decides to improve appearance.

Peer group: Main actor decides to have a party.

Job: Main actor decides to find a job.

Skill 45: Setting a Goal

Name _____ Date _____

SKILL STEPS

1. Figure out what goal you want to reach.
2. Find out all the information you can about how to reach your goal.
3. Think about the steps you will need to take to reach your goal.
4. Take the first step toward your goal.

FILL IN NOW

1. Where will you try the skill? _____

2. With whom will you try the skill? _____

3. When will you try the skill? _____

FILL IN AFTER YOU PRACTICE THE SKILL

1. What happened when you did the homework?

   _____

   _____

2. Which skill steps did you really follow?

   _____

   _____

3. How good a job did you do in using the skill? *(check one)*

   ☐ excellent   ☐ good   ☐ fair   ☐ poor

Skillstreaming From *Skillstreaming the Adolescent: A Guide for Teaching Prosocial Skills* (3rd ed.), © 2012 by E. McGinnis, Champaign, IL: Research Press (www.researchpress.com, 800-519-2707).

Skill 45: Setting a Goal

Name _____ Date _____

SKILL STEPS

1. Figure out what goal you want to reach.
2. Find out all the information you can about how to reach your goal.
3. Think about the steps you will need to take to reach your goal.
4. Take the first step toward your goal.

FILL IN NOW

1. Where will you try the skill? _____

2. With whom will you try the skill? _____

3. When will you try the skill? _____

4. If you do an excellent job, how will you reward yourself? _____

5. If you do a good job, how will you reward yourself? _____

6. If you do a fair job, how will you reward yourself? _____

FILL IN AFTER YOU PRACTICE THE SKILL

1. What happened when you did the homework?

   _____

   _____

2. Which skill steps did you really follow?

   _____

   _____

3. How good a job did you do in using the skill? *(check one)*

   ☐ excellent   ☐ good   ☐ fair   ☐ poor

4. What do you think your next homework assignment should be?

   _____

From *Skillstreaming the Adolescent: A Guide for Teaching Prosocial Skills* (3rd ed.), © 2012 by E. McGinnis, Champaign, IL: Research Press (www.researchpress.com, 800-519-2707).

Skill 46: Deciding on Your Abilities

SKILL STEPS

1. **Decide which abilities you might want to use.**

   Take the setting, circumstances, and goal into account.

2. **Think about how you have done in the past when you have tried to use these abilities.**

3. **Get other people's opinions about your abilities.**

   Ask others; take tests; check records.

4. **Think about what you found out and decide how well you use these abilities.**

   Consider the evidence from both Steps 2 and 3.

SUGGESTED MODELING DISPLAYS

School or neighborhood: Main actor decides type of school curriculum.

Home: Main actor evaluates ability to repair broken computer.

Peer group: Main actor decides whether to try out for team (play).

Job: Main actor decides how to do the job more efficiently.

COMMENTS

This skill is intended to help youngsters evaluate their capabilities realistically in view of available evidence. This skill is often tied to Skill 45 (Setting a Goal).

Skillstreaming

From *Skillstreaming the Adolescent: A Guide for Teaching Prosocial Skills* (3rd ed.), © 2012 by E. McGinnis, Champaign, IL: Research Press (www.researchpress.com, 800-519-2707).

Skill 46: Deciding on Your Abilities

Name _____ Date _____

SKILL STEPS

1. Decide which abilities you might want to use.

2. Think about how you have done in the past when you have tried to use these abilities.

3. Get other people's opinions about your abilities.

4. Think about what you found out and decide how well you use these abilities.

FILL IN NOW

1. Where will you try the skill? _____

2. With whom will you try the skill? _____

3. When will you try the skill? _____

FILL IN AFTER YOU PRACTICE THE SKILL

1. What happened when you did the homework?

   _____

   _____

2. Which skill steps did you really follow?

   _____

   _____

3. How good a job did you do in using the skill? *(check one)*

   ☐ excellent   ☐ good   ☐ fair   ☐ poor

From *Skillstreaming the Adolescent: A Guide for Teaching Prosocial Skills* (3rd ed.), © 2012 by E. McGinnis, Champaign, IL: Research Press (www.researchpress.com, 800-519-2707).

Skill 46: Deciding on Your Abilities

Name _____ Date _____

SKILL STEPS

1. Decide which abilities you might want to use.
2. Think about how you have done in the past when you have tried to use these abilities.
3. Get other people's opinions about your abilities.
4. Think about what you found out and decide how well you use these abilities.

FILL IN NOW

1. Where will you try the skill? _____

2. With whom will you try the skill? _____

3. When will you try the skill? _____

4. If you do an excellent job, how will you reward yourself? _____

5. If you do a good job, how will you reward yourself? _____

6. If you do a fair job, how will you reward yourself? _____

FILL IN AFTER YOU PRACTICE THE SKILL

1. What happened when you did the homework?

   _____

   _____

2. Which skill steps did you really follow?

   _____

   _____

3. How good a job did you do in using the skill? *(check one)*

   ☐ excellent   ☐ good   ☐ fair   ☐ poor

4. What do you think your next homework assignment should be?

   _____

Skillstreaming

From *Skillstreaming the Adolescent: A Guide for Teaching Prosocial Skills* (3rd ed.), © 2012 by E. McGinnis, Champaign, IL: Research Press (www.researchpress.com, 800-519-2707).

Skill 47: Gathering Information

SKILL STEPS

1. **Decide what information you need.**

2. **Decide how you can get the information.**

    You can get information from people, books, and so on.

3. **Do things to get the information.**

    Ask questions; make telephone calls; look in books or on the Internet.

SUGGESTED MODELING DISPLAYS

School or neighborhood: Main actor finds out information to complete a paper for a school assignment.

Home: Main actor gathers information on where to shop for particular item.

Peer group: Main actor finds out what kinds of things his/her date likes to do.

Job: Main actor gathers information on available jobs.

COMMENTS

This skill often precedes Skill 49 (Making a Decision). Although each constitutes a separate skill, when taken together they often compose an effective approach to problem solving.

Skill 47: Gathering Information

Name _____ Date _____

SKILL STEPS

1. Decide what information you need.
2. Decide how you can get the information.
3. Do things to get the information.

FILL IN NOW

1. Where will you try the skill? _____

2. With whom will you try the skill? _____

3. When will you try the skill? _____

FILL IN AFTER YOU PRACTICE THE SKILL

1. What happened when you did the homework?

   _____

   _____

2. Which skill steps did you really follow?

   _____

   _____

3. How good a job did you do in using the skill? *(check one)*

   ☐ excellent   ☐ good   ☐ fair   ☐ poor

Skillstreaming

From *Skillstreaming the Adolescent: A Guide for Teaching Prosocial Skills* (3rd ed.), © 2012 by E. McGinnis, Champaign, IL: Research Press (www.researchpress.com, 800-519-2707).

Skill 47: Gathering Information

Name _____ Date _____

SKILL STEPS

1. Decide what information you need.
2. Decide how you can get the information.
3. Do things to get the information.

FILL IN NOW

1. Where will you try the skill? _____

2. With whom will you try the skill? _____

3. When will you try the skill? _____

4. If you do an excellent job, how will you reward yourself? _____

5. If you do a good job, how will you reward yourself? _____

6. If you do a fair job, how will you reward yourself? _____

FILL IN AFTER YOU PRACTICE THE SKILL

1. What happened when you did the homework?

   _____

   _____

2. Which skill steps did you really follow?

   _____

   _____

3. How good a job did you do in using the skill? *(check one)*

   ☐ excellent ☐ good ☐ fair ☐ poor

4. What do you think your next homework assignment should be?

   _____

From *Skillstreaming the Adolescent: A Guide for Teaching Prosocial Skills* (3rd ed.), © 2012 by E. McGinnis, Champaign, IL: Research Press (www.researchpress.com, 800-519-2707).

Skill 48: Arranging Problems by Importance

SKILL STEPS

1. **Think about the problems that are bothering you.**

   Make a list; be inclusive.

2. **List these problems from most to least important.**

3. **Do what you can to hold off on your less important problems.**

   Delegate them; postpone them; avoid them.

4. **Go to work on your most important problems.**

   Plan first steps in dealing with the most important problem; rehearse these steps in your imagination.

SUGGESTED MODELING DISPLAYS

School or neighborhood: Main actor is worried about large number of school assignments.

Home: Parent tells main actor to take care of several chores before going out.

Peer group: Main actor has difficulty balancing school responsibilities, chores, and time with friends.

Job: Main actor decides which tasks are most important to get done with the time at work.

COMMENTS

This skill is intended to help the youth who feels overwhelmed by a number of difficulties. The youth is taught how to evaluate the relative urgency of the various problems and deal with each according to its priority.

From *Skillstreaming the Adolescent: A Guide for Teaching Prosocial Skills* (3rd ed.), © 2012 by E. McGinnis, Champaign, IL: Research Press (www.researchpress.com, 800-519-2707).

Skill 48: Arranging Problems by Importance

Name _____ Date _____

SKILL STEPS

1. Think about the problems that are bothering you.

2. List these problems from most to least important.

3. Do what you can to hold off on your less important problems.

4. Go to work on your most important problems.

FILL IN NOW

1. Where will you try the skill? _____

2. With whom will you try the skill? _____

3. When will you try the skill? _____

FILL IN AFTER YOU PRACTICE THE SKILL

1. What happened when you did the homework?

   _____

   _____

2. Which skill steps did you really follow?

   _____

   _____

3. How good a job did you do in using the skill? *(check one)*

   ☐ excellent   ☐ good   ☐ fair   ☐ poor

Skill 48: Arranging Problems by Importance

Name _____ Date _____

SKILL STEPS

1. Think about the problems that are bothering you.
2. List these problems from most to least important.
3. Do what you can to hold off on your less important problems.
4. Go to work on your most important problems.

FILL IN NOW

1. Where will you try the skill? _____

2. With whom will you try the skill? _____

3. When will you try the skill? _____

4. If you do an excellent job, how will you reward yourself? _____

5. If you do a good job, how will you reward yourself? _____

6. If you do a fair job, how will you reward yourself? _____

FILL IN AFTER YOU PRACTICE THE SKILL

1. What happened when you did the homework?

   _____

   _____

2. Which skill steps did you really follow?

   _____

   _____

3. How good a job did you do in using the skill? *(check one)*

   ☐ excellent   ☐ good   ☐ fair   ☐ poor

4. What do you think your next homework assignment should be?

   _____

Skillstreaming

From *Skillstreaming the Adolescent: A Guide for Teaching Prosocial Skills* (3rd ed.), © 2012 by E. McGinnis, Champaign, IL: Research Press (www.researchpress.com, 800-519-2707).

Skill 49: Making a Decision

SKILL STEPS

1. Think about the problem that requires you to make a decision.

2. Think about possible decisions you could make.

   Generate a number of possible alternatives; avoid premature closure.

3. Gather accurate information about these possible decisions.

   Ask others; read; observe.

4. Reconsider your possible decisions using the information you have gathered.

5. Make the best decision.

SUGGESTED MODELING DISPLAYS

School or neighborhood: Main actor decides which classes to take.

Home: Main actor decides how to spend money he/she has earned.

Peer group: Main actor decides whether to participate with friends in a weekend activity.

Job: Main actor decides what job to apply for.

COMMENTS

This skill follows Skill 47 (Gathering Information) to constitute the general skill of problem solving.

Skill 49: Making a Decision

Name _____ Date _____

SKILL STEPS

1. Think about the problem that requires you to make a decision.
2. Think about possible decisions you could make.
3. Gather accurate information about these possible decisions.
4. Reconsider your possible decisions using the information you have gathered.
5. Make the best decision.

FILL IN NOW

1. Where will you try the skill? _____

2. With whom will you try the skill? _____

3. When will you try the skill? _____

FILL IN AFTER YOU PRACTICE THE SKILL

1. What happened when you did the homework?

   _____

   _____

2. Which skill steps did you really follow?

   _____

   _____

3. How good a job did you do in using the skill? *(check one)*

   ☐ excellent   ☐ good   ☐ fair   ☐ poor

Skillstreaming

From *Skillstreaming the Adolescent: A Guide for Teaching Prosocial Skills* (3rd ed.), © 2012 by E. McGinnis, Champaign, IL: Research Press (www.researchpress.com, 800-519-2707).

Skill 49: Making a Decision

Name _____ Date _____

SKILL STEPS

1. Think about the problem that requires you to make a decision.
2. Think about possible decisions you could make.
3. Gather accurate information about these possible decisions.
4. Reconsider your possible decisions using the information you have gathered.
5. Make the best decision.

FILL IN NOW

1. Where will you try the skill? _____

2. With whom will you try the skill? _____

3. When will you try the skill? _____

4. If you do an excellent job, how will you reward yourself? _____

5. If you do a good job, how will you reward yourself? _____

6. If you do a fair job, how will you reward yourself? _____

FILL IN AFTER YOU PRACTICE THE SKILL

1. What happened when you did the homework?

   _____

   _____

2. Which skill steps did you really follow?

   _____

   _____

3. How good a job did you do in using the skill? *(check one)*

   ☐ excellent   ☐ good   ☐ fair   ☐ poor

4. What do you think your next homework assignment should be?

   _____

 From *Skillstreaming the Adolescent: A Guide for Teaching Prosocial Skills* (3rd ed.), © 2012 by E. McGinnis, Champaign, IL: Research Press (www.researchpress.com, 800-519-2707).

Skill 50: Concentrating on a Task

SKILL STEPS

1. **Decide what your task is.**

2. **Decide on a time to work on this task.**

   Consider when and how long to work.

3. **Gather the materials you need.**

4. **Decide on a place to work.**

   Consider where: Minimize noise level, people present, possible interruptions.

5. **Decide if you are ready to concentrate.**

SUGGESTED MODELING DISPLAYS

School or neighborhood: Main actor prepares to research and write a report.

Home: Main actor prepares to repair bicycle or appliance.

Peer group: Main actor gathers materials necessary for trip with friends.

Job: Main actor gathers materials and interview questions to interview for a job.

COMMENTS

This skill helps group members overcome problems with distractions by focusing on planning prior to undertaking a task. Planning, in this sense, involves scheduling and arranging materials and work environment.

.Skillstreaming

From *Skillstreaming the Adolescent: A Guide for Teaching Prosocial Skills* (3rd ed.), © 2012 by E. McGinnis, Champaign, IL: Research Press (www.researchpress.com, 800-519-2707).

Skill 50: Concentrating on a Task

Name _____ Date _____

SKILL STEPS

1. Decide what your task is.
2. Decide on a time to work on this task.
3. Gather the materials you need.
4. Decide on a place to work.
5. Decide if you are ready to concentrate.

FILL IN NOW

1. Where will you try the skill? _____

2. With whom will you try the skill? _____

3. When will you try the skill? _____

FILL IN AFTER YOU PRACTICE THE SKILL

1. What happened when you did the homework?

   _____

   _____

2. Which skill steps did you really follow?

   _____

   _____

3. How good a job did you do in using the skill? *(check one)*

   ☐ excellent   ☐ good   ☐ fair   ☐ poor

From *Skillstreaming the Adolescent: A Guide for Teaching Prosocial Skills* (3rd ed.), © 2012 by E. McGinnis, Champaign, IL: Research Press (www.researchpress.com, 800-519-2707).

Skill 50: Concentrating on a Task

Name _____ Date _____

SKILL STEPS

1. Decide what your task is.
2. Decide on a time to work on this task.
3. Gather the materials you need.
4. Decide on a place to work.
5. Decide if you are ready to concentrate.

FILL IN NOW

1. Where will you try the skill? _____

2. With whom will you try the skill? _____

3. When will you try the skill? _____

4. If you do an excellent job, how will you reward yourself? _____

5. If you do a good job, how will you reward yourself? _____

6. If you do a fair job, how will you reward yourself? _____

FILL IN AFTER YOU PRACTICE THE SKILL

1. What happened when you did the homework?

    _____

    _____

2. Which skill steps did you really follow?

    _____

    _____

3. How good a job did you do in using the skill? *(check one)*

    ☐ excellent   ☐ good   ☐ fair   ☐ poor

4. What do you think your next homework assignment should be?

    _____

Program Forms

LEADER/STAFF CHECKLIST

Student _____ Class/age _____

Leader/staff _____ Date _____

INSTRUCTIONS: Listed below are a number of skills that youth are more or less proficient in using. This checklist will help you evaluate how well each youth uses the various skills. For each youth, rate his or her use of each skill, based on your observations of the youth's behavior in various situations.

    Circle 1 if the youth is *almost never* good at using the skill.
    Circle 2 if the youth is *seldom* good at using the skill.
    Circle 3 if the youth is *sometimes* good at using the skill.
    Circle 4 if the youth is *often* good at using the skill.
    Circle 5 if the youth is *almost always* good at using the skill.

Please rate the youth on all skills listed. If you know of a situation in which the youth has particular difficulty using the skill well, please note it briefly in the space marked "Problem situation."

	almost never	seldom	sometimes	often	almost always
1. **Listening:** Does the youth pay attention to someone who is talking and make an effort to understand what is being said? Problem situation:	1	2	3	4	5
2. **Starting a Conversation:** Does the youth talk to others about light topics and then lead into more serious topics? Problem situation:	1	2	3	4	5
3. **Having a Conversation:** Does the youth talk to others about things of interest to both of them? Problem situation:	1	2	3	4	5
4. **Asking a Question:** Does the youth decide what information is needed and ask the right person for that information? Problem situation:	1	2	3	4	5
5. **Saying Thank You:** Does the youth let others know that he/she is grateful for favors, etc.? Problem situation:	1	2	3	4	5

 From *Skillstreaming the Adolescent: A Guide for Teaching Prosocial Skills* (3rd ed.), © 2012 by E. McGinnis, Champaign, IL: Research Press (www.researchpress.com, 800-519-2707).

6. **Introducing Yourself:** Does the youth become acquainted with new people on his/her own initiative?

     1   2   3   4   5

Problem situation:

7. **Introducing Other People:** Does the youth help others become acquainted with one another?

     1   2   3   4   5

Problem situation:

8. **Giving a Compliment:** Does the youth tell others that he/she likes something about them or their activities?

     1   2   3   4   5

Problem situation:

9. **Asking for Help:** Does the youth request assistance when he/she is having difficulty?

     1   2   3   4   5

Problem situation:

10. **Joining In:** Does the youth decide on the best way to become part of an ongoing activity or group?

     1   2   3   4   5

Problem situation:

11. **Giving Instructions:** Does the youth clearly explain to others how they are to do a specific task?

     1   2   3   4   5

Problem situation:

12. **Following Instructions:** Does the youth pay attention to instructions, give his/her reactions, and carry the instructions out adequately?

     1   2   3   4   5

Problem situation:

13. **Apologizing:** Does the youth tell others that he/she is sorry after doing something wrong?

     1   2   3   4   5

Problem situation:

	almost never	*seldom*	*sometimes*	*often*	*almost always*

14. **Convincing Others:** Does the youth attempt to persuade others that his/her ideas are better and will be more useful than those of the other person?

      1 2 3 4 5

Problem situation:

15. **Knowing Your Feelings:** Does the youth try to recognize which emotions he/she has at different times?

      1 2 3 4 5

Problem situation:

16. **Expressing Your Feelings:** Does the youth let others know which emotions he/she is feeling?

      1 2 3 4 5

Problem situation:

17. **Understanding the Feelings of Others:** Does the youth try to figure out what other people are feeling?

      1 2 3 4 5

Problem situation:

18. **Dealing with Someone Else's Anger:** Does the youth try to understand other people's angry feelings?

      1 2 3 4 5

Problem situation:

19. **Expressing Affection:** Does the youth let others know that he/she cares about them?

      1 2 3 4 5

Problem situation:

20. **Dealing with Fear:** Does the youth figure out why he/she is afraid and do something to reduce the fear?

      1 2 3 4 5

Problem situation:

21. **Rewarding Yourself:** Does the youth say and do nice things for himself/herself when the reward is deserved?

      1 2 3 4 5

Problem situation:

22. **Asking Permission:** Does the youth figure out when permission is needed to do something and then ask the right person for permission?

    1 2 3 4 5

    Problem situation:

23. **Sharing Something:** Does the youth offer to share what he/she has with others who might appreciate it?

    1 2 3 4 5

    Problem situation:

24. **Helping Others:** Does the youth give assistance to others who might need or want help?

    1 2 3 4 5

    Problem situation:

25. **Negotiating:** Does the youth arrive at a plan that satisfies both him/her and others who have taken different positions?

    1 2 3 4 5

    Problem situation:

26. **Using Self-Control:** Does the youth control his/her temper so that things do not get out of hand?

    1 2 3 4 5

    Problem situation:

27. **Standing Up for Your Rights:** Does the youth assert his/her rights by letting people know where he/she stands on an issue?

    1 2 3 4 5

    Problem situation:

28. **Responding to Teasing:** Does the youth deal with being teased by others in ways that allow him/her to remain in control of himself/herself?

    1 2 3 4 5

    Problem situation:

29. **Avoiding Trouble with Others:** Does the youth stay out of situations that might get him/her into trouble?

    1 2 3 4 5

    Problem situation:

	almost never	seldom	sometimes	often	almost always

30. **Keeping Out of Fights:** Does the youth figure out ways other than fighting to handle difficult situations?

    1   2   3   4   5

Problem situation:

31. **Making a Complaint:** Does the youth tell others when they are responsible for creating a particular problem for him/her and then attempt to find a solution for the problem?

    1   2   3   4   5

Problem situation:

32. **Answering a Complaint:** Does the youth try to arrive at a fair solution to someone's justified complaint?

    1   2   3   4   5

Problem situation:

33. **Being a Good Sport:** Does the youth express an honest compliment to others about how they played a game?

    1   2   3   4   5

Problem situation:

34. **Dealing with Embarrassment:** Does the youth do things that help him/her feel less embarrassed or self-conscious?

    1   2   3   4   5

Problem situation:

35. **Dealing with Being Left Out:** Does the youth decide whether he/she has been left out of some activity and then do things to feel better about the situation?

    1   2   3   4   5

Problem situation:

36. **Standing Up for a Friend:** Does the youth let other people know when a friend has not been treated fairly?

    1   2   3   4   5

Problem situation:

37. **Responding to Persuasion:** Does the youth carefully consider the position of another person, comparing it to his/her own, before deciding what to do?

    1   2   3   4   5

Problem situation:

38. **Responding to Failure:** Does the youth figure out the reason for failing in a particular situation and what he/she can do about it to be more successful in the future?

    1   2   3   4   5

Problem situation:

39. **Dealing with Contradictory Messages:** Does the youth recognize and deal with the confusion that results when others tell him/her one thing but say or do things that indicate that they mean something else?

    1   2   3   4   5

Problem situation:

40. **Dealing with an Accusation:** Does the youth figure out what he/she has been accused of and why, then decide on the best way to deal with the person who made the accusation?

    1   2   3   4   5

Problem situation:

41. **Getting Ready for a Difficult Conversation:** Does the youth plan on the best way to present his/her point of view prior to a stressful conversation?

    1   2   3   4   5

Problem situation:

42. **Dealing with Group Pressure:** Does the youth decide what he/she wants to do when others want him/her to do something else?

    1   2   3   4   5

Problem situation:

43. **Deciding on Something to Do:** Does the youth deal with feeling bored by starting an interesting activity?

    1   2   3   4   5

Problem situation:

44. **Deciding What Caused a Problem:** Does the youth find out whether an event was caused by something that was within his/her control?

    1   2   3   4   5

Problem situation:

45. **Setting a Goal:** Does the youth realistically decide on what he/she can accomplish prior to starting a task?   1 2 3 4 5

 Problem situation:

46. **Deciding on Your Abilities:** Does the youth realistically figure out how well he/she might do at a particular task?   1 2 3 4 5

 Problem situation:

47. **Gathering Information:** Does the youth decide what he/she needs to know and how to get that information?   1 2 3 4 5

 Problem situation:

48. **Arranging Problems by Importance:** Does the youth decide realistically which of a number of problems is most important and should be dealt with first?   1 2 3 4 5

 Problem situation:

49. **Making a Decision:** Does the youth consider possibilities and make choices that he/she feels will be best?   1 2 3 4 5

 Problem situation:

50. **Concentrating on a Task:** Does the youth make those preparations that will help him/her get a job done?   1 2 3 4 5

 Problem situation:

PARENT CHECKLIST

Name_____ Date_____

Child's name_____ Birth date_____

INSTRUCTIONS: Based on your observations in various situations, rate your child's use of the following skills.

Circle 1 if your child is *almost never* good at using the skill.
Circle 2 if your child is *seldom* good at using the skill.
Circle 3 if your child is *sometimes* good at using the skill.
Circle 4 if your child is *often* good at using the skill.
Circle 5 if your child is *almost always* good at using the skill.

	almost never	seldom	sometimes	often	almost always
1. **Listening:** Does your child listen when you or others talk to him/her? Comments:	1	2	3	4	5
2. **Starting a Conversation:** Does your child begin conversations with other people? Comments:	1	2	3	4	5
3. **Having a Conversation:** Does your child talk to others about things of interest to both of them? Comments:	1	2	3	4	5
4. **Asking a Question:** Does your child know how and when to ask questions of another person? Comments:	1	2	3	4	5
5. **Saying Thank You:** Does your child let others know that he/she is grateful for favors, etc.? Comments:	1	2	3	4	5
6. **Introducing Yourself:** Does your child become acquainted with new people on his/her own? Comments:	1	2	3	4	5

Skillstreaming

From *Skillstreaming the Adolescent: A Guide for Teaching Prosocial Skills* (3rd ed.), © 2012 by E. McGinnis, Champaign, IL: Research Press (www.researchpress.com, 800-519-2707).

Column headers (rotated): almost never | seldom | sometimes | often | almost always

7. **Introducing Other People:** Does your child help others become acquainted with one another?

    Comments:

    1   2   3   4   5

8. **Giving a Compliment:** Does your child tell others that he/she likes something about them or something they have done?

    Comments:

    1   2   3   4   5

9. **Asking for Help:** Does your child request assistance when he/she is having difficulty?

    Comments:

    1   2   3   4   5

10. **Joining In:** Does your child take steps to become part of an ongoing activity or group?

    Comments:

    1   2   3   4   5

11. **Giving Instructions:** Does your child clearly explain to others how and why they should do something?

    Comments:

    1   2   3   4   5

12. **Following Instructions:** Does your child carry out instructions from others quickly and correctly?

    Comments:

    1   2   3   4   5

13. **Apologizing:** Does your child tell others he/she is sorry after doing something wrong?

    Comments:

    1   2   3   4   5

14. **Convincing Others:** Does your child attempt to persuade others that his/her ideas are better than theirs?

    Comments:

    1   2   3   4   5

15. **Knowing Your Feelings:** Does your child recognize which emotions he/she has at different times?

            1   2   3   4   5

Comments:

16. **Expressing Your Feelings:** Does your child let others know which emotions he/she is feeling?

            1   2   3   4   5

Comments:

17. **Understanding the Feelings of Others:** Does your child understand what other people are feeling?

            1   2   3   4   5

Comments:

18. **Dealing with Someone Else's Anger:** Does your child try to understand someone else's anger without getting angry himself/herself?

            1   2   3   4   5

Comments:

19. **Expressing Affection:** Does your child let others know that he/she cares about them?

            1   2   3   4   5

Comments:

20. **Dealing with Fear:** Does your child figure out why he/she is afraid and do something to reduce the fear?

            1   2   3   4   5

Comments:

21. **Rewarding Yourself:** Does your child say and do nice things for himself/herself when it is deserved?

            1   2   3   4   5

Comments:

22. **Asking Permission:** Does your child understand when permission is needed and ask the right person for it?

            1   2   3   4   5

Comments:

	almost never	seldom	sometimes	often	almost always

23. **Sharing Something:** Does your child offer to share what he/she has with others?

   Comments:

   1 2 3 4 5

24. **Helping Others:** Does your child give assistance to others who might need or want it?

   Comments:

   1 2 3 4 5

25. **Negotiating:** Does your child help arrive at a plan that satisfies both himself/herself and others who have taken different positions?

   Comments:

   1 2 3 4 5

26. **Using Self-Control:** Does your child control his/her temper so things do not get out of hand?

   Comments:

   1 2 3 4 5

27. **Standing Up for Your Rights:** Does your child assert his/her rights by letting other people know where he/she stands on an issue?

   Comments:

   1 2 3 4 5

28. **Responding to Teasing:** Does your child deal in a constructive way with being teased?

   Comments:

   1 2 3 4 5

29. **Avoiding Trouble with Others:** Does your child stay out of situations that might get him/her in trouble?

   Comments:

   1 2 3 4 5

30. **Keeping Out of Fights:** Does your child figure out ways other than fighting to handle difficult situations?

   Comments:

   1 2 3 4 5

	almost never	seldom	sometimes	often	almost always

31. **Making a Complaint:** Does your child disagree with others in acceptable ways?

    1   2   3   4   5

Comments:

32. **Answering a Complaint:** Does your child try to arrive at a fair solution to someone else's justified complaint?

    1   2   3   4   5

Comments:

33. **Being a Good Sport:** Does your child express an honest compliment to others about how they played a game?

    1   2   3   4   5

Comments:

34. **Dealing with Embarrassment:** Does your child do things that help him/her feel less embarrassed or self-conscious?

    1   2   3   4   5

Comments:

35. **Dealing with Being Left Out:** Does your child deal positively with being left out of some activity?

    1   2   3   4   5

Comments:

36. **Standing Up for a Friend:** Does your child let other people know when a friend has not been treated fairly?

    1   2   3   4   5

Comments:

37. **Responding to Persuasion:** Does your child think alternatives through before responding to persuasion from others?

    1   2   3   4   5

Comments:

38. **Responding to Failure:** Does your child figure out the reasons he/she failed at something and how to correct the failure?

    1   2   3   4   5

Comments:

39. **Dealing with Contradictory Messages:** Does your child recognize and deal with it when others say or do one thing but also indicate they mean something else?

    Comments:

	almost never	seldom	sometimes	often	almost always
39.	1	2	3	4	5
40.	1	2	3	4	5
41.	1	2	3	4	5
42.	1	2	3	4	5
43.	1	2	3	4	5
44.	1	2	3	4	5
45.	1	2	3	4	5

40. **Dealing with an Accusation:** Does your child figure out what he/she has been accused of, then use constructive ways of dealing with it?

    Comments:

41. **Getting Ready for a Difficult Conversation:** Does your child plan on the best way to present his/her own point of view before a stressful conversation?

    Comments:

42. **Dealing with Group Pressure:** Does your child decide what he/she wants to do when others are urging him/her to do something else?

    Comments:

43. **Deciding on Something to Do:** Does your child deal with feeling bored by starting an interesting activity?

    Comments:

44. **Deciding What Caused a Problem:** Does your child try to find out whether an event was caused by something under his/her control?

    Comments:

45. **Setting a Goal:** Does your child realistically plan on what he/she would like to accomplish before starting a task?

    Comments:

46. **Deciding on Your Abilities:** Does your child accurately figure out how well he/she might do at a particular task?

    1   2   3   4   5

Comments:

47. **Gathering Information:** Does your child decide what he/she needs to know and how to get that information?

    1   2   3   4   5

Comments:

48. **Arranging Problems by Importance:** Does your child realistically decide which of a number of problems is most important and should be dealt with first?

    1   2   3   4   5

Comments:

49. **Making a Decision:** Does your child consider possibilities and make choices that he/she feels will be best?

    1   2   3   4   5

Comments:

50. **Concentrating on a Task:** Does your child pay full attention to the task on which he/she is working?

    1   2   3   4   5

Comments:

PARTICIPANT CHECKLIST

INSTRUCTIONS: Each of the questions will ask you about how well you do something. Next to each question is a number.

Circle number 1 if you *almost never* do what the question asks.
Circle number 2 if you *seldom* do it.
Circle number 3 if you *sometimes* do it.
Circle number 4 if you do it *often*.
Circle number 5 if you *almost always* do it.

There are no right or wrong answers to these questions. Answer the way you really feel about each question.

	almost never	seldom	sometimes	often	almost always
1. Do I listen to someone who is talking to me?	1	2	3	4	5
2. Do I start conversations with other people?	1	2	3	4	5
3. Do I talk with other people about things that interest both of us?	1	2	3	4	5
4. Do I ask questions when I need or want to know something?	1	2	3	4	5
5. Do I say thank you when someone does something for me?	1	2	3	4	5
6. Do I introduce myself to new people?	1	2	3	4	5
7. Do I introduce people who haven't met before to each other?	1	2	3	4	5
8. Do I tell other people when I like how they are or something they have done?	1	2	3	4	5
9. Do I ask for help when I am having difficulty doing something?	1	2	3	4	5
10. Do I try to join in when others are doing something I'd like to be part of?	1	2	3	4	5
11. Do I clearly explain to others how and why they should do something?	1	2	3	4	5
12. Do I carry out instructions from other people quickly and correctly?	1	2	3	4	5

Skillstreaming

From *Skillstreaming the Adolescent: A Guide for Teaching Prosocial Skills* (3rd ed.), © 2012 by E. McGinnis, Champaign, IL: Research Press (www.researchpress.com, 800-519-2707).

		almost never	seldom	sometimes	often	almost always

13. Do I apologize to others when I have done something wrong? 1 2 3 4 5

14. Do I try to convince others that my ideas are better than theirs? 1 2 3 4 5

15. Do I recognize the feelings I have at different times? 1 2 3 4 5

16. Do I let others know what I am feeling and do it in a good way? 1 2 3 4 5

17. Do I understand what other people are feeling? 1 2 3 4 5

18. Do I try to understand and not get angry when someone else is angry? 1 2 3 4 5

19. Do I let others know when I care about them? 1 2 3 4 5

20. Do I know what makes me afraid and do things so that I don't stay that way? 1 2 3 4 5

21. Do I say and do nice things for myself when I have earned it? 1 2 3 4 5

22. Do I understand when permission is needed to do something and ask the right person for it? 1 2 3 4 5

23. Do I offer to share what I have with others? 1 2 3 4 5

24. Do I help others who might need or want help? 1 2 3 4 5

25. Do I try to make both of us satisfied with the result when someone and I disagree? 1 2 3 4 5

26. Do I control my temper when I feel upset? 1 2 3 4 5

27. Do I stand up for my rights to let other people know what I think or feel? 1 2 3 4 5

28. Do I stay in control when someone teases me? 1 2 3 4 5

29. Do I try to stay out of situations that might get me in trouble? 1 2 3 4 5

30. Do I figure out ways other than fighting to handle difficult situations? 1 2 3 4 5

31. Do I make complaints I have about others in a fair way? 1 2 3 4 5

	almost never	seldom	sometimes	often	almost always

32. Do I handle complaints made against me in a fair way? 1 2 3 4 5

33. Do I say nice things to others after a game about how they played? 1 2 3 4 5

34. Do I do things that help me feel less embarrassed when difficulties happen? 1 2 3 4 5

35. Do I deal positively with being left out of some activity? 1 2 3 4 5

36. Do I let people know when I feel a friend has not been treated fairly? 1 2 3 4 5

37. Do I think choices through before answering when someone is trying to convince me about something? 1 2 3 4 5

38. Do I try to figure out the reasons it happened when I fail at something? 1 2 3 4 5

39. Do I deal with it well when someone says or does one thing but means something else? 1 2 3 4 5

40. Do I deal with it well when someone accuses me of doing something? 1 2 3 4 5

41. Do I plan ahead the best ways to handle it before I have a difficult conversation? 1 2 3 4 5

42. Do I decide what I want to do when others pressure me to do something else? 1 2 3 4 5

43. Do I think of good things to do and then do them when I feel bored? 1 2 3 4 5

44. When there is a problem, do I try to find out what caused it? 1 2 3 4 5

45. Do I think about what I would like to do before I start a new task? 1 2 3 4 5

46. Do I think about what I am really able to do before I start a new task? 1 2 3 4 5

47. Before doing something, do I decide what I need to know and how to find out?   1   2   3   4   5

48. Do I decide which problem is most important and should be handled first?   1   2   3   4   5

49. Do I think about different possibilities and choose the one that is best?   1   2   3   4   5

50. Do I pay full attention to whatever I am working on?   1   2   3   4   5

GROUPING CHART

	student names															
GROUP I: Beginning Social Skills																
1. Listening																
2. Starting a Conversation																
3. Having a Conversation																
4. Asking a Question																
5. Saying Thank You																
6. Introducing Yourself																
7. Introducing Other People																
8. Giving a Compliment																
GROUP II: Advanced Social Skills																
9. Asking for Help																
10. Joining In																
11. Giving Instructions																
12. Following Instructions																
13. Apologizing																
14. Convincing Others																
GROUP III: Skills for Dealing with Feelings																
15. Knowing Your Feelings																
16. Expressing Your Feelings																
17. Understanding the Feelings of Others																
18. Dealing with Someone Else's Anger																
19. Expressing Affection																
20. Dealing with Fear																
21. Rewarding Yourself																
GROUP IV: Skill Alternatives to Aggression																
22. Asking Permission																
23. Sharing Something																
24. Helping Others																

**Skillstreaming**

From *Skillstreaming the Adolescent: A Guide for Teaching Prosocial Skills* (3rd ed.), © 2012 by E. McGinnis, Champaign, IL: Research Press (www.researchpress.com, 800-519-2707).

	student names															
25. Negotiating																
26. Using Self-Control																
27. Standing Up for Your Rights																
28. Responding to Teasing																
29. Avoiding Trouble with Others																
30. Keeping Out of Fights																
GROUP V: **Skills for Dealing with Stress**																
31. Making a Complaint																
32. Answering a Complaint																
33. Being a Good Sport																
34. Dealing with Embarrassment																
35. Dealing with Being Left Out																
36. Standing Up for a Friend																
37. Responding to Persuasion																
38. Responding to Failure																
39. Dealing with Contradictory Messages																
40. Dealing with an Accusation																
41. Getting Ready for a Difficult Conversation																
42. Dealing with Group Pressure																
GROUP VI: Planning Skills																
43. Deciding on Something to Do																
44. Deciding What Caused a Problem																
45. Setting a Goal																
46. Deciding on Your Abilities																
47. Gathering Information																
48. Arranging Problems by Importance																
49. Making a Decision																
50. Concentrating on a Task																

HOMEWORK REPORT I

Name _____ Date _____

FILL IN NOW

1. What skill will you use? _____

2. What are the steps for the skill?

3. Where will you try the skill? _____

4. With whom will you try the skill? _____

5. When will you try the skill? _____

FILL IN AFTER YOU PRACTICE THE SKILL

1. What happened when you did the homework?

   _____

   _____

2. Which skill steps did you really follow?

   _____

   _____

3. How good a job did you do in using the skill? *(check one)*

   ☐ excellent   ☐ good   ☐ fair   ☐ poor

From *Skillstreaming the Adolescent: A Guide for Teaching Prosocial Skills* (3rd ed.), © 2012 by E. McGinnis, Champaign, IL: Research Press (www.researchpress.com, 800-519-2707).

293

HOMEWORK REPORT 2

Name _____ Date _____

FILL IN NOW

1. What skill will you use? _____

2. What are the steps for the skill?

3. Where will you try the skill? _____

4. With whom will you try the skill? _____

5. When will you try the skill? _____

6. If you do an excellent job, how will you reward yourself? _____

7. If you do a good job, how will you reward yourself? _____

8. If you do a fair job, how will you reward yourself? _____

FILL IN AFTER YOU PRACTICE THE SKILL

1. What happened when you did the homework?

   _____

   _____

2. Which skill steps did you really follow?

   _____

   _____

3. How good a job did you do in using the skill? *(check one)*

   ☐ excellent   ☐ good   ☐ fair   ☐ poor

4. What do you think your next homework assignment should be?

   _____

Skillstreaming

From *Skillstreaming the Adolescent: A Guide for Teaching Prosocial Skills* (3rd ed.), © 2012 by E. McGinnis, Champaign, IL: Research Press (www.researchpress.com, 800-519-2707).

SKILL CONTRACT

Name _____

Date(s) of contract _____

I agree to use the skill of _____

when _____

_____

If I do, then _____

_____

Participant signature _____

Leader/staff signature _____

Review date(s) _____

Name _____ Date _____

Skill _____

SKILL STEPS

NOTES

_____

_____

_____

_____

_____

_____

Skillstreaming

SELF-RECORDING FORM 1

Name _____ Date _____

INSTRUCTIONS: Each time you use the skill, write down when and how well you did.

Skill _____

When?	How well did you do?
	(excellent, good, fair, poor)

1. _____   _____

   _____

   _____

2. _____   _____

   _____

   _____

3. _____   _____

   _____

   _____

4. _____   _____

   _____

   _____

Name _____ Date _____

INSTRUCTIONS: Each time you use any of these skills (or skill combinations), write down when and how well you did.

SKILLS

_____

_____

When?	**How well did you do?** *(excellent, good, fair, poor)*

1. _____   _____

   _____

   _____

What happened as a result of your skill use?

_____

_____

When?	**How well did you do?** *(excellent, good, fair, poor)*

2. _____   _____

   _____

   _____

What happened as a result of your skill use?

_____

_____

Skillstreaming From *Skillstreaming the Adolescent: A Guide for Teaching Prosocial Skills* (3rd ed.), © 2012 by E. McGinnis, Champaign, IL: Research Press (www.researchpress.com, 800-519-2707).

Date _____

Dear Parent or Guardian:

Our class is learning to handle a variety of day-to-day concerns that face adolescents in positive, prosocial ways. Following instructions, understanding the feelings of others, negotiating, dealing with group pressure, and avoiding trouble with others are some of the skills we will be working on. We are all learning and practicing the specific steps to handle these skills in acceptable ways.

The process we are using to learn these skills is called Skillstreaming. First, students watch someone else use the skill. Then each student will try out the skill in a role-play situation and receive feedback about how well he or she performed the skill. Finally, each student will be asked to practice the skill in a real-life situation.

Every two weeks or so, whenever a new skill has been introduced, we will be e-mailing or sending a note to you that describes the skill and its steps. We hope that you will review this note with your student and help with practicing the skill at home.

Please feel free to call or e-mail me should you have questions.

Sincerely,

_____

Phone _____

E-mail _____

SCHOOL-HOME NOTE

Student _____ Date _____

DESCRIPTION OF LESSON

Skill name _____

Skill steps:

Skill purpose, use, value _____

_____

DESCRIPTION OF SKILL HOMEWORK

_____

_____

REQUEST TO PARENTS

1. Provide skill homework recognition and reward.

2. Respond positively to your child's skill use.

3. Return this note with your comments (on the back) about:

   • Quality of homework done

   • Rewards that work/don't work at home

   • Suggestions or questions regarding this skill, other skills, additional homework assignments, other ways to promote school-home collaboration, and so on

4. Please sign and return this form to _____

   by _____

Signature _____ Date _____

PARENT/STAFF SKILL RATING FORM

Date _____

_____ is learning
(participant)

the skill of _____

The steps involved in this skill are:

1. Did he or she demonstrate this skill in your presence?   ☐ yes   ☐ no

2. How would you rate his or her skill demonstration? *(check one)*

     ☐ poor   ☐ below average   ☐ average   ☐ above average   ☐ excellent

3. How sincere was he or she in performing the skill? *(check one)*

     ☐ not sincere   ☐ somewhat sincere   ☐ very sincere

Comments:

_____

_____

_____

Please sign and return this form to _____

by _____

Signature _____ Date _____

From *Skillstreaming the Adolescent: A Guide for Teaching Prosocial Skills* (3rd ed.), © 2012 by E. McGinnis, Champaign, IL: Research Press (www.researchpress.com, 800-519-2707).

Program Integrity Checklists

LEADER'S CHECKLIST

INSTRUCTIONS: Leader(s) may complete this checklist at the conclusion of the Skillstreaming group by marking "yes" or "no" relative to each procedure implemented.

Group leader(s) _____

Date of group _____ Time of group _____

	Yes	No
Step 1: Define the skill		
1. The skill to be taught was defined, and the group understood its meaning.	☐	☐
2. Skill steps were presented and discussed (via poster or skill cards).	☐	☐
(For all sessions after the first)		
3. Group members' skill homework was discussed.	☐	☐
4. Appropriate reinforcement was provided for group members who completed homework.	☐	☐
Step 2: Model the skill		
5. Two examples of the skill were modeled.	☐	☐
6. Each skill step was identified as the modeling unfolded.	☐	☐
7. Modeling displays were relevant to group members' real-life circumstances.	☐	☐
8. Group members were directed to watch for the steps being modeled.	☐	☐
9. The model was friendly and helpful.	☐	☐
10. A coping model was presented if indicated.	☐	☐
11. The model used self-talk to illustrate the steps and thinking about skill performance.	☐	☐
12. The modeling display depicted positive outcomes.	☐	☐
13. The model was rewarded for skill performance (following the skill steps).	☐	☐
Step 3: Establish student skill need		
14. Each group member's need for skill use was defined (when, where, and with whom) and listed.	☐	☐
Step 4: Select the first role-player		
15. The main actor was selected for role-play (e.g., "Who would like to go first?")	☐	☐
Step 5: Set up the role-play		
16. Main actor selected a coactor who reminded him/her most of the real-life person with whom he/she has the skill need.	☐	☐
17. Main actor described the physical setting, events preceding the problem, mood/manner of the person, and any other relevant information.	☐	☐

	Yes	No

Step 6: Conduct the role-play

		Yes	No
18.	Group members were assigned specific step(s) to observe.	☐	☐
19.	Main actor was instructed to follow the behavioral steps.	☐	☐
20.	Main actor was reminded to "think aloud."	☐	☐
21.	Coactor was reminded to stay in the role of the other person.	☐	☐
22.	Group leader assisted the main actor as needed (pointed to skill steps, coached).	☐	☐

Step 7: Provide performance feedback

		Yes	No
23.	Coactor was asked to provide feedback (e.g., how he/she felt, how well the main actor enacted the steps).	☐	☐
24.	Group members were asked if the main actor followed each step.	☐	☐
25.	Leaders provided appropriate feedback (praise, approval, encouragement), identifying specific aspects of the main actor's performance.	☐	☐
26.	Reinforcement in an amount consistent with the quality of role-play was provided.	☐	☐
27.	Main actor was invited to give comments.	☐	☐

Step 8: Select the next role-player

		Yes	No
28.	Volunteer participant was asked to act as the main actor in the next role-play and coached in Steps 5 through 7.	☐	☐
29.	All group members were given a chance to role-play, or plans were made to role-play for those who did not have a chance.	☐	☐

Step 9: Assign skill homework

		Yes	No
30.	Skill homework was assigned to each main actor.	☐	☐
31.	Assistance was provided as needed in identifying the day, place, with whom the skill will be used, and so forth.	☐	☐

TOTAL YES _____   **TOTAL NO** _____

OBSERVER'S CHECKLIST

INSTRUCTIONS: A highly skilled observer may complete this observation checklist as the Skillstreaming group is taking place. The observer will note whether leader(s) completed each procedure with a low level of competence (score 1), medium proficiency (score 2), or a high level of skill (score 3). At the conclusion of the observation, the observer may provide leader(s) with recommendations for specific steps needing improvement.

Group leader(s) _____ Observers _____

Date of group _____ Time of group _____

	Proficiency Level		
	1	2	3

Step 1: Define the skill

1. The skill to be taught was defined and the group understood its meaning. ☐ ☐ ☐
2. Skill steps were presented and discussed (via poster or skill cards). ☐ ☐ ☐

(For all sessions after the first)

3. Group members' skill homework was discussed. ☐ ☐ ☐
4. Appropriate reinforcement was provided for group members who completed homework. ☐ ☐ ☐

Step 2: Model the skill

5. Two examples of the skill were modeled. ☐ ☐ ☐
6. Each skill step was identified as the modeling unfolded. ☐ ☐ ☐
7. Modeling displays were relevant to group members' real-life circumstances. ☐ ☐ ☐
8. Group members were directed to watch for the steps being modeled. ☐ ☐ ☐
9. The model was friendly and helpful. ☐ ☐ ☐
10. A coping model was presented if indicated. ☐ ☐ ☐
11. The model used self-talk to illustrate the steps and thinking about skill performance. ☐ ☐ ☐
12. The modeling display depicted positive outcomes. ☐ ☐ ☐
13. The model was rewarded for skill performance (following the skill steps). ☐ ☐ ☐

Step 3: Establish student skill need

14. Each group member's need for skill use was defined (when, where, and with whom) and listed. ☐ ☐ ☐

Step 4: Select the first role-player

15. The main actor was selected for role-play (e.g., "Who would like to go first?") ☐ ☐ ☐

From *Skillstreaming the Adolescent: A Guide for Teaching Prosocial Skills* (3rd ed.), © 2012 by E. McGinnis, Champaign, IL: Research Press (www.researchpress.com, 800-519-2707).

	Proficiency Level		
	1	2	3

Step 5: Set up the role-play

16. Main actor selected a coactor who reminded him/her most of the real-life person with whom he/she has the skill need. ☐ ☐ ☐

17. Main actor described the physical setting, events preceding the problem, mood/manner of the person, and any other relevant information. ☐ ☐ ☐

Step 6: Conduct the role-play

18. Group members were assigned specific step(s) to observe. ☐ ☐ ☐

19. Main actor was instructed to follow the behavioral steps. ☐ ☐ ☐

20. Main actor was reminded to "think aloud." ☐ ☐ ☐

21. Coactor was reminded to stay in the role of the other person. ☐ ☐ ☐

22. Group leader assisted the main actor as needed (pointed to skill steps, coached). ☐ ☐ ☐

Step 7: Provide performance feedback

23. Coactor was asked to provide feedback (e.g., how he/she felt, how well the main actor enacted the steps). ☐ ☐ ☐

24. Group members were asked if the main actor followed each step. ☐ ☐ ☐

25. Leaders provided appropriate feedback (praise, approval, encouragement), identifying specific aspects of the main actor's performance. ☐ ☐ ☐

26. Reinforcement in an amount consistent with the quality of role-play was provided. ☐ ☐ ☐

27. Main actor was invited to give comments. ☐ ☐ ☐

Step 8: Select the next role-player

28. Volunteer participant asked to act as the main actor in the next role-play. Repeated Steps 5 through 7. ☐ ☐ ☐

29. All group members were given a chance to role-play, or plans were made to role-play for those who did not have a chance. ☐ ☐ ☐

Step 9: Assign skill homework

30. Skill homework was assigned to each main actor. ☐ ☐ ☐

31. Assistance was provided as needed in identifying the day, place, with whom the skill will be used, and so forth. ☐ ☐ ☐

TOTAL _____

59 points or below	Group leader intervention needed.
60–74 points	Continued monitoring of instruction necessary.
75–83 points	Consultation with master leader available.
84–93 points	Mastery of intervention demonstrated.

Comments:

Recommendations for improvement:

GENERALIZATION INTEGRITY CHECKLIST

Leader(s)_____

Group _____Date(s) of review _____ _____

INSTRUCTIONS: This self-rating checklist is designed to assist group leader(s) in enhancing generalization of student skill learning. While a numerical score is not computed, leader(s) may use this checklist to both plan instruction and evaluate the emphasis placed on generalization following instruction.

	Minimal	Average	Strong
Before session			
1. Instruction is provided to the same peers with whom the target students interact outside of the group.	☐	☐	☐
2. One instructor has ongoing, regular contact with the students.	☐	☐	☐
3. Skills likely to provide natural reinforcement are included.	☐	☐	☐
During session			
4. Students know the specific behavioral skill steps and can perform them well.	☐	☐	☐
5. Attempts made to create similarities between the instructional and real-life situations and settings.	☐	☐	☐
6. Numerous trials of correct skill performance provided.	☐	☐	☐
7. Variability of situations (range of settings, various people, variety of reasons for skill use, various cues) provided.	☐	☐	☐
8. When possible, instruction occured in the real-life environment where the skill is to be used.	☐	☐	☐
9. Some flexibility allowed to meet individual student needs and settings.	☐	☐	☐
After session			
10. Homework assignments provided after students competently performed the role-plays.	☐	☐	☐
11. Skill use prompted or coached when daily situations suggest skill use.	☐	☐	☐
12. Skill use reinforced with gradual thinning and delaying of reinforcement.	☐	☐	☐
13. Prompts and reminders gradually faded.	☐	☐	☐
14. Instruction in self-mediated generalization (e.g., self-recording, self-reinforcement) provided as appropriate to student need.	☐	☐	☐
15. Booster or coaching sessions provided as needed.	☐	☐	☐
16. Plan for addressing competing behaviors developed and implemented as needed.	☐	☐	☐
17. Strategies for parent involvement implemented.	☐	☐	☐

Skillstreaming

Behavior Management Techniques

Behaviors that both promote and inhibit skill learning can be influenced by behavior management techniques based on the principles of behavior modification. The effectiveness of behavior modification rests on a firm experimental foundation. Although not all of the techniques described in this appendix are equally valid for all age groups, a basic understanding of them is critical to managing the Skillstreaming group and to developing individual behavior intervention plans for those children and adolescents who need them. The techniques described are grouped under the behavioral principles of reinforcement and punishment.

Behavior modification techniques are derived from formal learning theory, systematically applied in an effort to change observable behavior and rigorously evaluated by experimental research. These procedures are based on the core premise that behavior is largely determined by its environmental consequences (Ferster & Skinner, 1957; Skinner, 1938, 1953). Operationally, this premise has been employed in techniques that contingently present or withdraw rewards or punishments (i.e., environmental consequences) to alter the behavior preceding these consequences. It is this contingent quality that has led to the use of the term *contingency management* to describe most of these activities.

REINFORCEMENT

Reinforcement can be of two types: positive or negative. Positive reinforcement is central to promoting enduring change in Skillstreaming and other learning efforts and is therefore discussed here at length. Negative reinforcement is far less common but does play a role in the classroom and Skillstreaming group.

Positive Reinforcement

A *positive reinforcer* is any event that increases the subsequent frequency of a behavior it follows. Presenting positive reinforcement to the student following and contingent upon the occurrence of appropriate behavior is an effective way to substitute appropriate for inappropriate behaviors. Teachers and other school-based staff have worked successfully with four types of positive reinforcers: material, social, activity, and token. (For a list of commonly used reinforcers, see Table 6 in chapter 6.)

Material reinforcers (sometimes called *tangible reinforcers*) are actual goods or objects presented to the individual contingent upon enactment of appropriate behaviors. An important subcategory of material reinforcement, *primary reinforcement,* occurs when the contingent event presented satisfies a basic biological need. Food is one such primary reinforcer.

Social reinforcers—most often expressed in the form of attention, praise, or approval—are particularly powerful and are frequently used in the Skillstreaming group. Both teacher experience and extensive experimental research testify to the potency of teacher-dispensed social reinforcement in influencing personal, interpersonal, and academic student behaviors.

Activity reinforcers are events a child or adolescent freely chooses when an opportunity exists to engage in several different activities. Given freedom to choose, many youth will watch television or spend time on the computer rather than complete their homework. The parent wishing to use this type of activity reinforcer may specify that the youth may watch television or use the computer for a given time period contingent upon the prior completion of the homework. Stated otherwise, the opportunity to perform a higher probability behavior (given free choice) can be used as a reinforcer for a lower probability behavior.

Token reinforcers, usually employed when more easily implemented social reinforcers prove insufficient, are symbolic items (chips, coupons, points, etc.) provided contingent upon the performance of appropriate or desirable behaviors. Tokens are then exchangeable for a wide range of material or activity reinforcers. A *token economy* is a system by which specific numbers of tokens are contingently gained and exchanged for the backup material or activity reinforcers.

In making decisions about which type of reinforcer to use with a given youth, the teacher should keep in mind that social reinforcement (e.g., attention, praise, approval) is easiest to implement on a continuing basis and is most likely to lead to enduring behavior change. Therefore, it is the type of reinforcement the teacher will wish to use most frequently. Unfortunately, in the initial stages of a behavior change effort—especially when aggressive, disruptive, and other inappropriate behaviors are probably being richly rewarded by teacher and peer attention, as well as by tangible reinforcers—the teacher will likely need to rely more on material and activity reinforcers.

A token reinforcement system may prove effective as the initial reinforcement strategy. Reinforcement preferences change over time, and teacher views of the appropriate reward value of desirable behaviors also change over time. Both variables are easily reflected in token-level adjustments. Some issues to be considered prior to implementing a token system (Kaplan & Carter, 2005) and are summarized as follows:

1. Identify what the student needs to do, the specific behaviors, to earn tokens.

2. Post a list of these contingent behaviors (e.g., somewhere in the classroom, on the student's desk) to remind him or her of the expectations.

3. Decide what the tokens will be. Tokens should be age appropriate and might include check marks, tallies, tickets, and so forth. Provisions need to be made to prevent students from having tokens that they have not earned (e.g., accept only tokens validated with the teacher's signature).

4. Determine how many tokens the students will earn for given behaviors and how much students will be charged (in tokens) for the reinforcers.

5. Determine the backup reinforcers—for example, prizes, entitlements (privileges students normally receive without having to earn them), other privileges.

6. Decide who will give the tokens (typically the teacher, associate, peer tutor).

7. Determine when the tokens will be given. Typically, tokens should be given as soon after the behavior is demonstrated as possible and according to the reinforcement schedule that is being followed with a particular student.

8. Determine how the tokens will be given (e.g., Given directly to the student? Marked

on a card? Placed in a bank?). This system should be kept simple.

9. Determine when the tokens will be redeemed. The primary consideration should be the student's needs (i.e., how long the student is able to wait before receiving the reinforcer). Activities or privileges that may be disruptive to the instructional setting will require additional consideration.

Tokens, as well as other tangible rewards, should be combined with social reinforcers. It is critical to remember that, with few exceptions, reliance on material, activity, or token reinforcement eventually should give way to reliance on more real-life social reinforcement.

The potency of many reinforcers is increased when the reward, in addition to being inherently desirable, also brings reinforcement from peers and others (e.g., ordering a DVD to watch as a group, earning extra gym or activity time for the class). A further benefit of certain activity reinforcers (e.g., playing a game with peers, helping in the principal's office) is the degree to which the activity, while serving as a reward, also helps the student practice one or more Skillstreaming skills.

Identifying Reinforcers

Identifying positive reinforcers for a given child or adolescent is often necessary prior to presenting such events contingently upon the occurrence of desirable behaviors. Given that almost any event may serve as a reinforcer for one individual but not another, how can the teacher decide which reinforcers may best be used? Simply, the youth may be asked straightforwardly which items he or she would like to earn. This direct approach may be insufficient because youth are unaware of the full range of reinforcers available to them or may discount in advance the possibility that a reinforcer will actually be given. When this is the case, other identification procedures must be employed. Carr (1981) and others have reported three procedures typically used for this purpose.

First, the teacher can often make an accurate determination of whether a given event is functioning as a reinforcer by carefully *observing effects* on the youth. The event probably is reinforcing if the youth (a) asks that the event be repeated, (b) seems happy during the event's occurrence, (c) seems unhappy when the event ends, or (d) will work to earn the event. If one or more of these reactions are observed, chances are good that the event is a positive reinforcer and that it can be contingently provided to strengthen appropriate, nonaggressive, or interactive behaviors. Second, *observing choices* can be helpful. As noted earlier in connection with activity reinforcers, when a youth is free to choose from among several equally available activities, which one the youth chooses and how long he or she engages in it are clues to whether an event is reinforcing. Finally, *questionnaires* have been effectively used to identify positive reinforcers.

As noted earlier, which objects or activities will in fact be reinforcing for a given youth will vary from individual to individual and from time to time. In addition, the strength of selected reinforcers often decreases the more frequently they are used. Some teachers therefore find it useful to create a "reinforcement menu," or a list of rewards from which the student can choose. Such a menu may be in the form of an actual list, or it may be in the form of coupons for tangible and activity rewards. Each coupon may be a voucher for a particular amount of a given reinforcer (e.g., five minutes of computer time, three-minute locker pass). Using a reinforcement menu prevents students from becoming satiated with one reward when it is offered over a period of time and also allows them to make their own reinforcement choices.

Presenting Positive Reinforcers

As noted, a basic principle of contingency management is that the presentation of a reinforcing event contingent upon the occurrence of a given behavior will function to increase the likelihood of the reoccurrence of that behavior. A number of considerations influence the success of the reinforcement effort and should be reflected in the actual presentation of reinforcers.

Contingency

The connection between the desirable behavior and the subsequent reward should be made explicit. As is true for all contingency management efforts, this description should be behaviorally specific—that is, the connection between particular behavioral acts and reinforcement should be emphasized over behaviorally ambiguous concepts like "good behavior" or "being well behaved." Instead, comments like "Good job taking turns" and "Good listening" will help the student understand what has gained him or her the desired reinforcement.

Immediacy

The more immediately the reinforcer follows the desirable behavior, the more likely it is to be effective. Rapid reinforcement augments the message that the immediately preceding behavior is desirable, whereas delayed reinforcement increases the risk that an inappropriate behavior will occur between the positive behavior and the reinforcement. In other words, the following sequence occurs: A (desirable behavior), B (undesirable behavior), and C (reinforcement intended for A that in actuality reinforces B).

Consistency

The effects of positive reinforcement on behavior are usually gradual, not dramatic, working slowly to strengthen behavior over a period of time. Thus, it is important that positive reinforcement be presented consistently. Consistency means not only that the teacher must be consistent but also that the teacher must attempt to match his or her reinforcement efforts with similar efforts from as many other important persons in the student's life as possible. This means, ideally, that when the student enacts the behavior to be reinforced—in school in the presence of other teachers, at home in the presence of parents or siblings, or at play in the presence of peers—such reinforcement will be forthcoming.

Frequency

When first trying to establish a new appropriate behavior, the teacher reinforces all or almost all instances of that behavior. This high frequency of reinforcement is necessary to establish the behavior in the individual's behavioral repertoire. Once it seems clear that the behavior has actually been acquired, the teacher thins the reinforcement schedule, decreasing presentation so that only some of the student's desirable behaviors are followed by the reinforcement. This schedule, known as *partial reinforcement,* contributes to the continuation of the appropriate behavior because it parallels the sometimes reinforced/sometimes not reaction the appropriate behavior will elicit in other settings from other people. Partial reinforcement of the appropriate behaviors may be on a fixed-time schedule (e.g., at the end of each Skillstreaming session), on a fixed-number-of-response schedule (e.g., every fifth instance of the appropriate behavior), or on variable-time or number-of-response schedules. In any event, the basic strategy for reinforcement frequency remains a rich level for initial learning and partial reinforcement to sustain performance.

Amount

Learning (i.e., acquiring knowledge about how to perform new behaviors) and performance (i.e., overtly using these behaviors) are different aspects of behavior. The amount of reinforcement provided influences performance much more than it does learning. Children and adolescents will learn new appropriate behaviors just about as fast for a small reward as for a large reward, but they are more likely to perform the behaviors on a continuing basis when large rewards are involved. Yet rewards can be too large, causing a *satiation effect* in which youth lose interest in seeking the reinforcement because it is "too much of a good thing." Or rewards can be too small: too little time on the computer, too few tokens, too thin a social reinforcement schedule. The optimal amount can be determined empirically. If a youth has in the past worked energetically to obtain a particular reinforcer but gradually slacks off and seems to lose interest in obtaining it, a satiation effect has probably occurred, and the amount of reinforcement should be reduced. On the other hand, if a youth seems unwilling to work for a reinforcer believed desirable, it can be given once or twice for free—that is, not contingent on a specific desirable behavior. If the youth seems to enjoy the reinforcer or wants more, the amount used may have been too little. The amount can be increased and made contingent; observations will then show whether it is yielding the desired effect. If so, the amount of reinforcement offered is appropriate.

Variety

A type of reinforcement satiation parallel to a satiation effect due to excessive reinforcement occurs when the teacher uses the same approving phrase or other reward over and over again. Students may perceive such reinforcement as mechanical, and they may lose interest in or decrease responsiveness to it. By varying the content of the reinforcer, the teacher can maintain its potency. Thus, instead of repeating "Nice job" four or five times, using a mix of comments (e.g., "Well done," "Good work," "You really listened") is more likely to yield a sustained effect.

Pairing with praise

As noted previously, social reinforcement is most germane to enduring behavior change, although there are circumstances under which material, activity, or token reinforcers are at least initially more appropriate. To move toward social reinforcement, the teacher pairs all presentations of material, activity, or token rewards with some expression of social reinforcement: an approving comment, a pat on the back, a wink, a smile, and so forth. Walker (1979) has noted a major benefit of this tactic:

By virtue of being consistently paired with reinforcement delivery, praise can take on the reinforcing properties of the actual reinforcer(s) used. This is especially important since teacher praise is not always initially effective. . . . By systematically increasing the incentive value of praise through pairing, the teacher is in a position to gradually reduce the frequency of (material, activity, or token) reinforcement and to substitute praise. After systematic pairing, the teacher's praise may be much more effective in maintaining the child's appropriate behavior. (p. 108)

Shaping

The first time a student practices an unfamiliar behavior, the performance may be rough or imperfect. This is true for classroom behaviors such as participating or paying attention, which a particular student may not have been exhibiting often. Therefore, even a partial or flawed performance should be reinforced early on. As the student becomes more confident and skilled in performing the behavior, rewards are given for the improved skill behaviors and eliminated for the earlier and less adequate approximations. Gradually, the rewarded performance will come to approximate the target behavior. The student's performance is thus "shaped" by the teacher. Social behavior can be shaped according to the following guidelines, developed by Sloane (1976):

1. Find some behavior in which the student is currently engaging that is a better approximation of your goal than the student's usual behavior and reinforce this approximation each time it occurs.

2. When an approximation has become more frequent for several days, select a slightly better one for reinforcement and stop reinforcing the first.

3. Ensure that each approximation is only slightly different from the last one.

4. Let a new approximation receive many reinforcements before moving on to another approximation.

5. Reinforce any behavior that is better than that currently required.

Behavior Contracting

Behavior contracting, sometimes known as contingency contracting, does not rely on the management of contingencies, but it can be effective in helping children and adolescents understand and change problem behaviors. A behavior contract is a written agreement between a leader and group member. It is a document each signs that specifies desirable behaviors and their contingent positive consequences, as well as undesirable behaviors and their contingent undesirable consequences. As Homme, Csanyi, Gonzales, & Rechs (1969) specify in their early description of this procedure, such contracts will more reliably lead to desirable behaviors when the contract payoff is immediate; approximations to the desirable behavior are rewarded; the contract rewards accomplishment rather than obedience; accomplishment precedes reward; and the contract is fair, clear, honest, positive, and systematically implemented.

Group Reinforcement

Children and adolescents are very responsive to the influence of their peers. This phenomenon can be used to encourage the performance of infrequent but desirable behaviors. In using group reinforcement, the teacher provides a reward (e.g., privilege, activity) to the entire group contingent on the cooperative behavior of individual group members. If the reward is meaningful and desirable to the entire group, group members are likely to put pressure on one another to behave appropriately. For example:

> For the last three sessions, Tammy has made statements about how "stupid and dumb" she thought the Skillstreaming group was. When Tammy made these remarks, other students joined in by adding their own de-

rogatory comments. The group leader decided to deal with this problem by telling the students that if, for the next three sessions, they encouraged one another's participation in the activities, they would earn a free-activity time. The teacher prepared a small chart on which he wrote the dates of the next three sessions and a space for marking how frequently encouraging statements were offered. The activity time was a desirable enough group reinforcer that when Tammy began her usual comments, the other students insisted that she stop disrupting the group.

Removing Positive Reinforcement

The teacher's behavior management goal with students who display aggressive or other problem behaviors is, in a general sense, twofold. Both sides of the behavioral coin—appropriate and inappropriate, prosocial and antisocial, desirable and undesirable—must be attended to. In a proper behavior change effort, procedures are simultaneously or sequentially employed to reduce and eliminate the inappropriate, antisocial, or undesirable components of the students' behavioral repertoires and to increase the quality and frequency of appropriate, prosocial, or desirable components. This latter task is served primarily by the direct teaching of prosocial behaviors via Skillstreaming participation and by the contingent presentation of positive reinforcement following skill use. Conversely, the contingent removal of positive reinforcement in response to aggressive, disruptive, or other negative behaviors is the major behavior management strategy for reducing or eliminating such behaviors. Therefore, in conjunction with the procedures discussed previously for presenting positive reinforcement, the teacher should also simultaneously or consecutively employ one or both of the following techniques for removing positive reinforcement.

Negative Reinforcement

Negative reinforcement is the removal of aversive stimuli contingent upon the occurrence of desirable behaviors. Negative reinforcement has seldom been used to modify behavior in a classroom context. The major exception to this rule is the contingent release of youth from time-out (an aversive environment), depending on such desirable behaviors as quietness and calmness. Such release serves as negative reinforcement for these behaviors. Unfortunately, negative reinforcement often proves important in a classroom context in a less constructive way. Consider a teacher–student interaction in which the student behaves disruptively (shouts, swears, fights), the teacher responds with anger and punishment, and the punishment brings about a temporary suppression of the youth's disruptiveness. The decrease in the student's disruptiveness may also be viewed by the teacher as a decrease in aversive stimulation, which functions to negatively reinforce the immediately preceding teacher behavior (in this case, punishment). The net effect of this sequence is to increase the likelihood that the teacher will use punishment in the future. Analogous sequences may occur and function to increase the likelihood of other ineffective or inappropriate teacher behaviors.

PUNISHMENT

Formally, punishment is the presentation of an aversive or negative stimulus contingent upon the performance of a given behavior, intended to decrease the future occurrences of that behavior. Two common forms are verbal punishment (e.g., reprimands) and physical punishment (e.g., paddling, spanking). Corporal punishment is no longer allowed in most schools, nor is it recommended in any setting, including the home.

In fact, it is a common finding that, when verbal and physical punishment does succeed in altering behavior, such effects are often temporary. A number of clinicians and researchers have assumed an antipunishment stance, seeing little place for punishment, especially in the classroom. This view corresponds to punishment research demonstrating such undesirable side effects as withdrawal from social contact, coun-

teraggression toward the punisher, violence, vandalism, modeling of punishing behavior, disruption of social relationships, failure of effects to generalize, selective avoidance (refraining from inappropriate behaviors only when under surveillance), and stigmatizing labeling effects (Azrin & Holz, 1966; Bandura, 1973; Mayer, 2001). Nelson, Lott, and Glenn (1993) state:

> Most teachers mean well when they administer punishment. They believe punishment is the best way to motivate students to behave properly. If the misbehavior stops for a while because of punishment, they may have been fooled into thinking they were right. However, when they become aware of the long-range effects of punishment on students, they naturally want to learn more respectful methods of motivating students to behave properly. (p. 78)

Because they are intended to reduce the frequency of behavior, extinction and time-out are, strictly speaking, also forms of punishment. These two techniques can be helpful in effecting behavior change in the Skillstreaming group if proper guidelines for their use are followed. Response cost and logical consequences can also have a place in helping children and adolescents decrease undesirable behavior.

Extinction

Extinction is the withdrawal or removal of positive reinforcement for aggressive or other undesirable behaviors that have been either deliberately or inadvertently reinforced in the past. This technique is the procedure of choice with milder forms of aggression (e.g., sarcasm, put-downs, or other low-level forms of verbal aggression).

Knowing When to Use Extinction

Determining when to use extinction is, of course, in part a function of each teacher's guiding group management philosophy and tolerance for deviant behavior. Each teacher will have to decide individually the range of undesirable behaviors that can be safely ignored. Taking a rather conservative stance, Walker (1979) suggests that extinction "should be applied only to those inappropriate behaviors that are minimally disruptive to classroom atmosphere" (p. 40). In any event, it is clear that the first step in applying extinction is knowing when to use it.

Providing Positive Reinforcement for Appropriate Behaviors

As noted earlier, attempts to reduce inappropriate behavior by reinforcement withdrawal should always be accompanied by efforts to increase appropriate behaviors by reinforcement provision. This combination of efforts will succeed especially well when the appropriate and inappropriate behaviors involved are opposite from, or at least incompatible with, each other (e.g., reward in-seat behavior, ignore out-of-seat behavior; reward talking at a conversational level, ignore talking loudly).

Identifying Positive Reinforcers Maintaining Inappropriate Behaviors

The reinforcers maintaining inappropriate behaviors are the ones to be withheld. The teacher should discern what the student is working for; what payoffs are involved; and what reinforcers are being sought or earned by aggression, disruptiveness, and similar behaviors. Very often, the answer will be attention. Looking, staring, yelling at, talking to, or turning toward are common teacher and peer reactions to a student's inappropriate behaviors. The withdrawal of such positive social reinforcement by ignoring the behaviors (by turning away and not yelling, talking, or looking at the perpetrator) is the teacher and peer behavior that will effect extinction.

Ignoring Low-Level Aggressive Behaviors

Carr (1981) has suggested guidelines for ignoring low-level aggressive behaviors (e.g., verbal comments). First, do not comment to the youth that you are ignoring. Long (or even short) explanations about why teachers, peers, or others are going to avoid attending to given behaviors pro-

vide precisely the type of social reinforcement that extinction is designed to withdraw. Ignoring behavior should simply occur with no forewarning, introduction, or explanation. Second, do not look away suddenly when the youth behaves inappropriately. Doing so may communicate the message that "I really noticed and was impelled to action by your behavior," the exact opposite of an extinction message. As Carr recommends, "It is best to ignore the behavior by reacting to it in a matter of fact way by continuing natural ongoing activities" (p. 38).

These guidelines should be followed only with behaviors that are not harmful to others. Observed incidents of verbal and physical aggression (or harassment) must be dealt with quickly and consistently to maintain a safe school environment. Thus, extinction is not supported as a method for dealing with behaviors that could cause harm to the student or others.

Using Extinction Consistently

As is true for the provision of reinforcement, removal of reinforcement must be consistent. Within a given Skillstreaming group, this rule of consistency means that the teacher and students must act in concert and that the teacher must be consistent across time. Within a given school, consistency means that, to the degree possible, all teachers having significant contact with a given student must strive to ignore the same inappropriate behaviors. In addition, to avoid the student's making the discrimination "I can't act up here, but I can out there," parent conferences should be held to bring parents, siblings, and other significant real-world figures in the student's life into the extinction effort.

Using Extinction Long Enough

Disruptive behaviors often have a long history of positive reinforcement. Especially if much of that history is one of intermittent reinforcement, efforts to undo these behaviors must be sustained. Teacher persistence in this regard will usually succeed. There are, however, two types of events to keep in mind when judging the effectiveness of extinction efforts. The first is what is known as the *extinction burst*. When extinction is first introduced, it is not uncommon for the rate or intensity of the aggressive behavior to increase sharply before it begins its more gradual decline toward zero. It is important that the teacher not be discouraged during this short detour. In fact, the meaning of the increase is that extinction is beginning to work. Second, inappropriate behaviors that have been successfully extinguished will reappear occasionally for reasons that are difficult to determine. Like the extinction burst, this *spontaneous recovery* is transitory and will disappear if the teacher persists in the extinction effort.

Time-Out

In time-out, a child or adolescent who engages in aggressive or other inappropriate behavior is removed from all sources of reinforcement for a specified time period. As with extinction, the purpose of time-out is to reduce the undesirable behavior. It differs from extinction in that extinction involves removing reinforcement from the person, whereas time-out usually involves removing the person from the reinforcing situation.

In school-based practice, time-out has typically taken three forms. *Isolation* or *seclusion time-out* requires that the youth be removed from the classroom to a time-out room. Because isolation or seclusion time-out is now considered to be a type of restraint, individuals considering this type of intervention should consult their state and district policies and procedures.

Exclusion time-out is somewhat less restrictive but also involves removing the youth from sources of reinforcement; it is perhaps the most common form of time-out used in school classrooms. Here the youth is required to go to a separate area of the classroom, which is sometimes behind a screen. The youth is not removed from the classroom but is excluded from classroom activities for a specified time period. *Nonexclusion*

time-out (also called *contingent observation*), the least restrictive time-out variant, requires the youth to sit and watch on the periphery of classroom activities to observe the appropriate behaviors of other students. This variant combines time-out with modeling opportunities and thus is the preferred approach for Skillstreaming group use. The implementation of time-out in any of its forms optimally employs the procedures next described.

Knowing When to Use Time-Out

As noted, extinction is the recommended procedure for undesirable behaviors that can be safely ignored. Behaviors potentially injurious to others require a more active teacher response, possibly time-out. Exclusion or nonexclusion time-out is also the procedure to use for less severe forms of problematic behavior when the combination of extinction and positive reinforcement for more positive behaviors has been attempted and failed.

Whenever possible, the student should be verbally directed to use the time-out area. If he or she refuses to go, the rest of the class or group may be removed instead of the student causing the problem. This will leave the student with the same response—time-out from positive reinforcement. In certain situations where student safety is at risk, it may be necessary to move a student physically to time-out. This may be the case for children age 2 to 12 who display high rates of potentially dangerous or aggressive behaviors. Such physical intervention should be used only as a last resort to protect the safety of the student or others—and only after attempts have been made to deescalate the student's behavior. Many times, after deescalation the student will move to the time-out area independently.

Providing Positive Reinforcement for Appropriate Behaviors

As is the case for extinction, positive reinforcement for appropriate behaviors should accompany any extinction procedure, including time-out. When possible, the behaviors positively reinforced should be opposite to, or at least incompatible with, those for which the time-out procedure is used. Carr (1981) recommends an additional basis combining these two techniques:

> Although one important reason for using positive reinforcement is to strengthen non-aggressive behaviors to the point where they replace aggressive behaviors, there is a second reason for using reinforcement procedures. If extensive use of positive reinforcement is made, then time-out will become all the more aversive since it would involve the temporary termination of a rich diversity of positive reinforcers. In this sense, then, the use of positive reinforcement helps to enhance the effectiveness of the time-out procedure. (pp. 41–42)

Arranging an Effective Time-Out Setting

Time-out must be a boring environment, with all reinforcers removed. With exclusionary time-out, there should be no attractive or distracting objects or opportunities—no books, posters, people, windows to look out, sounds to overhear, or other obvious or not-so-obvious potential reinforcers. When contingent observation is used, the youth will still hear the ongoing activity.

Sending a Student to Time-Out

The teacher can take a number of actions when initiating time-out to increase the likelihood of its effectiveness. As for positive reinforcement, immediacy is an issue. Time-out is best instituted immediately following the aggressive or other behavior to be modified. Having earlier explained to the student the nature of time-out, as well as when and why it will be used, the teacher should initiate the procedure in a more or less automatic manner following the undesirable behavior—that is, in a way that minimizes social reinforcement. This means sending the student to time-out without a lengthy explanation but with a brief description of the precipitating behavior. This process is best conducted in a calm and matter-of-fact manner. In addition, the effectiveness of time-out is further enhanced by its consistent application, when appropriate, by the same teacher on other occasions, as well as by other teachers.

Maintaining a Student in Time-Out

Two questions arise during a student's period in time-out: What is he or she doing? and How long should time-out last? Answering the first question by monitoring the student makes certain that the time-out experience is not in fact pleasant or positively reinforcing. For example, rather than being a removal from positive reinforcement, time-out may in reality help a youth avoid an aversive situation from which he or she would prefer to escape. Similarly, if monitoring reveals that the youth is singing or playing, time-out will be less effective. Unless the situation can be made essentially nonreinforcing, a different behavioral intervention may be required.

With regard to duration, most successful time-out implementations have been from 2 to 10 minutes long (2 to 3 minutes for preschoolers and kindergartners, 3 to 5 minutes for the elementary-age student, and 5 to 10 minutes for an adolescent), with clear preference for the shorter time spans in this range. If time-out periods are longer than necessary, the student may calm down and then act up again out of boredom or frustration. When experimenting to find the optimal duration for any given youth, it is best to begin with a shorter duration and to lengthen the time until an effective span is identified rather than to shorten an initially longer span. This latter approach would, again, risk the danger of introducing an event the student experiences as positive reinforcement when the teacher's intention is quite the opposite.

Excusing a Student from Time-Out

As noted earlier in connection with extinction, withdrawal of positive reinforcement frequently leads to an extinction burst in which more intense or more frequent problem behaviors appear before they begin to subside. This same pattern is evident with withdrawal from positive reinforcement—

that is, time-out. The first few times a student is directed to use time-out, what might be termed a *time-out burst* of heightened aggression or other problem behaviors may occur. These outbursts will usually subside, especially if the teacher requires the time-out to be served and the outburst does not result in the suspension of the time-out.

The student's release from time-out should be conducted in a matter-of-fact manner, and the student should be quickly returned to regular Skillstreaming activities. Lengthy teacher explanations or moralizing are, once again, tactically erroneous provisions of positive reinforcement that communicate to the student that acting out in the classroom will bring a short period of removal from reinforcement and then a (probably longer) period of undivided teacher attention.

It is important once the student returns to ongoing activities that the teacher quickly reinforce the student for subsequent positive behaviors. The Skillstreaming group must be a positive place—a place where the student wants to be—or time-out will be perceived as a reward instead of a negative consequence.

Providing Prosocial Alternatives

The responsible group leader will plan instruction in specific skills that could serve as prosocial ways of dealing with the problem that led to the use of time-out. For example, the student could be guided through the steps of Using Self-Control (Skill 26) or Dealing with Someone Else's Anger (Skill 18) to reduce the likelihood that the event will reoccur. In addition, the leader must attempt to deescalate future occurrences of such behavior through techniques like prompting.

Response Cost

Response cost involves the removal of previously acquired reinforcers to reduce future instances of inappropriate behavior. The previously acquired reinforcers may have been earned, as when response-cost procedures are a component of a token economy, or they may have simply been provided, as is the case with a freestand-ing response-cost system. In either instance, reinforcers are removed (the cost) whenever the undesirable behaviors occur (the response). Response-cost procedures can be effective, especially when combined with the provision of positive reinforcement via a token-economy system, for increasing prosocial behaviors. However, response-cost systems should never be a first choice in dealing with problem behaviors. Although the cost can be framed as a fine for breaking the rules or engaging in other actions for adolescents, this procedure has frequently shown to elicit aggressive responses on its own. Response cost is not appropriate for use with preschool or children in the early elementary grades.

Logical Consequences

An encouraging environment teaches students to respect themselves and others and treats all students with dignity. Rarely are students exposed to reprimands or other forms of harsh punishment; however, clear and consistent limits on unacceptable behavior are set and enforced so all students have the opportunity to learn. Logical consequences to reduce the frequency of undesirable behavior are most often recommended. Logical consequences are related to the individual's action, and they make sense (i.e., there is a cause-effect relationship; McLeod, Fisher, & Hoover, 2003). Consequences hold the student accountable yet maintain the student's dignity. McLeod, Fisher, & Hoover (2003) state:

> Punishment does not teach alternative acceptable behaviors; in fact, it models just the opposite. Teachers use punishment out of anger, frustration, or lack of other strategies. Consequences, however, teach students the connection between how they choose to behave and the outcomes of that behavior. (p. 114)

These authors suggest using restitution (fixing or replacing damaged, lost, or stolen items), restoration (giving the student a respite by being away from the group for a brief period of time), restriction (limiting privileges for a length of time), and reflection (reflecting on a problem and developing a plan through problem solving).

Dreikurs and Cassel (1972) further define logical consequences. Such consequences are related to the misbehavior; are planned, explained, and agreed on by students in advance; are administered in a neutral way; and are given consistently. In addition, consequences are reasonable and demonstrate respect by giving students a choice (i.e., to engage in the inappropriate behavior and receive an unpleasant consequence or to engage in the appropriate behavior and receive positive reinforcement).

When planning logical consequences, teachers will need to keep in mind that these consequences must be reasonable, related to the misbehavior, and respectful to the student (Nelson et al., 1993). Examples of logical consequences include the following:

- ▶ For choosing to talk instead of completing a class assignment, the student must complete the work during an enjoyable activity.

- ▶ For choosing to fight when provoked during passing period, the student must have a separate passing time.

- ▶ For choosing to take a notebook belonging to someone else, the student must make restitution.

Overcorrection

Overcorrection is a behavior modification approach developed by Foxx and Azrin (1973) for circumstances in which other behavioral strategies have failed and when few alternative appropriate behaviors are available to reinforce. Overcorrection is a two-part procedure, having restitution and positive practice as components. Restitution requires that the individual return the behavioral setting (e.g., the classroom) to its status prior to disruption or better. Thus, objects broken by an angry youth must be repaired, classmates struck in anger apologized to, papers scattered across the room picked up. The positive practice component of overcorrection requires that the youth then be made to repair objects broken by others, apologize to classmates who witnessed the classmate being struck, or clean up the rest of the classroom (including areas not disturbed by the youth). It is clear that the restitution and positive practice requirements serve both punitive and instructional functions.

References

Adams, M. B., Womack, S. A., Shatzer, R. H., & Caldarella, P. (2010). *Education, 130*(3), 513–528.

Advancement Project/Civil Rights Project. (2000, February). *Education denied: The negative impact of zero tolerance policies.* Testimony before the U.S. Commission on Civil Rights, Washington, DC.

Ahmad, Y., & Smith, P. K. (1994). Bullying in schools and the issue of sex differences. In John Archer (Ed.), *Male violence.* London: Routledge.

Alberto, P. S., & Troutman, A. C. (2006). *Applied behavior analysis for teachers: Influencing student performance.* Upper Saddle River, NJ: Merrill/Prentice Hall.

Andrews, S. P., Taylor, P. B., Martin, E. P., & Slate, J. R. (1998). *Evaluation of an alternative discipline program.* Chapel Hill: The University of North Carolina Press.

Applied Research Center. (1999). *Making the grade: A racial justice report card.* Washington, DC: Author.

Ascher, C. (1994). *Gaining control of violence in the schools: A view from the field* (ERIC Digest No. 100). New York: ERIC Clearinghouse on Urban Education.

Ayllon, T., & Azrin, N. H. (1968). *The token economy: A motivational system for therapy rehabilitation.* New York: Appleton-Century-Crofts.

Azrin, N. H., & Holz, W. C. (1966). Punishment. In W. K. Honig (Ed.), *Operant behavior: Areas of research and application.* New York: Appleton-Century-Crofts.

Bandura, A. (1973). *Aggression: A social learning analysis.* Englewood Cliffs, NJ: Prentice Hall.

Beane, A. (1999). *The bully-free classroom.* Minneapolis: Free Spirit.

Bender, W. N. (2009). Beyond the RTI pyramid: Solutions for the first years of implementation. Bloomington, IN: Solution Tree Press.

Blair, K. C., Fox, L., & Lentini, R. (2010). Use of positive behavior support to address the challenging behavior of young children within a community early childhood program. *Topics in Early Childhood Special Education, 30*(2), 68–79.

Blood, E., & Neel, R. S. (2007). From FBA to implementation: A look at what is actually being delivered. *Education and Treatment of Children, 30*(4), 67–80.

Bock, S. J., Tapscott, K. E., & Savner, J. L. (1998). Suspension and expulsion: Effective management for students? *Intervention in School and Clinic. 34*(1), 50–52.

Boyajian, A. E., DuPaul, G. J., Handler, M. W., Eckert, T. L., & McGoey, K. E. (2001). The use of classroom-based brief functional analyses with preschoolers at-risk for attention deficit hyperactivity disorder. *School Psychology Review, 30*(2), 278–293.

Brannon, D. (2008). Character education—A joint responsibility. *Kappa Delta Pi Record, 44*, 62–65.

Brendtro, L. K., Brokenleg, M., & Van Bockern, S. (2002). *Reclaiming youth at risk: Our hope for the future.* Bloomington, IN: National Educational Service.

Brownstein, R. (2010). Pushed out. *Teaching Tolerance,* March, 23–27.

Bruder, M. B. (2010). Early childhood intervention: A promise to children and families for their future. *Exceptional Children. 76*(3), 339–355.

Bryan, J. H., & Test, M. A. (1967). Models and helping: Naturalistic studies in aiding behavior. *Journal of Personality and Social Psychology, 6,* 400–407.

Camp, B. W., & Bash, M. A. S. (1981). Think Aloud: Increasing social and cognitive skills—A problem-solving program for children (Primary level). Champaign, IL: Research Press.

Canale, J. R. (1977). The effect of modeling and length of ownership on sharing behavior of children. *Social Behavior and Personality, 5,* 187–191.

Caprara, G. V., Barbaranelli, C., Pastorelli, C., Bandura, A., & Zimbardo, P. (2000). Prosocial foundation of children's academic achievement. *Psychological Science, 11,* 302–306.

Carr, E. G. (1981). Contingency management. In A. P. Goldstein, E. G. Carr, W. Davidson, & P. Wehr (Eds.), *In response to aggression.* New York: Pergamon.

Carr, E. G., Dunlap, G., Horner, R. H., Koegel, R. L., Turnbull, A. P., Sailor, W., Anderson, J. L., Albin, R. W., Koegel, L. K., & Fox, L. (2002). Positive behavior support: Evolution of an applied science. *Journal of Positive Behavior Interventions, 4*(1), 4–16.

Carter, D. R., & Horner, R. H. (2007). Adding function-based behavioral support to First Step to Success: Integrating individualized and manualized practices. *Journal of Positive Behavior Interventions, 11*(1), 22–34.

Cartledge, G. (2003, February 20). *Discipline, diversity and behavioral disorders: Issues and interventions.* Presentation made at the Midwest Symposium for Leadership in Behavioral Disorders, Kansas City, MO.

Cartledge, G., & Feng, H. (1996). The relationship of culture and social behavior. In G. Cartledge (Ed.), *Cultural diversity and social skills instruction: Understanding ethnic and gender differences.* Champaign, IL: Research Press.

Cartledge, G., & Johnson, S. (1997). Cultural sensitivity. In A. P. Goldstein & J. C. Conoley (Eds.), *School violence intervention: A practical handbook.* New York: Guilford.

Cartledge, G., & Kourea, L. (2008). Culturally responsive classrooms for culturally diverse students with and at risk for disabilities. *Exceptional Children, 74*(3), 351–371.

Cartledge, G., & Lo, Y. (2006). Teaching urban learners: Culturally responsive strategies for developing academic and behavioral competence. Champaign, IL: Research Press.

Cartledge, G., & Milburn, J. F. (1980). *Teaching social skills to children.* New York: Pergamon.

Cartledge, G., & Milburn, J. F. (1995). *Teaching social skills to children and youth.* Boston: Allyn & Bacon.

Cartledge, G., & Milburn, J. F. (1996). A model for teaching social skills. In G. Cartledge (Ed.), *Cultural diversity and social skills instruction: Understanding ethnic and gender differences.* Champaign, IL: Research Press.

Chapman, W. E. (1977). *Roots of character education.* Schenectady, NY: Character Research Press.

Chen, K. (2006). Social skills intervention for students with emotional/behavioral disorders: A literature review from the American perspective. *Educational Research and Reviews, 1*(3), 143–149.

Cochrane, W. S., & Laux, J. M. (2007). Investigating school psychologists' perceptions of treatment integrity in school-based interventions for children with academic and behavior concerns. *Preventing School Failure, 51*(4), 29–34.

Cohen, J., Pickeral, T., & McCloskey, M. (2009, April). Assessing school climate. *Education Digest, 74*(8), 45–48.

Coie, J. D., & Kupersmidt, J. B. (1983). A behavioral analysis of emerging social status in boys' groups. *Child Development, 54,* 1400–1416.

Cook, C. R., Crews, S. D., Wright, D. B., Mayer, G. R., Gale, B., Kramer, B., & Gresham, F. M. (2007). Establishing and evaluating the substantive adequacy of Positive Behavioral Support Plans. *Journal of Behavioral Education, 16,* 191–206.

Cook, C. R., Gresham, F. M., Kern, L., Barreras, R. B., & Crews, S. D. (2008). Social skills training for secondary students with emotional and/or behavioral disorders: A review and analysis of the meta-analytic literature. *Journal of Emotional and Behavioral Disorders, 16*(3), 131–144.

Costenbader, V., & Markson, S. (1998). School suspension: A study with secondary school students. *Journal of School Psychology, 36,* 59–82.

Crick, N. R., & Dodge, K. A. (1994). A review and reformulation of social information processing mechanisms in children's social adjustment. *Psychological Bulletin, 115,* 74-101.

Crone, D. A., Hawken, L. S., & Bergstrom, M. (2007). A demonstration of training, implementing, and using functional behavioral assessment in 10 elementary and middle school settings. *Journal of Positive Behavior Interventions, 9*(1), 15–29.

Crone, D. A., & Horner, R. H. (2003). Building positive behavior support systems in schools: Functional behavioral assessment. New York: Guilford.

Denham, A., Hatfield, S., Smethurst, J., Tan, E., & Tribe, C. (2006). The effect of social skills interventions in the primary school. *Educational Psychology in Practice, 22*(1), 33–51.

Denham, S. A. (1998). *Emotional development in young children.* New York: Guilford.

Dewey, J. (1938). *Experience and education.* New York: Collier.

Docksai, R. (2010). Teaching social skills. *Futurist, 44*(3), 12–13.

Donovan, M. S., & Cross, C. T. (Eds.). (2002). Minority students in special and gifted education. Washington, DC: National Academy Press.

Dreikurs, R., & Cassel, P. (1972). *Discipline without tears.* New York: Hawthorne.

Dupper, D. R., & Bosch, L. A. (1996). Reasons for school suspensions. *Journal for a Just and Caring Education, 2*(2), 140–150.

Dykeman, B. F. (2003). School-based interventions for treating social adjustment difficulties in children with Traumatic Brain Injury. *Journal of Instructional Psychology, 30*(3), 225–230.

Elksnin, L. K., & Elksnin, N. (2000). Teaching parents to teach their children to be prosocial. *Intervention in School and Clinic, 36*(1), 27–35.

Elliott, S. N., & Gresham, F. M. (1991). *Social skills intervention guide: Practical strategies for social skills training.* Circle Pines, MN: American Guidance Service.

Ellis, H. (1965). *The transfer of learning.* New York: Macmillan.

Epps, S., Thompson, B. J., & Lane, M. P. (1985). Procedures for incorporating generalization programming into interventions for behaviorally disordered students. Unpublished manuscript, Iowa State University, Ames.

Evers, W. L., & Schwartz, J. C. (1973). Modifying social withdrawal in preschoolers: The effects of filmed modeling and teacher praise. *Journal of Abnormal Child Psychology, 1,* 248–256.

Farmer, T. W., Farmer, E. M. Z., Estell, D. B., & Hutchins, B. C. (2007). The developmental dynamics of aggression and the prevention of school violence. *Journal of Emotional and Behavioral Disorders 15*(4), 197–208.

Feindler, E. L. (1979). *Cognitive and behavioral approaches to anger control training in explosive adolescents.* Unpublished doctoral dissertation, West Virginia University, Morgantown.

Feindler, E. L. (1995). An ideal treatment package for children and adolescents with anger disorders. In H. Kassinove (Ed.), *Anger disorders: Definition, diagnosis, and treatment.* New York: Taylor & Francis.

Feindler, E. L., & Ecton, R. B. (1986). *Adolescent anger control: Cognitive-behavioral techniques.* New York: Pergamon.

Ferster, C. B., & Skinner, B. F. (1957). *Schedules of reinforcement.* New York: Appleton-Century-Crofts.

Fialka, J., & Mikus, K. C. (1999). *Do you hear what I hear?* Ann Arbor, MI: Proctor.

Fox, C. L. & Boulton, M. J. (2005). The social skill problems of victims of bullying: Self, peer and teacher perceptions. *British Journal of Educational Psychology, 75,* 313–328.

Foxx, R. M., & Azrin, N. H. (1973). A method of eliminating aggressive-disruptive behavior for retarded and brain-damaged patients. *Behaviour Research and Therapy, 10,* 15–27.

Friesen, B. J., & Stephens, B. (1998). Expanding family roles in the system of care: Research and practice. In M. H. Epstein, K. Kutash, & A. Duchnowski (Eds.), *Outcomes for children and youth with behavioral and emotional disorders and their families.* Austin, TX: PRO-ED.

Galassi, J. P., & Galassi, M. D. (1984). Promoting transfer and maintenance of counseling outcomes. In S.D. Brown & R.W. Lent (Eds.), *Handbook of counseling psychology.* New York: Wiley.

Gibbs, J. C., Potter, G., & Goldstein, A. P. (1995). *The EQUIP program: Teaching youth to think and act responsibly through a peer-helping approach.* Champaign, IL: Research Press.

Gilliam, W. S. (2005). *Prekindergarteners left behind: Expulsion rates in state prekindergarten systems.* Retrieved May 22, 2011 from www.hartfordinfo.org/issues/wsd/education/NationalPreKExpulsionPaper

Glick, B., & Gibbs, J. C. (2010). *Aggression Replacement Training: A comprehensive intervention for aggressive youth* (3rd ed.). Champaign, IL: Research Press.

Goldstein, A. P. (1973). *Structured Learning Therapy: Toward a psychotherapy for the poor.* New York: Academic.

Goldstein, A. P. (1990). *The refusal skills video.* Champaign, IL: Research Press.

Goldstein, A. P. (1999a). *Low-level aggression: First steps on the ladder to violence.* Champaign, IL: Research Press.

Goldstein, A. P. (1999b). *The Prepare Curriculum: Teaching prosocial competencies* (2nd ed.). Champaign, IL: Research Press.

Goldstein, A. P., Glick, B., Carthan, W., & Blancero, D. (1994). *The prosocial gang.* Thousand Oaks, CA: Sage.

Goldstein, A. P., Glick, B., & Gibbs, J. C. (1998). *Aggression Replacement Training: A comprehensive intervention for aggressive youth* (2nd ed.). Champaign, IL: Research Press.

Goldstein, A. P., Glick, B., Irwin, M. J., Pask-McCartney, C., & Rubama, I. (1989). *Reducing delinquency: Intervention in the community.* New York: Pergamon.

Goldstein, A. P., Glick, B., Reiner, S., Zimmerman, D., & Coultry, T. (1986). *Aggression Replacement Training: A comprehensive program for aggressive youth.* Champaign, IL: Research Press.

Goldstein, A. P., & Kanfer, F. H. (1979). *Maximizing treatment gains.* New York: Academic.

Goldstein, A. P., & McGinnis, E. (1988). *The Skillstreaming video.* Champaign, IL: Research Press.

Goldstein, A. P., & McGinnis, E. (1997). Skillstreaming the adolescent: New strategies and perspectives for teaching prosocial skills (Rev. ed.). Champaign, IL: Research Press.

Goldstein, A. P., & Michaels, G. Y. (1985). *Empathy: Development, training and consequences.* Hillsdale, NJ: Erlbaum.

Goldstein, A. P., Palumbo, J., Striepling, S., & Voutsinas, A. M. (1995). *Break it up: A teacher's guide to managing student aggression.* Champaign, IL: Research Press.

Goldstein, A. P., Sprafkin, R. P., Gershaw, N. J., & Klein, P. (1980). *Skillstreaming the adolescent: A structured learning approach to teaching prosocial skills.* Champaign, IL: Research Press.

Goldstein, S. E., Young, A., & Boyd, C. (2008). Relational aggression at school: Associations with school safety and social climate. *Journal of Youth Adolescence, 37,* 641–654.

Greenbaum, S., Turner, B., & Stephens, R. D. (1989). *Set straight on bullies.* Malibu, CA: National School Safety Center.

Greenwood, C. R., Hops, H., Delquadri, J., & Guild, J. (1974). Group contingencies for group consequences in classroom management: A further analysis. *Journal of Applied Behavior Analysis, 7,* 413–425.

Gresham, F. M. (1998). Social skills training: Should we raze, remodel, or rebuild? *Behavioral Disorders, 24*(1), 19–25.

Gresham, F. M. (2002). Social skills assessment and instruction for students with emotional and behavioral disorders. In K. L. Lane, F. M. Gresham, & T. E. O'Shaughnessy (Eds.), *Interventions for children with or at risk for emotional and behavioral disorders.* Boston: Allyn & Bacon.

Gresham, F. M. (2005). Methodological issues in evaluating cognitive-behavioral treatments for students with behavioral disorders. *Behavioral Disorders, 30*(3), 213–215.

Gresham, F. M. (2009). Evolution of the treatment integrity concept: Current status and future directions. *School Psychology Review, 38*(4), 533–540.

Gresham, F. M., Cook, C. R., Crews, S. L., & Kern, L. (2004). Social skills training for children and youth with emotional and behavioral disorders: Validity considerations and future directions. *Behavioral Disorders, 30*(1), 32–46.

Gresham, F. M., & Gansle, K. A. (1993). Treatment integrity of school-based behavioral intervention studies: 1980–1990. *School Psychology Review, 22*(2), 254–272.

Gresham, F. M., MacMillan, M. E., Beebe-Frankenberger, M. E., & Bocian, K. M. (2000). Treatment integrity in learning disabilities intervention research: Do we really know how treatments are implemented: *Learning Disabilities Research and Practice, 15*(4), 198–205.

Gresham, F. M., Sugai, G., & Horner, R. H. (2001). Interpreting outcomes of social skills training for students with high-incidence disabilities. *Exceptional Children, 67,* 331–344.

Gresham, F. M., Van, M. B., & Cook, C. R. (2006). Social skills training for teaching replacement behaviors: Remediating acquisition deficits in at-risk students. *Behavioral Disorders, 31*(4), 363–377.

Gresham, F. M., Watson, T. S., & Skinner, C. H. (2001). Functional behavioral assessment: Principles, procedures, and future directions. *School Psychology Review, 30*(2), 156–172.

Grizenko, J., Zappitelli, M., Langevin, J. P., Hrychko, S., El-Messidi, A., Kaminester, D., Pawliuk, N., & Stepanian, M. T. (2000). Effectiveness of a social skills training program using self/other perspective-taking: A nine month follow-up. *American Journal of Orthopsychiatry, 70*(4), 501–509.

Guzzetta, R. A. (1974). Acquisition and transfer of empathy by the parents of early adolescents through structured learning training. Unpublished doctoral dissertation, Syracuse University, New York.

Harry, B., & Klingner, J. (2006). *Why are so many minority students in special education?* New York: Teachers College Press.

Hickman, G. P., Bartholomew, M., Mathwig, J., & Heinrichs, R. S. (2008). Differential developmental pathways of high school dropouts and graduates. *Journal of Educational Research, 102*(1), 3–14.

Homme, L., Csanyi, A. P., Gonzales, M. A., & Rechs, J. R. (1969). *How to use contingency contracting in the classroom.* Champaign, IL: Research Press.

Hoover, J. H., & Oliver, R. (1996). The bullying prevention handbook: A guide for principals, teachers, and counselors. Bloomington, IN: National Education Service.

Horner, R. H., & Carr, E. G. (1997). Behavioral support for students with severe disabilities: Functional assessment and comprehensive intervention. *The Journal of Special Education, 31*(1), 84–104.

Horner, R. H., Sugai, G., Todd, A. W., & Lewis-Palmer, T. (2000). Elements of behavior support plans: A technical brief. *Exceptionality, 8*(3), 205–215.

Individuals with Disabilities Education Act Amendments of 1997, Pub. L. No. 105-17.

Individuals with Disabilities Education Act Amendments of 2004, Pub. L. No. 180-446.

Ingram, K., Lewis-Palmer, T., & Sugai, G. (2005). Function-based intervention planning: Comparing the effectiveness of FBA function-based and non-function based intervention plans. *Journal of Positive Behavior Interventions, 7*(4), 224–236.

Jewett, J. (1992). *Aggression and cooperation: Helping young children develop constructive strategies.*

(ERIC Document Reproduction Service No. ED351147)

Johns, B. H., Carr, V. G., & Hoots, C. W. (1995). *Reduction of school violence: Alternatives to suspension.* Horsham, PA: LRP.

Johnson, S. L. (2009). Improving the school environment to reduce school violence: A review of the literature. *Journal of School Health, 79*(10), 451–465.

Jolivette, K., Scott, T. M., & Nelson, C. M. (2000). *The link between Functional Behavioral Assessments (FBAs) and Behavioral Intervention Plans (BIPs)* (ERIC Digest E592). Reston, VA: Council for Exceptional Children.

Jones, K. M., Young, M. M., & Friman, P. C. (2000). Increasing peer praise of socially rejected delinquent youth: Effects on cooperation and acceptance. *School Psychology Review, 15,* 30–39.

Jones, V. F., & Jones, L. S. (2000). *Comprehensive classroom management.* Needham, MA: Allyn & Bacon.

Jung, L. A., Gomez, C., Baird, S. M., & Keramidas, C. L. G. (2008). Designing intervention plans: Bridging the gap between individualized education programs and implentation. *Teaching Exceptional Children, 41*(1), 26–33.

Kame'enui, E. J., & Simmons, D. C. (1990). Designing instructional strategies: The prevention of academic learning problems. Columbus, OH: Merrill.

Kaplan, J. S., & Carter, J. (2005). Beyond behavior modification: A cognitive behavioral approach to behavior management in the school (3rd ed.) Austin, TX: PRO-ED.

Karoly, P., & Steffen, J. J. (Eds.). (1980). *Improving the long term effects of psychotherapy.* New York: Gardner.

Kauffman, J. M. (2005). *Characteristics of emotional and behavioral disorders of children and youth* (9th ed.). Upper Saddle River, NJ: Pearson.

Kauffman, J. M., Mostert, M. P., Trent, S. C., & Hallahan, D. P. (1998). *Managing classroom behavior: A reflective case-based approach* (2nd ed.). Boston: Allyn & Bacon.

Kavale, K. A. & Forness, S. R. (1996). Learning disability grows up: Rehabilitation issues for individuals with learning disabilities. *Journal of Rehabilitation, 62*(1), 34–42.

Kazdin, A. E. (1975). *Behavior modification in applied settings.* Homewood, IL: Dorsey.

Keeley, S. M., Shemberg, K. M., & Carbonell, J. (1976). Operant clinical intervention: Behavior management or beyond? Where are the data? *Behavior Therapy, 7,* 292–305.

Kendall, P. C., & Braswell, L. (1985). *Cognitive behavioral therapy for children.* New York: Guilford.

Kern, L., Hilt, A. M., & Gresham, F. (2004). An evaluation of the functional behavioral assessment process used with students with or at-risk for emotional and behavioral disorders. *Education and Treatment of Children, 27*(4), 440–452.

Knight, B. J., & West, D. J. (1975). Temporary and continuing delinquency. *British Journal of Criminology,* 15, 43–50.

Kohlberg, L. (1969). Stage and sequence: The cognitive-developmental approach to socialization. In D. A. Goslin (Ed.), *Handbook of socialization theory and research.* Chicago: Rand McNally.

Kohlberg, L. (Ed.). (1973). *Collected papers on moral development and moral education.* Cambridge, MA: Harvard University, Center for Moral Education.

Kounin, J. (1970). *Discipline and group management in classrooms.* New York: Holt, Rinehart and Winston.

Kulli, K. (2008). Developing effective behavior intervention plans: Suggestions for school personnel. *Intervention in School and Clinic, 43*(3), 140–149.

Kurtz, M. M., & Mueser, K. T. (2008). A meta-analysis of controlled research on social skills training for schizophrenia. *Journal of Consulting and Clinical Psychology, 76*(3), 491–504.

Ladd, G. W., & Mize, J. (1983). A cognitive-social learning model of social skill training. *Psychological Review, 90,* 127–157.

Lane, K. L., Menzies, H. M., Barton-Arwood, S. M., Doukas, G. L., Munton, S. M. (2005). Designing, implementing, and evaluating social skills interventions for elementary students: Step-by-step procedures based on actual school-based investigations. *Preventing School Failure, 49*(2), 18–26.

Lane, K. L., Wehby, J. H., & Cooley, C. (2006). Teacher expectations of students' classroom behavior across the grade span: Which social skills are necessary for success? *Exceptional Children, 72*(2), 153–167.

LaRue, R. H., Jr., Weiss, M. J., & Ferraioli, S. J. (2008). State of the art procedures for assessment and treatment of learners with behavioral problems. *International Journal of Behavioral Consultation and Therapy, 4*(2), 250–263.

Lassen, S. R., Steele, M. M., & Sailor, W. (2006). The relationship of school-wide positive behavior support to academic achievement in an urban middle school. *Psychology in the Schools, 43*(6), 701–712.

Little, V. L., & Kendall, P. C. (1979). Cognitive-behavioral interventions with delinquents: Problem solving, role-taking, and self-control. In P. C. Kendall & S. D. Hollon (Eds.), *Cognitive-behavioral interventions.* Orlando, FL: Academic.

Lo, Y., Loe, S. A., & Cartledge, G. (2002). The effects of social skills instruction on the social behaviors of students at risk for emotional or behavioral disorders. *Behavioral Disorders, 27*(4), 371–385.

Loeber, R., & Dishion, T. (1983). Early predictors of male delinquency: A review. *Psychological Bulletin, 94,* 68–99.

Lopata, C., Thomeer, M. L., Volker, M. A., & Nida, R. E. (2006). Effectiveness of a cognitive-behavioral treatment on the social behaviors of children with Asperger Disorder. *Focus on Autism and Other Developmental Disabilities, 21*(4), 237–244.

Luria, A. R. (1961). The role of speech in the regulation of normal and abnormal behavior. New York: Liveright.

Maag, J. W. (2005). Social skills training for youth with emotional and behavioral disorders and learning disabilities: Problems, conclusions, and suggestions. *Exceptionality, 13,* 155–172.

Maag, J. W. (2006). Social skills training for students with emotional and behavioral disorders: A review of reviews. *Behavioral Disorders, 32*(1), 5–17.

MacNeil, A. J., Prater, D. L., & Busch, S. (2009). The effects of school culture and climate on student achievement. *International Journal of Leadership in Education, 12*(1), 73–84.

Maddern, L., Franey, J., McLaughlin, V., & Cox, S. (2004). An evaluation of the impact of an interagency programme to promote social skills in primary school children. *Educational Psychology in Practice, 20*(2), 135–155.

Mann, J. H. (1956). Experimental evaluations of role playing. *Psychological Bulletin, 53,* 227–234.

Manning, M., Heron, J., & Marshall, T. (1978). Styles of hostility and of social interactions at nursery, at school and at home: An extended study of children. In L. A. Hersov & M. Berger (Eds.), *Aggression and anti-social behavior in childhood and adolescence.* Oxford, UK: Pergamon.

Marx, G. (2006). *An overview of sixteen trends: Their profound impact on our future—Implications for students, education, communities, and whole of society.* Alexandria, VA: Educational Research Service.

Marzano, R. J., & Haystead, M. W. (2008). *Making standards useful in the classroom.* Alexandria, VA: Association for Supervision and Curriculum Development.

Mayer, G. R. (2001). Antisocial behavior: Its causes and prevention within our schools. *Education and Treatment of Children, 245*(4), 414–429.

Mayer, M., Lochman, J., & Van Acker, R. (2005). Introduction to the special issue: Cognitive-behavioral interventions with students with EBD. *Behavioral Disorders, 30*(3), 197–212.

McConnell, S. R. (1987). Entrapment effects and the generalization and maintenance of social skills training for elementary school students with behavioral disorders. *Behavioral Disorders, 12,* 252–263.

McGinnis, E., & Goldstein, A. P. (1984). *Skillstreaming the elementary school child: A guide for teaching prosocial skills.* Champaign, IL: Research Press.

McGinnis, E., & Goldstein, A. P. (1990). *Skillstreaming in early childhood: Teaching prosocial skills to the preschool and kindergarten child.* Champaign, IL: Research Press.

McGinnis, E., & Goldstein, A. P. (1997). *Skillstreaming the elementary school child: New strategies and perpectives for teaching prosocial skills* (Rev. ed.). Champaign, IL: Research Press.

McGinnis, E., & Goldstein, A. P. (2003). *Skillstreaming in early childhood: New strategies and perpectives for teaching prosocial skills* (Rev. ed.). Champaign, IL: Research Press.

McIntosh, K., Flannery, K. B., Sugai, G., Braun, D. H., & Cochrane, K. L. (2008). Relationship between academic and problem behavior in the transition from middle school to high school. *Journal of Positive Behavior Interventions, 10*(4), 243–255.

McIntosh, K., & Mackay, L. D. (2008, Fall). Enhancing generalization of social skills: Making social skills curricula effective after the lesson. *Beyond Behavior,* pp. 18–25.

McIntosh, R., Vaughn, S., & Zaragoza, N. (1991). A review of social interventions for students with learning disabilities. *Journal of Learning Disabilities, 24,* 451–458.

McLaren, E. M., & Nelson, C. M. (2009). Using functional behavior assessment to develop behavior interventions for students in Head Start. *Journal of Positive Behavior Interventions, 11*(1), 3–21.

McLeod, J., Fisher, J., & Hoover, G. (2003). *The key elements of classroom management: Managing time and space, student behavior, and instructional strategies.* Alexandria, VA: Association for Supervision and Curriculum Development.

Meichenbaum, D. H. (1977). Cognitive-behavior modification: An integrative approach. New York: Plenum.

Meier, C. R., DiPerna, J. C., & Oster, M. M. (2006). Importance of social skills in the elementary grades. *Education and Treatment of Children, 29*(3), 409–419.

Mendler, A. N., & Curwin, R. L. (1999). *Discipline with dignity for challenging youth.* Bloomington, IN: National Educational Service.

Mercer, C. D., & Pullen, P. C. (2005). *Students with learning disabilities.* Upper Saddle River, NJ: Pearon Education.

Miller, J. P. (1976). *Humanizing the classroom.* New York: Praeger.

Modro, M. (1995). *Safekeeping: Adult responsibility, children's right.* Providence: Behavioral Health Resource.

Moroz, K. B., & Jones, K. M. (2002). The effects of positive peer reporting on children's social involvement. *School Psychology Review, 31*(2), 235–245.

Morrison, R. L., & Bellack, A. S. (1981). The role of social perception in social skills. *Behavior Therapy, 12,* 69–70.

Mruzek, D. W., Cohen, C., & Smith, T. (2007). Contingency contracting with students on the autism spectrum. *Journal of Developmental and Physical Disabilities, 19,* 103–114.

Neilans, T. H., & Israel, A. C. (1981). Towards maintenance and generalization of behavior change: Teaching children self-regulation and self-instructional skills. *Cognitive Therapy and Research, 5,* 189–195.

Nelson, J., Lott, L., & Glenn, H. S. (1993). Positive discipline in the classroom: How to effectively use class meetings and other positive discipline strategies. Rocklin, CA: Prima.

Newman, D. A., Horne, A. M., & Bartolomucci, C. L. (2000). *Bully busters: A teacher's manual for helping bullies, victims, and bystanders.* Champaign, IL: Research Press.

Nickerson, A. B., & Martens, M. P. (2008). School violence: Associations with control, security/enforcement, educational/therapeutic approaches, and demographic factors. *School Psychology Review, 37*(2), 228–241.

Nowicki, S., Jr., & Duke, M. P. (1992). *Helping the child who doesn't fit in.* Atlanta, GA: Peachtree.

Olweus, D. (1991). Bully/victim problems among school children: Basic facts and effects of a school-based intervention program. In D. Pepler & K. H. Rubin (Eds.), *The development and treatment of childhood aggression.* Hillsdale, NJ: Erlbaum.

Olweus, D. (1993). Bullying at school: What we know and what we can do. Oxford, UK: Blackwell.

Osgood, C. E. (1953). *Method and theory in experimental psychology.* New York: Oxford University Press.

Partnership for 21st Century Skills. (2008). *21st century skills, education, and competitiveness: A resource policy guide.* Retrieved July 18, 2011, from www.21st centuryskills.org

Patterson, G. R. (1982). *Coercive family process.* Eugene, OR: Castalia.

Patterson, G. R., Reid, J. B., Jones, R. R., & Conger, R. E. (1975). *A social learning approach to family intervention* (Vol. 1). Eugene, OR: Castalia.

Pelco, L. E., & Reed-Victor, E. (2007). Self-regulation and learning-related social skills: Intervention ideas for elementary school students. *Preventing School Failure, 51*(3), 36–41.

Perea, S. (2004). *The New America: The America of the moo-shoo burrito.* Denver, CO: HIS Ministries Publications.

Public Health Service. (2001). *Youth violence: A report of the Surgeon General.* Retrieved May 22, 2011, from www.surgeongeneral.gov/library/youthviolence/toc.html

Quinn, M. M., Osher, D., Warger, C. L., Hanley, T. V., Bader, B. D., & Hoffman, C. C. (2000). *Teaching and working with children who have emotional and behavioral challenges.* Longmont, CO: Sopris West.

Raine, A., Dodge, K., Loeber, R., Gatzke-Kopp, L., Lynam, D., Reynolds, C., Stouthamer-Loeber, M., & Liu, J. (2006). The Reactive-Proactive Aggression Questionnaire: Differential correlates of reactive and proactive aggression in adolescent boys. *Aggressive Behavior, 32,* 159–171.

Reid, M. J., Webster-Stratton, C., & Hammond, M. (2007). Enhancing a classroom social competence and problem-solving curriculum by offering parent training to families of moderate- to high-risk elementary school children. *Journal of Clinical Child and Adolescent Psychology, 36*(4), 605–620.

Robins, K. N., Lindsey, R. B., Lindsey, D. B., & Terrell, R. D. (2006). *Culturally proficient instruction: A guide for people who teach* (2nd ed.). Thousand Oaks, CA: Corwin Press.

Robins, L. N., West, P. A., & Herjanic, B. L. (1975). Arrests and delinquency in two generations: A study of black urban families and their children. *Journal of Child Psychology and Psychiatry, 16,* 125–140.

Rock, E. E., Fessler, M. A., & Church, R. P. (1997). The concomitance of learning disabilities and emotional/behavioral disorders: A conceptual model. *Journal of Learning Disabilities, 30,* 245–263.

Rose, L. C., & Gallup, A. M. (2004). *The 36th Annual Phi Delta Kappa/Gallup poll of the public's attitude toward public schools.* Bloomington, IN: Phi Delta Kappa International.

Sanetti, L. M., & Kratochwill, T. R. (2008). Treatment integrity in behavioral consultation: Measurement, promotion, and outcomes. *International Journal of Behavioral Consultation and Therapy, 4*(1), 95–114.

Sanetti, L. M., & Kratochwill, T. R. (2009). Toward developing a science of treatment integrity: Introduction to a special series. *School Psychology Review, 38*(4), 445–459.

Sarason, I. G., Glaser, E. M., & Fargo, G. A. (1972). *Reinforcing productive classroom behavior.* New York: Behavioral Publications.

Schoenfeld, N. A., Rutherford, R. B., Jr., Gable, R. A., & Rock, M. L. (2008). *ENGAGE: A blueprint for incorporating social skills training into daily academic instruction.* Birmingham, AL: Heldref.

Scott, T. M., Anderson, C. M., & Spaulding, S. A. (2008). Strategies for developing and carrying out functional assessment and behavior intervention planning. *Preventing School Failure, 52*(3), 39–49.

Simon, S. G., Howe, L. W., & Kirschenbaum, H. (1972). *Values clarification.* New York: Hart.

Skiba, R. J., Peterson, R. L., & Williams, T. (1997). Office referrals and suspension: Disciplinary intervention in middle schools. *Education and Treatment of Children, 20*(3), 295–315.

Skiba, R. J., & Sprague, J. (2008). Safety without suspension. *Educational Leadership, 66*(1), 38–43.

Skinner, B. F. (1938). *The behavior of organisms: An experimental analysis.* New York: Appleton-Century-Crofts.

Skinner, B. F. (1953). *Science and human behavior.* New York: Macmillan.

Skinner, C. H., Cashwell, T. H., & Skinner, A. L. (2000). Increasing tootling: Effects of a peer-monitored group contingency program on students' reports of peers' prosocial behaviors. *Psychology in the Schools, 37,* 263–270.

Slavin, R. E. (1980). *Using student team learning* (Rev. ed.). Baltimore, MD: Johns Hopkins University, Center for Social Organization of Schools.

Slim, L., Whiteside, S. P., Dittner, C. A., & Mellon, M. (2006). Effectiveness of a social skills training program with school age children: Transition to clinical setting. *Journal of Child and Family Studies, 15,* 409–418.

Sloane, H. N. (1976). Classroom management: Remediation and prevention. New York: Wiley.

Smith, P. K., & Levan, S. (1995). Perceptions and experiences of bullying in younger pupils. *British Journal of Educational Psychology, 65,* 489–500.

Smith, S. W., & Gilles, D. L. (2003). Using key instructional elements to systematically promote social skill generalization for students with challenging behavior. *Intervention in School and Clinic, 39*(1), 30–37.

Spivack, G. E., Platt, J. J., & Shure, M. B. (1976). *The problem-solving approach to adjustment.* San Francisco: Jossey-Bass.

Spivack, G. E., & Shure, M. B. (1974). *Social adjustment of young children.* San Francisco: Jossey-Bass.

Sprague, J., & Walker, H. (2000). Early identification and intervention for youth with antisocial and violent behavior. *Exceptional Children, 66*(3), 367–379.

Stokes, T. F., & Baer, D. M. (1977). An implicit technology of generalization. *Journal of Applied Behavior Analysis, 10,* 349–367.

Strain, P. S., & Timm, M. A. (2001). Remediation and prevention of aggression: An evaluation of the region-al intervention program over a quarter century. *Behavioral Disorders, 26*(4), 297–313.

Sugai, G., Guardino, D., & Lathrop, M. (2007). Response to intervention: Examining classroom behavior support in second grade. *Exceptional Children, 73*(3), 288–310.

Thorndike, E. L., & Woodworth, R. S. (1901). The influence of improvement in one mental function upon the efficiency of other functions. *Psychological Review, 8,* 247–261.

Trussell, R. P., Lewis, T. J., & Stichter, J. P. (2008). The impact of targeted classroom interventions and function-based behavior interventions on problem behaviors of students with emotional/behavioral disorders. *Behavioral Disorders, 33*(3), 153–166.

Trzesniewski, K. H., Moffit, T. E., Caspi, A., Taylor, A., & Maughan, B. (2006). Revisiting the association between reading and antisocial behavior: New evidence of an environmental explanation from a twin study. *Child Development, 77,* 72–88.

Tse, J., Strulovitch, J., Tagalakis, V., Meng, L., & Fombonne, E. (2007). Social skills training for adolescents with Asperger Syndrome and High Functioning Autism. *Journal of Autism and Developmental Disorders, 37,* 1960–1968.

Turner, N. D. (2003). Preparing preservice teachers for inclusion in secondary classrooms. *Education, 123*(3), 491–495.

Voltz, D. L., Sims, M. J., & Nelson, B. (2010). *Connecting teachers, students, and standards: Strategies for success in diverse and inclusive classrooms.* Alexandria, VA: Association for Supervision and Curriculum Development.

Walker, H. M. (1979). The acting-out child: Coping with classroom disruption. Boston: Allyn & Bacon.

Walker, H. M., Colvin, G., & Ramsey, E. (1995). *Antisocial behavior in school: Strategies and best practices.* Pacific Grove, CA: Brooks/Cole.

Walker, H. M., Ramsey, E., & Gresham, F. M. (2004). *Antisocial behavior in school: Evidence-based practices* (2nd ed.). Belmont, CA: Wadsworth/Thomson Learning.

Werner, E. E., & Smith, R. S. (1982). *Vulnerable but invincible.* New York: McGraw-Hill.

Wood, B. K., Umbreit, J., Liaupsin, C. J., & Gresham, F. M. (2007). A treatment integrity analysis of function-based intervention. *Education and Treatment of Children, 30*(40), 105–120.

Zins, J. E., Bloodworth, M. R., Weissberg, R. P., & Walberg, H. J. (2004). The scientific base linking social and emotional learning to school success. In J. Zins, M. Bloodworth, R. Weissberg, & G. Walberg (Eds.), *Building academic success on social and emotional learning: What does the research say?* New York: Teachers College Press.

About the Author

Ellen McGinnis earned her Ph.D. from the University of Iowa in 1986. She holds degrees in elementary education, special education, and school administration. She has taught elementary and secondary students in the public schools in Minnesota, Iowa, and Arizona. In addition, she has served as a special education consultant in both public and hospital schools and as assistant professor of special education at the University of Wisconsin–Eau Claire. Dr. McGinnis also served with the Des Moines Public Schools as the principal of the education program at Orchard Place, a residential and day treatment facility for children and adolescents with emotional/behavioral disorders. She has been an executive director of student support services in both Iowa and Colorado and is currently a private consultant. The author of numerous articles on identifying and teaching youth with emotional/behavioral disorders, Dr. McGinnis collaborated with Dr. Arnold P. Goldstein on earlier Skillstreaming books and is author of the newly released third editions of *Skillstreaming the Elementary School Child* and *Skillstreaming in Early Childhood*.

Skillstreaming

The widely acclaimed and evidence-based social skills teaching method developed by Dr. Arnold P. Goldstein and colleagues

SKILLSTREAMING IN EARLY CHILDHOOD

A Guide for Teaching Prosocial Skills

Dr. Ellen McGinnis

PROGRAM BOOK

A complete description of the *Skillstreaming* program, with instructions for teaching 40 prosocial skills.

Skill Areas

- Beginning Social Skills
- School-Related Skills
- Friendship-Making Skills
- Dealing with Stress
- Alternatives to Aggression
- Dealing with Feelings

8 ½ × 11, 352 pages (CD included)

SKILL CARDS

Convenient 3 × 5 cards, illustrated for nonreaders, listing the behavioral steps for each of the 40 early childhood skills. Eight cards provided for each skill—a total of 320 cards.

SKILL POSTERS

A set of 40 12 × 18 posters, illustrated for nonreaders and displaying the behavioral steps in each of the skills for preschool and kindergarten.

SKILLSTREAMING THE ELEMENTARY SCHOOL CHILD

A Guide for Teaching Prosocial Skills

Dr. Ellen McGinnis

PROGRAM BOOK

Instructions for teaching 60 prosocial skills, plus complete guidelines for running the *Skillstreaming* program.

Skill Areas

- Classroom Survival Skills
- Friendship-Making Skills
- Skills for Dealing with Feelings
- Skill Alternatives to Aggression
- Skills for Dealing with Stress

8 ½ × 11, 408 pages (CD included)

SKILLSTREAMING IN THE ELEMENTARY SCHOOL

Lesson Plans and Activities

Make *Skillstreaming* even more fun! This book provides supplementary activities for at least one week of additional instruction for each of the 60 elementary skills. Features 600 easy-to-use lesson plans and a CD including over 200 printable forms necessary to implement the lesson plans.

8½ × 11, 312 pages (CD included)

STUDENT MANUAL

Written for the elementary-age student, a concise guide describing the program, designed to promote active involvement in the *Skillstreaming* group. A useful reference and organizer.

8½ × 11, 80 pages

SKILL CARDS

In a convenient 3 × 5 format, cards list the behavioral steps for each of the 60 elementary *Skillstreaming* skills. Eight cards provided for each skill—480 cards total.

POSTERS

A set of 60 18 × 12 posters displaying the behavioral steps in each of the skills for elementary-age students.

DVD—For Student Viewing
PEOPLE SKILLS: DOING 'EM RIGHT!

A quick and easy way to show your students what *Skillstreaming* is all about. Illustrates the process of teacher modeling, student role-playing, and feedback to clarify the benefits of using skills and motivate students to participate.

Elementary DVD, 17 minutes (closed captioned)

SKILLSTREAMING THE ADOLESCENT

A Guide for Teaching Prosocial Skills

Dr. Ellen McGinnis with Dr. Robert P. Sprafkin, Dr. N. Jane Gershaw, and Paul Klein

PROGRAM BOOK

A complete description of the *Skillstreaming* program, with detailed instructions for teaching 50 prosocial skills.

Skill Areas

- Beginning Social Skills
- Advanced Social Skills
- Skills for Dealing with Feelings
- Skill Alternatives to Aggression
- Skills for Dealing with Stress
- Planning Skills

8½ × 11, 360 pages (CD included)

SKILL CARDS

Convenient 3 × 5 cards listing the behavioral steps for each of the 50 adolescent Skillstreaming skills. Eight cards provided for each skill—400 cards total.

AGGRESSION REPLACEMENT TRAINING®

A Comprehensive Intervention for Aggressive Youth

Third Edition

Dr. Barry Glick and Dr. John C. Gibbs

Identified as a promising or model program by the Office of Juvenile Justice and Delinquency Prevention, Office of Safe and Drug-Free Schools, and National Center for Mental Health Promotion and Youth Violence Prevention

A new edition of the groundbreaking ART approach originally developed by Dr. Arnold P. Goldstein and Dr. Barry Glick, employing social skills training, anger control training, and moral reasoning. Updated and reorganized, with session-by-session instructions. Completely new moral reasoning problem situations, along with photocopiable skill cards, participant handouts, parent materials, and evaluation forms.

8½ × 11, 426 pages (CD included)

STUDENT MANUAL

A concise description of the program written in language adolescents can understand. Promotes active involvement in the *Skillstreaming* group and serves as a useful reference and organizer.

8½ × 11, 64 pages

POSTERS

A set of 50 18 × 12 posters displaying the behavioral steps for each of the adolescent skills.

DVD—For Student Viewing
PEOPLE SKILLS: DOING 'EM RIGHT!

A quick and easy way to show your students what *Skillstreaming* is all about. Illustrates the process of teacher modeling, student role-playing, and feedback to clarify the benefits of using skills and motivate students to participate.

Adolescent DVD, 17 minutes (closed captioned)

THE SKILLSTREAMING DVD

How to Teach Students Prosocial Skills

Shows Drs. Arnold P. Goldstein and Ellen McGinnis in actual training sessions with educators and small groups of adolescents and elementary-age children. Clearly demonstrates the *Skillstreaming* teaching model and procedures. Purchase includes a copy of the *Skillstreaming the Adolescent* and *Skillstreaming the Elementary School Child* program books.

26 minutes (closed captioned)

Contact Research Press for current prices and ordering information.

RESEARCH PRESS
PUBLISHERS

2612 N. Mattis Avenue ♦ Champaign, IL 61822
www.researchpress.com ♦ (800) 519-2707

Visit www.skillstreaming.com for details on research support for the program, sample lessons, and more.